Best wi
Nick

CW00421599

l   ,

THE LAST PATROL

Allen Forster

(fiction, adult humour)

Chapter One

The dull grey boat rode the, for once, calm waters with ease and stayed at periscope level, her skipper rubbing his bleary dawn eyes and wondering what had happened to the last few hours en route from the Breton coast. Still, any lull in this war of attrition and nerves gave his crew time to snatch a precious few hours of rest.

He looked around, and the crew on watch began to stir as well. Surely they couldn't have all drifted off to sleep? They were mostly good men, reliable, and far too professional for that. The skipper checked the boat's compass and position on the chart. They were drifting and had to be careful in these treacherous waters.

Looking through the periscope, he scanned the still early morning waters around him. Nothing moved on the surface of the sea. He scanned landwards a few short miles to the south. A distinctive lighthouse stood away on a rock to the west. He knew where he was just by observing that. Lighthouses were tall and were impossible to keep hidden from view.

By now the rest of the crew had awoken and assumed their stations. The skipper, Kapitanleutnant Otto Von Diesel, rubbed his grisly ginger beard. His head felt a bit fuzzy. He looked at his duty officer.

"Hans, what has happened? Why are all the men in a state of torpor?"

"I know not why, Herr Kapitan. Perhaps the boat's ration of the strong stuff went to their heads last night."

Von Diesel thought Hans was an imbecile who shouldn't be in charge of a child's toy boat in a bath. However, he was stuck with the young Leutnant. The rest of the crew were much better, he consoled himself. Von Diesel looked through the periscope again.

"This is very strange, Hans. Make sure the men are now fully alert. We are in dangerous waters. Stay at periscope level and be very vigilant."

The Kapitan paused and observed the grey Atlantic waters carefully.

"By my reckoning, Hans, there should be minefields here about, but there does not seem much evidence of this. How very odd."

Hans Krieger hadn't a clue where they were. Somewhere off the north Cornish coast, he guessed, such were their secret orders.

"So, where exactly are we, Herr Kapitan?"

"Just west of a small fishing village going by the name of Porth Branven. It is just over there. It has the most wunderbar little tea and gift shop that sells Cornish cream teas, piskies and tea towels depicting the rather ample fräuleins in scanty beach attire."

"You know this place then, Herr Kapitan? How?"

Hans paused before continuing his questioning.

"Our superior German intelligence in Berlin is right up there on the ball, so to speak?"

"Nein," replied the skipper. "I went there for my holidays in 1937 and 1938. I have a distant cousin who lives in Truro. I also went to St Ives and Falmouth. In Falmouth I took some wunderbar snaps with my glorious Swiss camera. I will show them to you later in the wardroom. There are some especially good ones of several big ships in Falmouth harbour."

"Herr Kapitan, I thought the British banned the taking of photos before the war started."

Hans wondered why they would be so stupid not to.

"They did, Hans, but only when they believed the war with the Fatherland would happen. I took these in 1937. It was a good summer, Hans. I met this fräulein called Molly. She wore these exciting--"

The skipper was interrupted by Schwartz, a seaman using the hydrophones.

"Herr Kapitan, I hear the engines of a small vessel that I don't recognise. The engines must be of some new secret design."

The man, Schwartz, continued to listen carefully. The skipper looked through the periscope.

"Ah, yes. Hans, take a look. I see her. Tell me what you see also."

Hans scanned the sea's surface and focused on a small fishing trawler approaching their position from the west. It was surrounded by gulls. Hans kept it in view and handed back to the Kapitan.

"A small fishing smack, Herr Kapitan, and obviously British. Maybe some one thousand meters away and heading towards us. Maybe it is a Q-boat sent to attack us. It is of strange design as Schwartz described its engine noises, the like I also have never heard before. Shall I prepare torpedoes for attack, Herr Kapitan?"

Von Diesel continued to observe the small craft as it approached at steady speed, keeping the same course.

Hans thought briefly about his beautiful Helga back in Düsseldorf. He always did when danger threatened. He prayed that she, and little Willy and Helmut, were safe from the air raids.

"Hold our position, Hans. Do not order the firing of the torpedoes. Remember our secret orders? We are not to reveal ourselves to anyone."

The Kapitan wondered what to do next. They could be about to be attacked by a British Q-boat disguised as a trawler. It might even be some cleverly designed prototype attack vessel.

"They must know our position, Herr Kapitan."

Hans sweated a little while the Kapitan kept his nerve.

"For some reason, Hans, we have lost radio contact with Naval Command. This is getting worrying. We are not supposed to attack vessels but stick to our secret orders. Our mission is simple and we must obey orders."

"But, Herr Kapitan, she approaches with speed, no more than eight hundred metres away."

"Hans, I do not wish to waste a valuable torpedo on such a puny craft. Still, we must do something. We could surface and use the deck gun to blast them out of the water and save a torpedo for bigger fish, if we need to, but we will also alert half the British Navy and the RAF to our presence."

Schultz, a lowly seaman, held his breath and approached the senior officer.

"Herr Kapitan, I was going to make you a bacon sandwich for your breakfast, but we are out of bacon. Forgive the intrusion, Herr Kapitan, but I have a suggestion to make."

"What is it, Schultz?" said the Kapitan, turning to look at the man.

"Well, Herr Kapitan, we are low on supplies, particularly biccies and fresh food. A fishing smack might have on board some fresh fish, ja? I know how the Kapitan is partial to some smoked kipper for breakfast when it becomes available. Maybe we could capture this vessel and take the spoils of war. Then we could send her to the bottom. They could have lunch with Herr Davey Jones in his locker and the great Kapitan of this proud vessel could have the fresh fish for breakfast."

The Kapitan thought about Schultz's suggestion and then spoke.

"Good thinking, Schultz, but they won't have the smoked kippers on board; maybe some mackerel or pollack."

The Kapitan then gave orders to surface at a range of two hundred metres from the fishing boat. The gun crew prepared to man the powerful deck gun. Von Diesel thought that Schultz would make a better first officer then that imbecile, Hans Krieger from Düsseldorf, masquerading as an officer on one of the German Navy's finest small coastal submarines.

When UB-AF9, the pride of the German Kriegsmarine, was at a range of two hundred metres, she surfaced, the cold Atlantic waters cascading down her conning tower.

Leutnant Franz Spiegel prepared to emerge with the deck gun firing party. His yellow oil-skinned figure rapidly came out from the conning tower, dripping wet. The gun crew followed him, scaling the metal ladder down onto the deck, and prepared the big gun ready to fire.

On board the small trawler, *The Two Inbred Sisters*, the first mate was at the wheel and immediately cut the boat's engines and gestured to the skipper, who was on deck checking the catch.

"Hey, Bert, you aren't going to believe this. Come and see for yourself. Come take a look!"

Bert, the boat's skipper, stopped what he was doing and entered the open door of the wheel house. He looked ahead to see the menacing grey steel tube of war right there in their path, with an enormous deck gun pointing straight at them. The three men aboard *The Two Inbred Sisters*, which included 17-year-old deck hand, John Thomas, looked at it.

"Jeez! Is this some kind of war film being made?" shouted Bert.

The two men in the wheel house plus John Thomas went out onto the fore deck.

Leutnant Spiegel had a loud hailer.

"Herr Kapitan! I order you to surrender your vessel to the victorious German Navy at once! Resistance is futile! We are heavily armed and coming aboard!"

Bert looked at Arthur Pengelly in utter amazement.

"It's a bloody German U-boat! It can't be. What Navy museum did they get that from? Look, it's even flying a swastika flag. It must have something to do with the celebrations tomorrow."

"Bloody funny way of showing friendship," said Arthur Pengelly. "The big gun looks real enough though."

The men stood and watched, and let their boat drift on the slight swell.

On board UB-AF9, the officer had prepared a boarding party of himself and three hands, and all were armed.

The fishermen stood motionless as the black rubber inflatable dinghy made its way towards the trawler. It came alongside the bobbing vessel.

"Guten Morgen, gentlemen. Now throw down the mooring rope to secure this boat," ordered the German officer, waving his Luger pistol.

With guns trained on them, the fishermen responded.

The German Navy boarding party secured the flimsy dinghy to the side of the trawler and hauled themselves aboard.

"Who is your Kapitan?" demanded Spiegel with authority in his voice.

"That'll be me," announced Big Bert. "But I don't understand. You are pointing a great big gun at us, you fuckin' half wits."

Bert clenched his fists in anger, ready to attack, but then he thought better of it when the guns were brandished more menacingly.

"What is this? Is it a film or something? Or, if it's a joke, it's a fuckin' sick one. You frightened the shit out of us. What's your game, dressed up as wartime Germans?"

"I am Leutnant Spiegel of the German Kriegsmarine, and on behalf of Kapitanleutnant Otto Von Diesel of the U-boat, AF9, I am taking this vessel as spoils of war, and its cargo, under the rules of war."

"What war? And what cargo?" asked Bert. "We only have four boxes of fish, a few crabs and lobsters."

"Das ist gut," said the officer commanding the boarding party. "The Kapitan will be pleased. Now show me this fishy catch, ja?"

Back on board the U-boat, Kapitanleutnant Von Diesel watched the boarding scene through binoculars from the top of the conning tower. He ordered a few other seamen to have their guns trained directly on the target opposite. He was taking no chances with this strange vessel, which looked like a fishing smack. He knew from experience that these Cornish could be crafty people who couldn't always be trusted.

Leutnant Spiegel was efficient and quickly scoured the trawler for anything valuable to take. He didn't have the time in the early morning light to deprive the vessel of its fuel. He opted to seize the fish and the prisoners, and had them transferred across to the waiting submarine, where another boarding party on a second inflatable boat was summoned over. The trawler was a small craft, he decided, and one almost unworthy of plundering and sending to the bottom, but they were at war, and the rules of normal seamanship were suspended. He ordered one of his men to scuttle *The Two Inbred Sisters*, when he, the rest of the boarding parties and the prisoners were all ready to leave.

One of the German ratings opened up the sea cocks and *The Two Inbred Sisters* listed to port and began to sink. The rating got back on board the second inflatable and pushed her off as the trawler made strange death throe gurgling sounds and could be seen sinking speedily.

"Better get out of here quickly," ordered Leutnant Spiegel. "We don't want to be dragged down also with the Cornish fishing smack."

The three prisoners sat quietly in the first boat, looking completely dejected and bemused, under armed guard. Big Bert, the trawler's skipper, turned around to look at his vessel consigned to her fate in the waters, which had begun to chop up a bit. He sadly saw her slipping below the surface.

"My boat, my precious boat. You foolish bastards have sunk her with your stupid war games. You'll pay for this when I report you to the police and coastguard for piracy on the high seas!"

He was almost in tears at the loss.

"Never mind the boat, Herr Kapitan. These things are expected to happen in war. Be thankful I spared your lives and didn't shoot you."

A half smile appeared on the German officer's face, and then an expression of alarm as he jumped up and almost capsized the inflatable, with its occupants a whisker away from all being thrown into the sea.

"Ralf! Watch that big lobster! His claws are sharp so be careful with him, or his razor claw will sink us!"

The boarding party with their prisoners returned safely to the UB-AF9.

Kapitanleutnant Von Diesel was overseeing things from the top of the conning tower.

"Get the boats stowed away quickly, men, and get those prisoners and the fresh provisions below as well. We need to get out of here quickly. It's a minor miracle how enemy aircraft haven't spotted us already."

Arthur Pengelly and Big Bert looked at each other with some amazement and wished to proclaim that the man was a lunatic. He might be, they decided, but he and his men were heavily armed and they were on the business end of those weapons.

The sailors prodded the prisoners down into the submarine and they obeyed without question. Young John Thomas was terrified and kept his mouth shut tight.

The Kapitanleutnant scanned the coast and sky with his binoculars for signs of enemy activity but saw none. This was so strange, he thought. The last time he had sailed these dangerous waters, he had encountered a minefield and he and his crew had only just escaped with their lives and some minor damage to their vessel. On that last trip they had also been depth charged and strafed by enemy aircraft fire. It was a miracle they hadn't been sent to spend their final minutes or hours on the bottom.

He ordered the boat to cruise just below the periscope level, and on a course a bit further out to sea and well away from dangerous reefs that guarded this stretch of the coast. Once they were out at a safe distance, he would interrogate the three prisoners.

The Two Inbred Sisters lay on the bottom, one hundred and fifty feet down, and her catch provided some well received fresh fish rations for the hungry crew. The smell of cooked mackerel wafted through the boat as it vied with the heady mixture of diesel fumes and damp smelling clothes and body odours usually associated with a submerged submarine on a patrol. The Kapitan was the first to be served up fresh fish. It was a pleasant change for breakfast.

When the Kapitan had eaten and the boat was in safer, deeper waters and just drifting with the current, he went to the control room and looked at his three prisoners carefully. He could tell that they were just ordinary fishermen. He had a healthy respect for mariners of all nationalities. The sea could be a cruel mistress with the changing moods of a woman, on which they all shared their collective danger, particularly in wartime.

"Turn out your pockets, gentlemen, please," ordered the Kapitanleutnant.

11

The men did as ordered. The U-boat skipper watched as tobacco, an assortment of coins, and keys were produced. The Kapitan picked up and examined some of the coins.

"Here is the King's shilling, ja? And here is something called the one new pence. And what is this? A strange shaped fifty pence piece? I have never heard of such coins; they must be some secret wartime local coinage to fool our agents."

The Kapitan quizzed the men about naval and coastal defences in the area. He wanted to know what defences there were around these parts in particular.

Big Bert didn't have a clue what was going on here and thought that maybe their best hope of survival might be served by going along with these weirdoes in old German submariner uniforms. If this was a film they had encroached, then where were the cameras?

"Well, Captain, the beaches are obviously mined and the coast all the way around is heavily fortified, particularly at my port."

"Which is?" asked the German captain.

"Porth Branven," came the answer from Bert.

"Ja, Porth Branven."

The U-boat skipper smiled knowingly.

"You know it?" asked Big Bert.

"I know it well, my friend, but it is I who is doing the asking of the questions here."

The loaded gun held by a nearby German rating got closer to Bert's head; it concentrated his mind much more clearly.

"Tell me, Kapitan Bert Whatever-Your-Name-Is, I need some vital wartime intelligence information. Is the wunderbar Atlantic Tea Rooms Und Gift Shop still there?"

Bert looked at an equally puzzled Arthur and then back at the Captain of the U-boat.

"Why, yes, it is. Molly, a lady I know, runs it. But how do you know about The Atlantic Tea Rooms And Gift Shop, Captain?"

The German U-boat commander smiled and didn't answer. He looked at Hans Krieger.

"Hans, arrange for these prisoners to have some fresh fish and steaming hot German Navy regulation coffee, and then secure them somewhere where they can do no harm while I decide on what to do with them. It's only fair to give them breakfast as our guests, Hans, considering I was responsible for the demise of their vessel and its

12

catch. Let no one accuse us Germans of being barbarians on the high seas."

"But, Herr Kapitan, it was Seaman Holsteig who scuttled the British boat."

Hans looked at the Kapitan.

"What an absolute cretinous lentil brain," thought Kapitanleutnant Von Diesel as he retired to his tiny cabin.

If this boat ever made it safely back to Bremerhaven, he would recommend to the Admiralty that Leutnant Hans Krieger was posted on a supply submarine to the Antarctic weather station, where he could do no harm. The man was an absolute dummkopf who he sometimes thought might be a Royal Navy spy sent to infiltrate and cause havoc amongst the German Kriegsmarine.

The Commander relaxed in his cabin. He alerted his steward to fetch Leutnant Franz Spiegel to his cabin. The Kapitan's instructions were clear.

"You know my orders, Franz. Keep the prisoners out of mischief and cast an eye over that idiot, Hans, or we will probably end up on a beach, stuck amongst the mines and barbed wire."

"Jawohl, Herr Kapitan," replied the smart and efficient officer, smiling, knowing that the Kapitan had little time for the 'Dummkopf from Düsseldorf', as Commander Von Diesel referred privately to Leutnant Hans Krieger.

Von Diesel was aware that the boat was in the safest hands possible. The steward had brought him a fresh cup of coffee, and he gave some thought to his mission. It had been simple. The UB-AF9 was to rendezvous later that night off an isolated cove on this coast to pick up a German agent with top secret information operating in Cornwall.

It would also give him the opportunity to replenish the U-boat with supplies of diesel fuel, which was stored at a nearby secret location, and which had been organised and set up since 1939 by Cornish fifth columnists, Cornish right wing nationalists who wanted political freedom from London.

That was the simple plan, but the strange thing was that Kapitanleutnant Von Diesel could remember leaving the Breton coast two days before, but the events leading up until early dawn were a complete blur to him. It had been as if time itself had been snatched from him and his crew.

Another mystery had presented itself. For some unknown reason, no radio or signal contact could be made to, or received from, Naval Command, or to any other operating friendly vessel in these enemy waters. Kapitanleutnant Von Diesel wondered if the British had some sort of secret sonar weapon that was somehow blocking all means of communication.

Why hadn't they encountered any minefields, or seen any signs of enemy ships or aircraft? Von Diesel would have at least expected to have encountered a fast armed patrol boat along this coast. It was all so strange.

Maybe the British were cleverer than they made out and knew where he was all along, and were just playing a cat and mouse waiting game before they struck.

Von Diesel was normally a stickler for routine and obeying orders, which had flown in the face of how he had operated that morning. He should not have broken cover to seize the fishing boat, and especially not to take prisoners. That was an error of judgement on his part. At least Naval Command wouldn't get to hear about it as he wouldn't register it later as a 'kill' when he got back home. The fresh mackerel for breakfast at least made it seem worthwhile though.

But what was he to do with the three prisoners on board? They had compromised his mission. Shooting them in cold blood wasn't an option for Kapitanleutnant Otto Von Diesel of the German Navy's Kriegsmarine.

Some of his men felt a little differently, and he was aware of their feelings, but he had given precise orders for the prisoners to be detained and not to be harmed in any way but treated as prisoners of war in transit.

The Kapitan consoled himself with the fact that he didn't have any crew members who were Nazis aboard. Now that was rare for a serving U-boat of the line but a blessing. He was a good old fashioned German Naval Officer doing his duty and would have no truck with that sort. These SS and Gestapo people could make life extremely difficult and unpleasant, even for a U-boat commander, if they had a mind to.

There was a sudden shout from a familiar voice.

"Herr Kapitan! Come quick!"

The Commander arose from his bunk at action stations speed.

"What is it, Hans? Are we under enemy attack?"

14

Leutnant Krieger stood facing the Kapitan outside his cabin.

"Nein, Herr Kapitan. Herman has escaped!"

The U-boat Commander rubbed his tired eyes some more. He was now convinced beyond all doubt that Hans Krieger, the Düsseldorf Dummkopf, was an utter lunatic.

"Who is this Herman? Has a man gone missing?"

The Commander had said the words without really thinking about how one of his men could have gone missing from a submerged U-boat on a patrol.

"Herman the lobster, Herr Kapitan. Horst, the cook, gave him the name in affectionate terms before he was about to cook him for the Kapitan's supper this evening. Now he has escaped somewhere. Apart from his big sharp saw claw, he has the fine running legs also."

The Kapitan followed Leutnant Krieger into the control room. It was as if they were at action stations. The Commander had to assume order before this idiot, and a lobster, sank this boat. The pride of the German Navy, sent to the bottom by a lobster called Herman. It was the stuff of movies and oceanic nightmares.

The three Cornish prisoners, handcuffed securely to some pipes, watched in some amusement but didn't show it too much on account of their captors taking this matter rather more seriously.

"Where is Leutnant Spiegel?" asked the Commander.

"The Chief Engineer wanted him to look at a small problem we have been having in the engine room, Herr Kapitan," said Hans Krieger, who the Kapitan believed was more scared of Herman the lobster than a sudden enemy attack with depth charges, or their running suddenly into a minefield.

"Very well, Leutnant Krieger. I will take command once more while you and two detailed men organise a search party to find Herman. If he discovers a wrong place to hide, he could cause some damage to this boat. He might even block some vital equipment and cause us to sink."

Leutnant Krieger set to with some gusto. He didn't fancy ending his days on the bottom of the Cornish coast, having been sent there by a lobster called Herman.

The prisoners looked on and, if the notion had not scared them as well, they would have thought it delicious irony that their boat's sinking had been avenged by a lobster; a lobster adopted as Herman the German, but who they had captured from the depths in the first place.

A little while later, it was discovered that Herman had somehow scuttled away from the galley and found his way down to the engine room, where he almost nipped the Chief Engineer on the leg. There was always sea water splashing around down there and Herman had made himself quite at home, hidden behind some pipes, daring anyone to put their hand in and yank him out. Here was one lobster not yet ready for the cooking pot.

With the Kapitan making the trip down to the engine room, he looked at the Chief Engineer and shook his head in amazement.

Leutnant Spiegel, who had been assessing an engineering problem brought to his attention, acknowledged the Kapitan and returned to the control room.

The Kapitan looked first at Hans Krieger, who was keeping a safe distance from the lobster, and then at the Chief Engineer.

"Can he do any damage down here, Fritz?"

The big, portly Chief Engineer rubbed his oily hands with and equally oily rag that made his hands more oily.

"Nein, Herr Kapitan. He is safe for the moment. He has no food supply but plenty of water; enough to keep him alive for hours. I will keep my eye on him and entice him out with some food nearer to supper time. He seems to have taken a liking to my leg."

"Wunderbar!" said the Kapitan. "Order is restored, and now I return to the control room. I have much more important things to attend to than hunt for a lobster who escapes from the boat's galley. Hans, come also, and stand down the men on the lobster search party."

Soon, in the control room, Leutnant Franz Spiegel had kept the boat trimmed and on course to their safer position out in deeper waters away from the coast. He decided that the Kapitan was right about Hans Krieger. The man was a complete and utter dolt with the brain the size of Herman the lobster's.

The Leutnant ordered his men on duty to be exceptionally vigilant as, for some unknown reason, the British had been far too quiet for his liking too.

While he studied the charts, he wondered whether the Kapitan would enter any of this lobster nonsense in the boat's log. If German Naval Command or even the Führer himself got to hear of this business, then Kapitanleutnant Otto Von Diesel would be relieved of his command and taken to the Verschoten Naval Psychiatric Assessment Hospital Facility at Bremerhaven. It was a place that Hans Krieger should have been sent to years ago.

How he wished the war would recommence, to maintain his own sanity.

Chapter Two

Major Robert Beere, The Duke of Cornwall's Light Infantry, retired, was a long-term resident of The Bluebells Residential Home in Porth Branven. The Major was a sprightly old gentleman with a shock of white hair and a neat moustache, and still had an obvious military bearing.

The good Major was, from his old army days, a creature of habit. Every day of his life, whatever the weather, he would take a constitutional walk out on to the cliffs to the north of the Porth Branven cove. Once there, he would spend a little while looking out to sea with a beautiful old brass ship's telescope. The Major loved scanning the waters before returning to The Bluebells for breakfast.

This particular morning, he saw something totally unexpected. Major Beere, alone on the cliff tops, hurried as quickly as he could back to The Bluebells to tell the story to someone. Eventually, very breathless, he came through the doors of the establishment.

"Matron! Matron! Better call the police and the coastguard! A German U-boat has just surfaced to the north and seized Big Bert's boat, *The Two Inbred Sisters*. They sunk the boat and captured the crew!"

The Major had to sit down in the hallway. One of the home's carers came and picked up his telescope, which had slipped out of his hand on to the floor. The Matron came to see what the fuss was about.

"Why, Major Beere, you've gone a funny colour. I think you need to lie down for a while and take it easy. I can arrange for you to have your breakfast a bit later, if you wish?"

"But, Matron, you don't understand!" he blurted out. "We have to take action to stop these people before they strike again. You have to call the coastguard and police!"

The Major tried to catch his breath.

"Call the police and coastguard immediately, there's a good lady. Matron, I have just witnessed an outrageous act of piracy on the high seas."

"There, there, Major Beere. You've been looking out to sea again with your telescope."

"I saw them with my own eyes, Matron. My eyes have never let me down yet. There they were, the German scoundrels. It was a U-boat and it came up right next to Big Bert's boat, and then they boarded her and stole his catch. Then they sank her!"

"Who boarded Big Bert's boat?" asked the Matron.

"Why, the Jerries of course, Matron. The Jerry sailors from the submarine."

The Matron smiled and made a face at the carer and gestured as if to ask her whether the Major had taken his medication that morning. Hadn't the Major once claimed to have seen a pirate ship pass by one morning out to sea? He had, but the Matron was unaware that a replica sailing ship used in a film had, in fact, passed through these waters early morning en route from Bristol to the Spanish coast.

Meanwhile, out at sea, UB-AF9 lay low and Kapitanleutnant Von Diesel ordered the boat to the surface as no other vessels were in the vicinity. It was a chance for her batteries to be recharged and for the whole crew to take it in rotation to get some well needed fresh air.

Down in the engine room, Herman the lobster was staying put in his safe place behind the pipes. The Chief Engineer kept a half-eye on him while he worked. He didn't want that thing taking a liking to his leg again.

The prisoners were restless and placed in a tiny maintenance store room, and allowed to use the heads (or toilet bucket) once every four hours. They demanded to know what was to become of them but were told to keep quiet and were given no answers. The Kapitan thought they were better suited in there, out of the way of hearing his orders and from seeing the crew at first hand operating stations.

The boat stank of mackerel, diesel fumes and sweat. Duty personnel kept a watchful eye on the sea and on the skies above.

Several small fishing vessels passed a mile or so away from their position, but the U-boat ignored them. The Kapitan decided that the British must have acquired a whole new fleet of ultra modern fishing boats, because neither he nor any member of his crew had seen their design before.

He questioned the prisoners, but got no information that was remotely useful. He decided they knew nothing anyway and thought that later that night he would put them ashore after he had successfully accomplished his mission.

The watchmen kept a careful eye on passing fishing boats and the Kapitan gave orders for no further engagement until one of them shouted to him.

"Herr Kapitan! Possible enemy aircraft sighted! Approaching us on the port bow!"

The action stations sirens were sounded and a flurry of activity took place above and below decks.

There was no time to dive before the small single-prop plane approached. The crew on deck got ready to fire the deck gun whilst others prepared to use small arms fire, and a machine gun was aimed at the plane.

"It looks like a small spotter plane," said the Commander. "I do not recognise such a design. It must be a more modern British aircraft than our intelligence is aware of. Prepare to open fire!"

"It is towing something, Herr Kapitan," said Leutnant Spiegel from the top of the conning tower alongside the Commander.

"It must be some new anti-submarine tracking device."

Both men were equally puzzled and watched with hearts beating quickly as the rickety light aircraft rocked in the sky as the pilot strived to keep its wings steady. It appeared as if the pilot was doing a circular sweep of land and sea.

"Fire!" ordered the Kapitan, and the gunners opened up, sending a heavy shell skywards and just missing the tail of the small aircraft.

The plane was towing a big, long banner behind it. The banner was raked with machine gun fire and it hung in tattered rags behind the plane. The pilot had difficulty in righting the aircraft and flew off inland with a sharp turn to starboard.

"We missed him but got the secret anti-submarine device he was towing!" shouted the gunner to the Kapitan.

The Commander gave the immediate order to evacuate the deck and "dive, dive, dive!".

The men covered up the deck gun and ran to their stations, climbing at speed down through the hatches. The Kapitan was last below. He barked out more orders.

"Dive to twenty metres and steer a course away from here to the north west. He will have alerted the Royal Navy and the RAF to our presence by now. We need to get away from here as soon as the hell is possible, and lie low further out to sea until darkness falls."

It seemed like an eternity before the U-boat submerged and she moved away from the danger area. The Commander was relieved that there were no signs of follow up by the enemy, but why were the British so thin on the ground on this part of the coast? Maybe they were concentrating their defence forces in other areas.

He had to contact Naval Command about this position, but all means of communication still appeared to be jammed despite all the other equipment on board appearing to work satisfactorily. As hard as they tried, they could not make contact with the rest of the German Navy.

Kapitanleutnant Von Diesel knew of at least four other U-boats operating in these waters. Without communication, they could end up being attacked by their own side. He was not alone in living on his nerves.

The Kapitan calmed down when they were safely further out to sea. He could feel the waters around the submarine getting noticeably rougher. Bad weather was not expected in this part of the world for at least another week, but the weather, he knew, was like the fräuleins from back home - fickle and unpredictable.

Nothing much of note happened that day on the patrol of UB-AF9. Kapitanleutnant Von Diesel wrote up his log with no mention of Herman, who remained firmly ensconced behind the pipes in the watery engine room, and who showed reluctance to emerge despite the best efforts of the Chief Engineer trying occasionally to tempt him out with a piece of chocolate ration. How long was he intending to hide there? The Chief Engineer shouted to a rating above the incessant noise associated with below deck.

"Baumgarten, what do these crustaceans usually eat? They don't seem to like the regulation German Navy ration chocolate. Go see if you can find out what they eat, boy."

A few minutes later the young rating returned to the engine room.

"The cook says the hummer eats the live food - the small fish, the molluscs and worms."

The Chief Engineer rubbed his oily rag across his sweating forehead.

"Have we any of these things on board?"

The answer came back with a smirk on the young rating's face.

"Well, Herr Engineer, Seaman Wolfgang had the crabs and passed them on to half of the crew, but he no longer has them."

The Chief Engineer shook his bald and oily head in amazement.

"Not those crabs, you dummkopf. Crabs that live in the sea."

The Chief was informed that the crabs taken from the Cornish fishermen's catch had all gone in the pot, but there were some mackerel left over.

"Get me a strip of mackerel then," said the Chief, losing his patience with the young rating.

The younger man went back to the galley to fetch the fish. The Chief sloshed the water around his boots and stooped down to speak to Herman.

"Herman, my crustacean friend. I soon give you the tasty mackerel, when that idiot returns from the galley."

Herman remained firmly behind the pipes and was in no hurry to come out.

The U-boat lay silently beneath the swirling waters of the Atlantic. The Commander relaxed and listened to some Strauss records on his wind-up gramophone. It helped him to concentrate on the mission in hand. He was aware that the saga of Herman was still occurring under his command, but the morale of his crew was important to him, as long as such events did not get in the way of efficiency and discipline when it really counted. If Herman the lobster was keeping some of them amused, then so be it. Herman, he decided, would make a better sailor than that oaf of a Leutnant going by the name of Hans Krieger. He wondered how the man had even managed to join the Kriegsmarine in the first place.

Down in the engine room, the Chief Engineer was having no luck in enticing Herman out from under the pipes. Even a strip of mackerel did not do the trick. The Chief believed that Herman was aware of the fate that awaited him should he decide to come out from his hideout.

And then things changed the mood on board. The ratings on watch were alert, which was just as well because Hans Krieger was near the controls. One of the ratings shouted to the Leutnant.

"Herr Leutnant, have a look at this! It must be the enemy! I have never set eyes upon a vessel looking anything like this before!"

The man was in awe of what he had seen. Leutnant Krieger took over the periscope. There, about one thousand five hundred metres away, was the largest warship he had ever seen. For once, the Leutnant was sensible.

"Better call the Kapitan and give Leutnant Spiegel a shout also."

The two men were disturbed in their bunks without ceremony.

"What is it, man? Have you captured Herman?" said the Kapitan, stirring.

"Nein, nein, Herr Kapitan. Herman is no fish, but if he were, then this one would be much bigger. You had better come and see this for yourself, Herr Kapitan!"

Reluctantly, the Commander came to the control room and took over from Hans and looked through the periscope himself. He couldn't believe what he was seeing.

There, ahead, on the starboard bow, was the biggest warship he had ever seen, and one that defied description. It looked like nothing that the British had in their Navy, and yet it flew the white ensign. He spoke the ship's number on her bows to himself.

"F230."

He studied the big ship carefully. This was no HMS *Prince of Wales*, or HMS *Rodney*, or HMS *Hood*, but obviously something far more powerful and menacing.

The large aircraft carrier had many planes aboard, and they too looked futuristic. She was heavily armed and had a bristling array of what Von Diesel believed might be some hitherto unknown communications system with numerous antennae. Her huge funnel belched out a black plume of diesel smoke. He could see a large contingent of crew aboard who were practising some kind of drill.

This vessel made the *Bismarck* look like a toy.

"Mein Gott im Himmel, Hans! This is the biggest warship I have ever encountered. No wonder the British have been scarce in these waters with that vessel. They have a ship that we could only dream of."

The Commander continued to observe the ship at periscope level and from what he believed to be a safe distance. He decided to act quickly and efficiently.

"Hans, go below to the engine room and check on Herman. See that he is behaving his crustacean self, ja?"

"Jawohl, Herr Kapitan," replied Hans, not really seeing the significance of his being ordered below deck.

The Commander spoke to the officer he could most trust - Leutnant Franz Spiegel, his right hand man. The Leutnant observed the enemy ship.

"What do you think, Franz?"

The Leutnant took a long, hard look and replied.

"Herr Kapitan, I would estimate this vessel, obviously an aircraft carrier, to be some eighty to one hundred thousand tons in weight. She carries at least forty aircraft, and maybe more below decks. I, too, have never seen the like of this before. It is strange how the glorious German Navy has been unaware of this vessel before. There is something about this ship, Herr Kapitan that worries me, and all is not quite right here. Surely she is far too big for us to attack, Herr Kapitan? And we are supposed not to break cover, of course."

"I agree," said the Kapitan. "However, Franz, what a prize she would be if we were to sink her. I would probably be promoted to Admiral of the Fleet, and you would do well also. It does seem also that she is unaware of our presence. Give orders to close the distance between us to eight hundred metres."

"Jawohl, Herr Kapitan."

Von Diesel was not normally a man to disobey orders, and had already done so once today, but this potential prize of war was far too inviting to turn down.

The U-boat prepared herself to attack the British warship to their starboard bow.

Von Diesel pondered over his dilemma. Here was a monster prize to be claimed, but his orders were not to break cover by attacking enemy vessels.

The boat was put at action stations, but the Commander ordered that the prisoner known as Big Bert be brought to the control room. The big man was brought under armed guard, and said silent prayers as he believed they were going to shoot him. The Commander could sense the prisoner's deep fears.

"Don't worry, fisherman. I only brought you here because I need you. Look through the periscope and tell me what you see."

Bert did as he was ordered.

"It's a warship, Captain."

"Yes, I know this, but I want to know which warship. Help me with this identification and I will let you and your two friends live to see another mackerel day."

"So how am I to do that when you sank my boat?"

Bert was annoyed but still held at gunpoint.

"You will get another boat, my friend. This war will end someday soon. Now tell me what you see!"

Bert looked again through the periscope and wondered what to tell the German Captain, who was taking all this stuff very seriously and had obviously escaped from some secure unit somewhere. It was best to humour him, Bert thought.

"She's HMS *Bosun*, the pride and the flagship of The Royal Navy. She is the most advanced and powerful warship in the world."

The Commander rubbed his chin and looked puzzled.

"I have never heard of this ship before. Where have the British been hiding her? Our intelligence knows the whereabouts of all your surface vessels."

"Nowhere, Captain," replied Bert. "There is no need to hide her. She is on a courtesy visit to Falmouth."

Both men were now deeply confused but for totally differing reasons. Bert suddenly felt uneasy.

"Surely not. You are, aren't you? You are going to attack the British flagship."

The Commander said nothing for a few seconds and then questioned Bert again.

"So, how big is this HMS *Bosun*? Her tonnage?"

"Around one hundred thousand tons," said Bert, knowing that he was not divulging any state secrets; it was common knowledge that HMS *Bosun* was the world's most advanced and powerful warship.

"Closing in to nine hundred metres, Herr Kapitan," came a confident voice from a rating near to the Commander.

"Prepare torpedoes for firing. She will make a nice, juicy kill. Naval Command will forgive me for deviating from my orders to sink such a prize."

The Kapitan steeled himself for combat.

Bert put his head in his hands and wondered where these people who were waiting to wage war had actually come from.

"Can we three prisoners please leave your boat now, Captain, before this madness is the last thing we ever see in this life?" said Bert, sensing the end of the world, at least their world, was nigh.

"Nein," replied the Commander. "You stay put and witness your glorious warship being sent to the ocean floor. Our glorious German Navy will show your HMS *Bosun*, who is the boss in these waters."

Bert was flabbergasted.

"But she has weapons systems that will..."

He stopped in mid sentence. It was no use. The German Captain was determined to attack the British warship with this leaky museum exhibit that could well be their tomb.

"Well, that's the end of us all," said Bert. "And it will happen very quickly. I'm surprised they haven't spotted you in our waters already. Your weapons are mere peashooters compared with the fire power they have on that ship."

"We shall see," said the German Commander confidently overseeing battle stations.

Leutnant Hans Krieger had returned from checking on Herman.

"Crustacean report, Herr Kapitan. He is well, but still refuses to emerge from the pipes in the engine room. The Chief Engineer has no far not been able to tempt him out with the mackerel."

"Thank you, Hans," said the Commander. "Now make sure you check up on Herman every two hours on the hour. I do not want him running amok when we are facing such dangers. The last thing we need is the Herman on the loose."

Big Bert scratched his head.

"Who the hell is Herman?"

"You should know, big fisherman. You kindly donated him to us," said the Kapitan.

"Herr Kapitan," said Hans, puzzled. "What is a peashooter?"

The Kapitanleutnant wanted to place his regulation Navy sea boot up the Leutnant's jacksie. What was a peashooter? It was the only weapon that he would trust Hans to be in charge of. The man was a complete dunderhead. If he was a light bulb, he wouldn't even register as one watt.

UB-AF9 closed to eight hundred metres and the Kapitan gave the order to fire the number one torpedo, followed shortly by a second silver fish. He tracked their early progress through the periscope. Judging the warship's speed and course, he believed he had aimed true, and as accurately as his Swiss watch kept time. The two torpedoes sped towards the target through the choppy waters of the August day.

Big Bert broke into song.

"*Nearer, my God, to thee...*"

The Germans did not join in but laughed nervously.

On board HMS *Bosun*, which was cruising sedately down the coast to round Land's End, half of the ship's complement was on deck practising a ceremonial drill.

Up on the ship's bridge, a junior officer on watch alerted the Captain much as if he had just seen a Martian shopping in Woolworths for pick 'n' mix sweets.

"Captain! Torpedo approaching on our port side! A fucking torpedo is heading for us! It's followed by a second! We must take evasive action!"

An unimpressed Captain admonished the junior officer.

"Have you been on the rum, man? Get a grip of yourself. This is the north Cornish coast. There are no enemy submarines in these waters, and if there were, we would have no difficulty tracking them with our sophisticated defence systems on this ship."

The Captain decided to take a look anyway. Maybe the junior officer had mistaken dolphins for torpedoes. He almost dropped his binoculars in alarm and couldn't believe what he was seeing.

"What the fuckin'...? We are being attacked! Increase to full speed ahead!" he screamed to the engine room. "Two torpedoes are heading for us. Take evasive action. Now! Do it, man! Now!"

The action stations alarms sounded all over the huge ship, and up on the flight deck the men broke off what they were doing and rushed to battle stations, thinking to themselves that here was another bloody training drill. Many thoughts raced through the Captain's brain.

"What conventional submarine was operating in our coastal waters? And why was it attacking? Maybe it was one of ours attacking them on a surprise exercise to check their efficiency?"

Their state of the art defensive systems had completely failed on the Navy's newest and grandest ship. It was too late to take evasive action. Heads would roll over this, the Captain told himself.

It quickly became obvious that the huge ship couldn't evade the torpedoes and the first was about to hit amidships. The Captain steeled himself for the explosion.

It never came. Going over to the starboard side of the bridge, he saw the first torpedo appear to go right underneath HMS *Bosun*. How could it? It must have struck. There was no doubt about this because he could gauge the depth of the torpedo accurately, and it was less than the known draught of the ship.

The second torpedo appeared to follow the first right under the keel. Then, a few metres away to the ship's starboard stern, they exploded, sending a white plume of water skywards with two enormous bangs.

By now the warship was beginning to change course and was at full battle stations. A flurry of signals was exchanged between the vessel and the Fleet Commander and the Admiralty. What the hell was going on? Maybe a Soviet conventional rogue submarine had been responsible for the attack.

The signals continued to be exchanged between ship and shore, and the big warship began the hunt for the submarine that had attacked it.

Aboard UB-AF9, Kapitanleutnant Von Diesel was a deeply disappointed man when he became aware that the kill he'd expected hadn't happened. He was convinced the two torpedoes had struck their massive target.

"Dive, dive, dive!" he ordered. "We must leave this area immediately. They will make life very uncomfortable for us if we stay in these waters!"

The words were shouted with some disgust in his voice at what he saw as a failure, and he wondered how it had happened. The U-boat slithered away to safety after altering her course.

"Herr Kapitan, you never told me what a peashooter was," said Hans Krieger.

The Commander never answered, and if he had a peashooter, he would have stuck it up Hans where the sun didn't shine.

Chapter Three

HMS *Bosun* was ordered to proceed on her original course to Falmouth.

The frigate, HMS *Alison*, already in the Western Approaches, and the minesweeper, HMS *Morton*, arrived in the area later that night from duties elsewhere, to maintain a temporary presence in the area. A Nimrod reconnaissance aircraft from RAF St Mawgan in Cornwall also searched for the intruder but with no success.

The Commander of HMS *Bosun* was summoned to London when his ship docked during her five-day visit to Falmouth. The Admiralty wanted answers. The Captain didn't have any but had to come up with some plausible explanation. He was also livid that his ship's defences had failed so miserably. It shouldn't have happened. But, this being the Navy, they acted on facts and not stories better suited to schoolboy comics.

He could see his long term chances of becoming an Admiral of the Fleet diminishing. He knew how these things worked. Probably a psychiatric assessment and then a new posting to HMS *Oban*, an isolated concrete land ship located in the highlands of Scotland at some God-forsaken place.

It was a glorious August night on the north coast. The sun eventually sunk into the west like the clichéd big orange ball slowly disappearing below the horizon to signal a brand new day across the other side of the world.

Kapitanleutnant Von Diesel made final preparations for the execution of his top secret mission sanctioned on high from Berlin. The agent he was designated to pick up was, according to his orders on setting out from the Breton coast, in possession of detailed plans of Cornwall's entire north coast defences and troop strengths. This information would be vital to the German war effort.

He became aware of two smaller British warships scouring the coast, and they too seemed to be of a differing design from any ship in the German Navy. He didn't underestimate the British because they had superior looking ships to what he had been told by Naval Intelligence, but their submarine detection systems did not appear that good. The boat lay on the surface in the darkness, undisturbed, and watched the enemy's lights from a distance.

He thought about missing the prize of HMS *Bosun*. He was hugely disappointed, of course, not to claim her as a kill, but, on the other hand, he was glad that she had left the area. He decided that the British must be gearing up for a big naval battle out in the Atlantic somewhere. Well, they could get on with it and leave him to his business here off the Cornish coast.

Darkness fell and the land appeared to merge with the sea. The Commander watched as the two British vessels slowly disappeared over the horizon and patrolled elsewhere. This was good. He made sure all the crew remained in a state of readiness for sudden attack. There was still the menace of mines and maybe a British submarine in the area.

He discussed with his other officers the puzzle of why they had remained unhindered so far on their mission. Where were all the minefields and anti-submarine defences he knew existed along this coastline? It was all a deepening mystery.

"Have you also noticed, Herr Kapitan, there has been little merchant Navy shipping activity also? No signs of any merchant vessels," said Leutnant Spiegel.

The Kapitan thought about this and rubbed his beard.

"This is true, Franz, and I have no answers. Go below and see what the fat engineer is up to. See if he has any problems with the boat that he is aware of. Report back to me with a full account."

"Jawohl, Herr Kapitan."

The officer left the wardroom. The Kapitan looked at Hans.

"Leutnant Krieger, I have an important task for you when we go ashore in the early hours of the morning. Leutnant Spiegel knows his orders. He will be in charge of the leading inflatable dinghy with three chosen ratings. They will land on the beach at the isolated cove and pick up the agent, bringing him back here to the boat. I want you to command the second boat, the wooden skiff, which is prepared for launch. Four detailed ratings will go ashore under your command and ferry back the drums of fuel. While they do that, you have an equally important mission. You are to scour the rocks of the cove and collect a bucket of food for Herman. He must be hungry by now."

"Food, Herr Kapitan? So what food does he eat?"

"Look for the mussels clinging to the rocks, Hans. Knock some limpets also off the rocks with a large pebble. These creatures are stubborn, just like the fräuleins in the brothels of Hamburg, and drive a hard bargain. They will not shift unless you knock them off their perches very hard. Collect up a big bucketful, enough to keep Herman happy for a while, ja? And, Hans..."

"Yes, Herr Kapitan?"

"Collect also a fresh bucket of sea water. Herman's water supply must be stagnant by now. We will give him some fresh water. Sea water that is, Hans, you understand?"

The Kapitan knew that Hans had never been in a brothel in Hamburg in his life and wouldn't know what to do if he ever was. Keeping him occupied with something away from the mission, as such, would keep him out of mischief. Surely even Hans Krieger couldn't cause much trouble on a Cornish beach at 0200 hours on a warm August night.

"Can I leave that with you, Hans? I am relying on you, as is Herman, who has become a very important member of this crew."

The young Leutnant understood his duties and acknowledged his superior officer.

Meanwhile, Herman flexed his claws and hissed and acted menacingly towards any slight movement in his direction. The Chief Engineer could eat the mackerel himself, he decided. The man was so fat it looked like he'd already eaten a shoal for his last meal. Herman wondered how the man had ever managed to get out through the submarine hatches.

Everything was ready for the mission to go ahead. Lying almost four miles off the coast, the Commander was up on the conning tower looking landwards. Leutnant Franz Spiegel joined him. Then Von Diesel spoke as he breathed in the fresh sea air.

"Such a beautiful night, Franz. Look at all the stars up in the sky. It is said that there is one for each of us."

Franz looked skywards.

"That one is mine, Herr Kapitan."

Franz pointed up to a bright star to the west.

"Franz, take a look towards land. Does not something strike you as being a little bit strange?"

The Leutnant looked landwards.

"Why, lights, Herr Kapitan. That is the fishing town of Porth Branven, ja? Yet she is lit up like the St Nicholas tree in the middle of Berlin before the war started. Along the coast, Herr Kapitan, I can see other lights also. What are these fools playing at, Herr Kapitan? What happened to the blackout? It is as if they are inviting our glorious Luftwaffe to find them in the middle of the night."

The Kapitan had been observing the shore closely.

"This is true, Franz, but these British cannot possibly be as stupid as this. They must have a plan up their sleeves to invite our bombers to attack. A trap of some sort. Maybe they have some other secret weapon that we know nothing about. Maybe our intelligence is not as good as we think it is. Remember, we knew nothing about that huge warship or the design of that fishing smack."

The Kapitan paused and rubbed his bristly beard, which had collected salt from the sea air.

"We will find out the truth when you pick up the agent from the beach, Franz."

He continued to scan the land through binoculars.

"I know these Cornish, Franz, so be careful. The ones I have met are far from stupid, but they are completely untrustworthy, and some of them would steal your auntie's ball bearings from her powder bag. And when you land on the beach, make sure you keep an eye on that Leutnant Krieger. I set him the task of providing food for Herman, so he should keep out of trouble."

"Jawohl, mein Kapitan," answered the junior officer.

UB-AF9 began to move towards its offshore rendezvous position, where it was to set off and pick up the boats again. It was a position just to the west of Porth Branven, a sheltered and hidden spot under some three-hundred-foot cliffs.

The beach was a small, inaccessible cove, except to those who knew how to get down to its glorious sands.

Exploring old mine workings before the war had commenced with agents already in Cornwall, the Germans had managed to set up a secret small fuel dump hidden away in deep caves in the cliffs.

An access raise, or near vertical tunnel, dropped all the way from the surface most of the way down to the beach and it was lined with

32

rusted old ladder ways. Its entrance on the top of the cliffs had been concealed quite cleverly.

Kapitanleutnant Von Diesel had made two successful pick-ups here in the past couple of years, so felt confident that tonight's mission would also be a success. He did not envisage any problems.

It was 0130 hours on the morning of 7th August 1941, a Thursday. The U-boat reached its position offshore, avoiding the dangerous reef that lay in wait across most of the cove, and which had torn the guts out of many an unknowing and hapless vessel in the past.

The Kapitan prayed that the good weather would hold for a bit longer. So far Mother Nature had been kind to him, and long may it continue. He watched carefully as the lights of what seemed to be three small trawlers moved slowly back towards port from their fishing grounds off The Scillies.

The trawlers would have to be ignored. They were not too important to chase when this mission was much more vital for the war effort.

The prisoners were restless and cramped. They had been fed and given regular drinks of coffee. All they could do was snatch sleep and wait whilst keeping a low profile, while their captors scurried about this dripping, claustrophobic tin can with engines.

The whole sub stank of diesel fumes, oil and sweat, and was a potential death trap. So much depended on secure brass fittings and nuts and bolts, and the hope that the engineer knew what he was doing. Plus, of course, there were all the usual dangers associated with the sea, and, as a bonus, they had these lunatics re-enacting the war in their submariner uniforms. It was best, the captives decided, to keep a low profile and to hope they got out of this weird mess alive.

John Thomas had harboured thoughts of joining the Navy, but he had now changed his mind.

These Germans, thought Big Bert quietly to himself, were up to something. They were definitely up to something. The prisoners were powerless to find out what that was, incarcerated in their small metal lock-up.

"It is just like the night that the *Titanic* sank, Herr Kapitan," said Hans Krieger, breathing in the early morning air. "A lovely starry, starry night but not half so cold."

The Kapitan shook his head in silence. After a pause, he spoke.

"Hans, from this moment on, you are to maintain silence. When you reach the beach at the cove, be careful to only keep the chatter down to essential minimum. Remember that the sounds they travel in the night air and darkness."

Hans went silent and still wondered what a peashooter was.

The two designated crews quickly and efficiently launched the boats off the side of the submarine, which rolled gently in the waves, a quarter of a mile off the coast.

Leutnant Franz Spiegel, in charge of the operation, remembered his orders. They were to land, pick up the waiting agent and not delay in getting him back to the submarine. The second party would load two drums of diesel and return to the submarine with due speed also. They would make four trips in all before dawn broke. The skiff, which was more stable and much easier to row, would hold the drums no problem. If they encountered resistance, they were armed and were to return fire and get back to their vessel in haste. They would wait one hour for the agent and if he did not show, then there was obviously a problem and they would leave, and the diesel refuel operation would cease at that point with however much fuel they had managed to collect.

In the fishing town of Porth Branven, the town council had been burning the midnight oil preparing for the big day tomorrow. They all needed their beds badly after meticulous planning and hard work, which had taken weeks, and they were all determined that their German visitors would be given a warm welcome. It would be a welcome that their hosts from across the North Sea would never forget. Be they young, old or in between, the residents of, and visitors to, Porth Branven were in for a treat of Cornish proportions. They really knew how to do celebrations in this town in West Cornwall.

The Mayor, a big, jolly fellow called Roger (and Jolly Roger to the locals) was also at the meeting. He wondered where his wife, Molly, some years younger than himself, had got to. She was one of the

Chief organisers and had worked hard on these forthcoming celebrations. However, tonight she had been conspicuous by her absence. Jolly Roger sighed and forgave her. After all, she had put a great deal of effort into this event to be held all tomorrow; or today, he told himself, looking at the ancient clock on the wall of The People's Rooms in the main street.

Strangely missing from the meeting that night was Jake Harvey, who had organised the fireworks for the occasion. Now where was he tonight?

Jolly Roger and the town council leader wound down the meeting and the self-appointed congratulators sloped off into the night. Tomorrow, or rather today, would be the longest in the fishing port's calendar.

"Are the fireworks secure?" enquired Jolly Roger as he walked the short distance to his harbour side cottage.

A councillor walking home with him answered.

"Yes, Roger, that's all sorted. Jake Harvey organised it all and has given them to Al at the garage for storage in his MOT bay. They're safe as houses at Al's garage, alongside all his old oil and diesel drums, and not a million miles away from the forecourt, under which are stored the petrol and diesel tanks. Yes, they are safe enough there; all half a ton of them. Al's as good as gold and will look after them. Funny though, Jake buggering off tonight."

Roger had been thinking that as well. He made it home and wondered if Big Bert and the lads had had a good fishing trip to the west of the Scillies. They were due back tomorrow.. Roger remembered that the last time Bert fished those grounds, he had almost sunk the boat under the enormous weight of fish caught.

Upon entering his kitchen, the Mayor switched on the light and saw the note on the table. Now, where was Molly? He picked up the note and read her neat writing.

Dear Roger,

I have gone over to meet Alice in Truro for a catch up and drink. Staying with her overnight and will be back early tomorrow morning in plenty of time for the big day's celebrations.

There's a sandwich in the fridge.

Love you,
Molly XX

Roger ate his sandwich and drank a mug of hot cocoa before letting his dog out for a pee. The hound was extremely grateful and bursting at the seams. He and Roger settled down for the rest of the night.

The boats had left the UB-AF9, slipping away silently with the darkened coast invitingly clear in the near distance. The high cliffs looked foreboding. In the sky above, to the west, Franz Spiegel's special star in the sky kept a bright watchful eye over him. The star's close companions were out in support on what was a glorious night by any standards.

The leading boat approached cautiously and rode the gentle surf as it swept the flimsy inflatable in between the jagged rocks that acted like protecting teeth to the beach.

The ocean made beautiful whooshing sounds as its waves swept up the sands of the cove. The bladder wrack and limpets sighed with renewed vigour as they were refreshed by the incoming tide once more.

The two sailors aboard paddled cautiously and skilfully manoeuvred their way on to the beach. Leutnant Spiegel steadied his craft up and onto the sand. Leutnant Krieger followed in the light wooden skiff.

The sailors not paddling in his boat kept a careful watch and their fingers on the triggers of their weapons. The men involved in this mission were all tense and fearful that something unpleasant might happen at any moment. They were prepared as best they could be. More than one stomach groaned in unwanted protest. Fear of the unexpected could cause a dread all of its own making.

They got ashore using the surge of the turning tide, negotiated carefully in between the guarding rocks and beached the skiff alongside the inflatable.

The moon retreated temporarily behind some clouds, which violated the starry sky, but which came as a relief to Kapitanleutnant

Von Diesel back on board the UB-AF9. He wished the night would become cloudy to make it safer for the men ashore.

Leutnant Krieger felt his heavy boots making virgin imprints on the golden sand, which looked white in the darkness.

The two boats were secured and the men went about their respective business.

Leutnant Krieger's eyes had adjusted to the dark and he set about scouring the nearby rocks glistening with bladder wrack and other weed for the limpets he had been ordered to collect. He couldn't see any mussels at the moment, but there were limpets aplenty. Picking up a hand-sized white pebble, he proceeded to hack the limpets unceremoniously off the jagged rocks. They protested with resistance, not used to being disturbed, and sighed as they were made homeless.

The other sailors made their way up to the darkened caves and old mine workings under the cliffs, breathing quietly and being alert to any sudden danger that presented itself. They were probably the only Germans who were ashore on the British mainland at this time in the war.

At The Bluebells Residential Home, Major Beere couldn't sleep. No-one had believed his story about the U-boat sinking Bert's boat, taking him and his crew prisoner and seizing his catch. He knew what he had seen. The world was going mad and he felt like he was on a child's roundabout going more and more quickly until he was spun off. It was only a question of when. He wasn't too keen on all of this friendship nonsense, but, being a gentleman, he would be polite tomorrow, if called on to be so.

He took a swig from his secret bottle of the hard stuff he kept secreted under his bed away from Matron. He knew though that it would be extremely difficult for him to be civil tomorrow, seeing how he knew full well about these people's previous generations and their behaviour. He vowed to do his best. It only ate into a person to harbour grudges.

The Major looked at his watch. It was just after 2AM. It was no use. He just didn't feel tired. All was quiet. He wondered whether the Countess was awake as well. He dressed quickly and made his way quietly down the corridor on the ground floor and knocked gently on her door.

"Countess Olga, are you awake?"

The Major waited patiently for a few seconds outside the door and then it opened slowly.

He was greeted by the Countess Olga Trovanovich, who was of unknown age but very elderly. However, she was the most sprightly old lady the Major had ever known, and had some fight in her. She was a real Russian-born lady who called herself the Countess, and everybody knew her as such. Whether she was or not, nobody knew for sure. She told tales of how she was a small child when the Bolsheviks came. Countess Olga was a good friend of the Major, and one of The Bluebells' great characters. She spoke softly.

"What is it, Major? Do you wish for me to beat you at cards again?"

"No, dear lady," replied the Major, smiling. "How would you like to have some real fun, Olga? An early morning adventure, just the two of us. Better bring something for us to sit down on."

The Countess Olga was always up for something that broke up the dreary routine of the residential home. The Major and she had been residents and friends for years and often took tea together in the afternoon at The Atlantic Tea Rooms And Gift Shop.

"Let me slip into something warm," she said with her distinctive Russian lilt.

"I'll wait for you in my room," said the Major before disappearing back down the corridor.

All was quiet in the home and no-one stirred. A few minutes later, the Countess knocked gently and entered the Major's room, which was very tidy and ordered. He led her over to the big wooden sash window. Despite being an elderly man, he could get in and out of the window with no problems, and out into the garden.

"Here is your telescope, Major," said the Countess, accepting his hand to aid her on getting through the open window.

They stepped down onto the early morning grass covered in dew. The Major quietly lowered the window down and placed a wedge of an old fir cone under the wood to stop it shutting completely. The garden was a mass of bushes and ordered shrubs, and no-one was around.

"Don't worry, old girl," said the Major, leading the way. "If we get cold, I have my hip flask."

His eyes twinkled as if he was a naughty boy being caught having a midnight bean feast in the dorm of his old public school.

"I too have my flask also," said the Countess, feeling for the flask through her coat.

"I bet I know what's inside it," said the Major, smiling. "Vodka?"

Olga just smiled and the pair walked quietly away through the garden and out onto the deserted road beyond. When they had reached the path that wended its way through short scrub up to the top of the cliffs to the west of the cove, Olga stopped for breath.

"The Matron, Major, won't she be missing us?"

Major Beere caught his breath as well.

"That miserable old bag. I know her well and she's a real creature of habit like me. Know your enemy, Olga. Once she retires for the night, she always sleeps in that back room behind her office with the help of that big bottle of vodka she buys daily from the off-licence. She will be well gone now. Her assistant only ever checks residents if they ring the bell for attention. Once she does her rounds at eleven o' clock, she doesn't come around until 6AM."

"Or unless there is a fire," said Olga.

"Well, let's pray there is no fire then," replied the Major. "Come on, let's have ourselves an early morning walk up on the cliffs. Look at the stars in the sky. Makes you glad to be alive."

"It certainly does," said Countess Olga, appreciating the beauty. "It reminds me of the skies over Russia when I was little, before the Bolsheviks came."

The Major looked at his luminous watch dial and mentally calculated how long they could stay out for what he had in mind, and made sure they could get back in good time before The Bluebells' day staff arrived in the morning.

They reached a spot a little later that was one of the Major's favourites, but usually for his slightly later on early morning constitutional.

"Here we are, Countess. Put down your blanket and make yourself comfortable while I set up the telescope."

He went about this and breathed in the fresh morning air. It was surprisingly mild for the time of the morning. All they could hear was the background rushing noise of the sea, and a lone taxi arriving in Porth Branven. The vehicle dropped off its passenger amidst much slamming of doors, and then roared off. All was quiet once more.

"Come and have a look through the telescope and tell me what you can see. I might have to focus it for you because your eyesight is different from mine."

The Countess looked through the glass while Major Beere took a swig from his hip flask. He offered it first to Olga, but she declined, saying, "Maybe later, Major, dear boy. After I have finished off my ration of vodka."

"So what can you see, Olga?" repeated the Major.

The Countess scanned the sea and then looked closer, down at the beach. She steadied the old brass instrument as the moon threw down silvery light, casting shadows on the sand far below where the rocks jutted out to meet the water.

"I see two, no, maybe three men down there on the beach. How did they get down there, Major? And what are they doing at this time of the morning?"

The Countess looked puzzled, looked at the Major, and then back down through the telescope to the beach. She allowed Major Beere to see for himself. He gasped.

"By Jove, you are right, old girl!"

He studied the beach carefully. He couldn't pick out Leutnant Krieger, who was hidden by shadows of the cliff cast over him, but he could clearly make out the group of men in uniforms who stood on the sand nearby, and their two boats. He studied them for a few long seconds.

"Are they smugglers, Major? Is that why you have brought me up here, to see them land their contraband on the beach below? Maybe they will let us have some spirits from the continent cheap if we promise not to tell the police and the revenue men."

"They are not smugglers, Olga, but they are up to no good. I saw them yesterday morning. They are German sailors!"

"Are you sure they are not the Bolsheviks coming for me?" said Olga, having a short flashback amidst early morning confusion.

"No, they are definitely Jerries," said the Major. "By Gad, they are, madam!"

The Major trained the telescope a little way out to sea and honed in on a darkened shape that, even in the night, was distinctive, its

40

conning tower breaking the sleek form of its half submerged hull. The sea lapped around her bows.

"And there's that bally U-boat of theirs. Can't make out from here what her identification number is, and she doesn't look modern. That Matron doubted my sanity yesterday. I knew I had seen a German U-boat. I wonder what happened to Bert and his two crew. Maybe the ghastly blighters murdered them and dumped them at sea."

The Major scanned the beach again.

"Bert?" said Olga, her mind becoming lucid again. "Do you mean that lovely Big Bert who sometimes fetches the fresh fish he catches from his boat?"

"The same Bert," replied Major Beere.

The Countess thought about the situation for a few seconds and then became overcome with emotion.

"Germans? The Bosch? I'll remind them of Stalingrad and our glorious Red Army!"

She shook her frail fist in anger. Knowing about the visit of the Germans later that day had only fuelled her imagination and confused her some more. She took a big shot of vodka from her hip flask and offered the Major some. He accepted.

Down on the beach, Leutnant Spiegel was a worried man. He kept his weapon close to him and scanned the darkened cove very cautiously. A rating came up to him.

"Herr Leutnant, we have searched the caves and there is no sign of the fuel dump. The Kapitan must have been mistaken or got the wrong cove. And there is no sign of the agent also."

The Leutnant decided to look for himself and the small party disappeared once more up into the caves under the cliffs, and only then shone their torches around. The wet, dripping caves were black in the early morning and very cold. The rating pointed out the iron ladder way that stretched upwards.

"We have climbed it, Herr Leutnant, but it appears to be blocked near the top. That is all there is here. No sign of any fuel drums; in fact, nothing."

Leutnant Krieger was busy filling up his bucket with limpets and had even managed to find a few clumps of decent sized mussels, which proved difficult to twist off the rocks. He let out a yelp of pain as a disturbed small shore crab nipped him on the finger.

A few feet away from him, around on the other side of the rock formation, the sounds muffled from Krieger's ears by the sound of sea, were unmistakeable.

"Yes! Oh, yes! More, more! Shove it in deeper, Jake! Harder! Oh!"

The woman underneath the man was in the throes of passion as he humped away between her spread-eagled legs, thrusting and groaning for all his worth. Their sounds were drowned out by the waves rushing into the tiny cove.

Jake suddenly stopped in mid stream and placed a firm hand over Molly's mouth and whispered to her.

"Did you hear that, Molly? I heard someone; I'm sure I did. We are not alone down here."

The words chilled the woman, Molly, as Jake got up, made himself half decent and looked around.

Molly too got up and wiped her bottom clean of wet, gritty sand with a tissue brought for the purpose. She made herself decent too and couldn't help herself breathing too heavily.

"You... you don't think...? No. Roger?"

Jake continued to look around.

"Roger? I don't think so. He's too fat to ever get down here. He'll be tucked up in bed now, dreaming of strong German lager and ringing his bell, shouting, 'Oyez! Oyez!'; a bit like what you were saying just now!"

Molly laughed at the joke but was mortified that someone might have seen them together, and down here of all places.

The pair crept cautiously around the edge of the rocks and then quietly made their way further back to some darker rocks hidden under the towering cliffs. From there they could make out the lone figure standing on the rocks just a few feet away from where they had been going at it so passionately with the old in-out.

Jake looked at Molly and scratched his head. What they witnessed was unmistakable.

Here was a man in a sailor's uniform, possibly an officer, and he appeared to be collecting limpets and mussels from the rocks. That was hard to believe. Even harder to believe would have been the reason why he was doing it, not that they would ever find that out.

The pair remained still and quiet in their darkened hideaway. Then they saw the group of sailors emerging from the larger cave on the other side of those rocks. They could make out their distinctive figures in the moonlight, which threw down tall black shadows, making them look like ghosts that had just come from the sea.

"It is no use, Herr Leutnant," said the leading rating. "There definitely is no fuel and no agent."

Annoyed, the Leutnant took the decision to leave.

"Right, men, we are leaving here right now. We have spent far too long at this place. We are wasting our precious time."

They made their way back to their two boats.

"Hey, wait for me," said Leutnant Krieger, clutching his precious pail and almost spilling the whole contents back onto the slippery rocks as he followed.

His pail was half full and survived against the odds, and he rejoined the main party. He got into the stern of the skiff with his cargo.

"They are leaving," said the Major. "Take a look. Their boats are heading back to the U-boat out there off Spurdog Point. What have they been up to down there? The blighters!"

The boats began to move through the tricky surf and Krieger got a face full of sea water for his troubles. He filled his second bucket up with fresh sea water and steadied the two cargoes with his boots as his men rowed away out towards the submarine.

Jake and Molly emerged from their hiding place and watched them leave, hidden from the Germans' view by the darkened mass of the high cliffs.

"Well, how strange," said Jake. "They sounded like Germans. Maybe it's some kind of film being made, or something to do with the celebrations later today. Never mind, Molly, whoever they were, they have buggered off now and we are alone once more. And we have some unfinished business."

He nudged her ear and whispered an obscenity into it.

"Oh, Jake, I couldn't possibly do that again when..."

"So that's a yes then?" he said, leading her by the hand as she protested half-heartedly.

They got back down onto the sand once more and, after removing their lower garments, got on with it like hammer and tongs, their cries being applauded by the music made by the sea orchestra in the background, its foamy white fingers stretching up and almost touching them, and sounding so much closer in the moonlight.

Up on the cliff top, the Major scanned the Germans in their boats, making steady progress back out to their submarine.

"What are they up to now, Major?" asked the Countess.

The Major coughed and needed a large swig of fortifying drink from his hip flask, plus some more vodka from Olga for good measure.

"Oh, nothing, old thing. Nothing that you would wish to see, dear girl. They have left two of them down there and they are doing some kind of night time exercise, the like of which I haven't seen for donkey's years."

The Major picked up his telescope.

"I think we had better be making tracks, Countess. It is getting a bit chilly now."

The Countess agreed and they packed up to leave.

A little later, when Jake and Molly had completed their tryst, they made their way home, taking another route up from the cove, one which only a few knew about.

Jake mentally thanked the Cornish miners of old for providing the numerous tracks and tunnels they had hewed out of the hard rock of the imposing and not-for-the-faint-hearted cliffs.

By then, the Countess and the Major had sneaked back to their rooms at The Bluebells.

Molly spent the rest of the night at Jake's, and at breakfast time, 'arrived back from Truro by taxi'.

Roger slept soundly all night in blissful ignorance of the events that took place in the sleepy Cornish fishing hamlet where nothing much ever happened.

Chapter Four

The leading boat, the rubber inflatable dinghy, made its way steadily towards its mother boat. The skiff behind seemed to be dragging its heels in the current.

Leutnant Krieger felt a sudden lurch and wondered if the shallow keel of the skiff had scraped a submerged rock or hit some underwater obstruction. The flimsy craft was definitely dragging something. Krieger decided it was probably a big clump of floating seaweed that had tangled itself around the tiller. The crew struggled to row against the obstruction and the current.

The leading boat made it alongside the U-boat where the boarding party was relieved to be back aboard hard metal. They were helped aboard by other ratings. The occupants were soon on the firm, if slippery, deck and the Kapitan ordered that the boat remain secured to the hull of the U-boat. He spoke the obvious.

"Where is the agent, Leutnant Spiegel? He is not with you. Is he in the other boat with Leutnant Krieger?"

"Nein," replied Leutnant Spiegel, steeling himself.

He believed the Kapitan would not be best pleased that the mission had to be aborted. He briefly explained to him what had happened. The Kapitan was surprisingly calm.

"Something is very wrong here, Franz. That cove is the right one, I can assure you. I know it from my last visit here on board a sister vessel, and from my time spent here in Cornwall before the war. I took a fräulein named Molly there once."

The Kapitan looked out to the second boat.

"Why is that idiot, Krieger, taking so long to get his boat here, Franz?"

They both looked to where the skiff gradually drew closer to the U-boat, obviously making heavy weather of it.

When it did dock against the U-boat hull, ratings helped to moor the skiff and helped Leutnant Krieger out with his two metal buckets, one slopping sea water around as he tried to keep his balance and not spill any.

Kapitanleutnant Von Diesel had noticed that the Leutnant had brought the full bucket of sea water all the way over from the cove when he could have filled the bucket up here and saved himself the trouble.

"Dummkopf," he said under his breath. "The lentil brain only had to dip the bucket into the water."

He was pleased however that the Leutnant had brought Herman a bucket full of fresh nourishment that would surely entice him from under the pipes in the engine room.

The Kapitan gave the order for the two buckets to be taken down to the engine room and handed over to the Chief Engineer.

"Right, men, get the skiff out of the water and stowed away. We need to get out of here quickly. We must not hang around in these waters any longer than necessary. Our mission has been aborted. Hans, why did the boat seem to labour in the water?"

"Mein Kapitan, I believe the tiller got caught up by the big clump of seaweed."

The ratings dragged the boat from the water but met resistance. They discovered that a rusted chain had wedged itself between the tiller and the boat and would need to be cut free. There was a loud clang under the water's surface. Worried seamen believed they knew exactly what it was. The chain was attached to a mine. It bumped again, making the same sound.

"Minen!" said the Kapitan, placing his fingers in his ears.

The mine didn't go off, much to his instant relief, but the danger was still present. The thing could go off at any second.

"Hans, you dummkopf! You have dragged a mine with the boat and brought it back to this vessel. It could go off at any time."

Leutnant Spiegel, alert to the danger, had acted immediately and sent orders to the engine room for cutting equipment to be brought up on deck.

The sweating rating arrived on deck and proceeded to free the chain from the skiff. The crew on deck shut their eyes for a few seconds while he worked away. Then the chain parted and the mine dropped away. These were variable waters in depth, and all they could hope for was that the mine, when striking the sea bed, didn't go off. It hit the hull once more on the way down without exploding.

The Kapitan breathed a huge sigh of relief.

"I need to go below and change my underwear, Herr Kapitan," said Leutnant Krieger.

The Kapitan said nothing and ordered the submarine to leave these waters immediately after the prisoners were released. He still had visions of the mine exploding underneath his vessel.

Kapitanleutnant Von Diesel ordered the prisoners to be brought on to the deck.

"What is that horrible smell?" said Big Bert, covering his nose with his hand as they passed by Leutnant Krieger's curtained off bunk, where he was getting changed.

Then a shriek echoed right through the vessel, as the crab from the shore had hitched a lift in Krieger's uniform and nipped him again for good measure.

Up on the conning tower the Kapitan had heard the noise.

"What is that idiot, Krieger, doing now? He will alert the enemy with his screams."

The prisoners were glad to be able to stretch their legs and climb up out of the steel coffin into the clear, fresh night air. They made their way, under armed guard, out on to the deck.

"I guess this is the parting of the ways, gentlemen," said the Kapitan from the top of the conning tower.

The prisoners drew in deep breaths and were then scared, particularly John Thomas, whose legs almost buckled as he trembled. Big Bert held him together like a father figure and supported him.

"Have courage, lad," said Bert as he looked up at the German. "I suppose this is where you are going to shoot us, Kapitan."

There was a short pause of silence. Von Diesel waved his arm aloft.

"We Germans are not pirates or savages, Herr Kapitan. There is the rubber boat with the paddles. Get in it and go with some haste unless, of course, you wish to be blown up by your own British mine, which sits a few feet below our keel. Maybe when this war is over, we can have a drink together in The Anchor Inn, ja? And no hard feelings over the loss of your boat. These things are unpleasant, but they happen in war. Now go before I change my mind!"

A rating helped the men aboard the dinghy with the aid of an extended boat hook. They almost tipped it up as they got into it. The German sailor untied the mooring rope and gave them a gentle shove away from the hull of the U-boat. They began to slowly drift away into the night on the bobbing sea.

"Keep the town lights in your vision, Herr Kapitan, and you will be OK and on the shore within the hour. Good luck and God speed. Auf Wiedersehen, my British friends."

The Kapitan gave the order for the sub to move away on the surface when the men in the dinghy had reached a safe distance. He then ordered his boat to dive. He wanted to be far away from that mine. Where there was one mine, there were probably many more.

As the small dinghy drifted with the current, John Thomas sat while the two older men paddled. They all had a suspicion that they had been tricked, and that the Germans would fire on them in the water. They wouldn't want anybody alive to witness what they were up to. They were definitely not part of a war film and those guns were for real. They tensed themselves for the gunfire to commence. It didn't. The German Kapitan was as good as his word; an honourable man in that respect.

"Fuckin' Germans fighting their own private war," said Bert in disgust. "They sunk my fuckin' boat and they want to have a drink with me in The Anchor, and with no hard feelings!"

"How does he know The Anchor?" asked Arthur Pengelly, paddling steadily in rhythm with Bert. "He talked as if he had been there. What has gone on out here tonight, Bert? This is like a nightmare and we have just been part of it."

"With a difference," said Bert. "My boat's on the bottom of the sea and we are awake. I suppose it *was* a nightmare, but not the usual one. C'mon, keep paddling. We need to get ashore as quickly as possible and report those German pirates to the authorities."

"Who do we report them to, Bert?" asked John Thomas.

"I dunno," was the reply. "The police? The coastguard? The Navy? Come on, paddle harder, Arthur. We are drifting with the current over to Spurdog Point."

The lights of Porth Branven appeared to be drifting away to the east.

"What was that smell when they freed us?" said Bert, who was remembering it all too well. "Anybody would think somebody had shit themselves."

"Well, I nearly did when they pointed those guns at us," said Arthur.

John Thomas said nothing. They would never know how close he had come to crapping himself as well. He looked out to sea. There was no sign of the U-boat.

"And what was all that stuff about a mine under the U-boat? Do you think he was serious?"

Bert didn't know what to think. He knew it was every fisherman's nightmare to drag up a mine.

"Who was Herman?" asked John Thomas.

The two other men looked at each other as they paddled towards land.

"Herman? Why, he's the big lobster they stole from us. Appropriate, I suppose - Herman the German."

Kapitanleutnant Von Diesel and his crew did not leave the Cornish coast that morning. A minor problem in the engine room needed some repairs.

The duty watch kept a close eye out for enemy vessels or aircraft, but the early morning hours were deathly quiet.

"I have some good news and some bad news," said the Chief Engineer, covered in oil and sweating profusely.

"So what is the bad news?" asked the Kapitan.

"The bad news, Herr Kapitan, is that we have a small problem in the engine room with the electrics. It is fixable, but it will take a little time."

"And the good news?" asked the Kapitan.

"The good news, Herr Kapitan, is that the crustacean is coming out of his hiding place and is eating the mussels and the limpets. I chucked the bucket of fresh sea water on him and he is quite happy down there with me and the other seamen. I will make sure that the Kapitan has him for tea later."

Von Diesel was horrified.

"I will keel haul any man who harms an inch of his shell. Herman is now a valuable member of the crew. He is our lucky mascot, and no harm is to come to him. Do you understand, Fritz?"

"Jawohl, Herr Kapitan," said the Chief Engineer, completely baffled by the Kapitan's decision.

The Chief Engineer suddenly turned up his nose.

"What is that awful smell?"

Leutnant Hans Krieger went quietly about his duties. He had cleaned himself up and changed his uniform, but his personal bunk still had the pervasive smell hovering around.

The Chief Engineer went back down below deck to see what Herman was up to.

"Herman must have shit himself," he said, shaking his big, oily head as he disappeared below, clutching a big spanner tightly.

With that idiot, Krieger, aboard, it would seem that the Kapitan was adopting a similar position, he thought. This boat was becoming a madhouse. What would German Naval Command make of all this? A U-boat with a pet lobster aboard.

The Chief went back amidst the heavy diesel fumes to sort out the problem in the engine room.

Kapitanleutnant Von Diesel ordered the crew on watch to be extra vigilant to the danger of enemy activity because, until the Chief Engineer did his repairs, they were going nowhere, and dawn would be breaking soon. He summoned his officers to the wardroom. He poured them all a small tot of German spirit.

"Gentlemen, you are all aware of our dilemma. We have no contact with anyone and we have a technical problem in the engine room. Our mission has had to be aborted and we have six torpedoes and some deck gun ammunition left. I am proposing we do not waste these torpedoes, but when we get going again, we look for some merchant shipping to sink. That way, we won't return home empty handed, ja?"

The three men in the black dinghy had travelled westwards with the current, and the cliffs loomed large ahead, menacing and foreboding in the early morning.

The paddlers put in extra effort and, gradually, the small boat was rocked by the incoming surf that surged into the deserted isolated cove. Their boat almost overturned, but they managed to reach the shore just in time to see the inflatable lose air as it got ripped on the jagged rocks that had provided Herman's dinner. The boat was a black mass of sinking rubber.

The three waded through the last few feet of the white surf and up onto the sand.

"So, how do we make our way up there? Those cliffs are fuckin' massive," said Big Bert, looking up.

The moon came back out to greet them.

"I know a way up to the top," said John Thomas, beckoning them with this hand.

"So, the lad is not completely useless," thought Bert.

The two older men followed John Thomas up the beach and then Bert stopped them.

"Look, you two. There are fresh boot imprints here. So, it's obvious we are not the only ones stomping around here tonight. There are loads of them, and in pairs. I reckon these are German boots. So our pirate friends have been here as well."

"Have they got little swastikas on their boot treads?" said John Thomas.

They ignored him.

"Now, I wonder why there are loads of boot imprints here."

Big Bert was mystified.

That wasn't the only discovery they made on that beach. Arthur suddenly stooped and picked up the item of clothing and examined it closely.

"I'd recognise these anywhere. These knickers belong to Molly! Now, what was she doing here tonight, and all those boot prints?"

Big Bert kept quiet. He also recognised the pair of Molly's knickers, with their distinctive little heart patterns on them. He should do, because he had removed them several times in the past. Maybe not down here but in other places where they had managed to sneak off together.

When that idiot of a Mayor she called her husband wasn't around, he was too busy dressing up, ringing his bell and shouting, "Oyez! Oyez!" to largely disinterested and amused public. And he was also a Morris man, which put him on a par with a rusty old Hillman Imp that wouldn't start in the morning.

If Molly fancied some German bratwurst, then why couldn't she wait until later that day when the celebrations commenced?

Chapter Five

Dawn was breaking off the Cornish coast. It was going to be a beautiful day. The weather was holding, much to the relief of all concerned.

HMS *Bosun* was moored in the Carrick Roads off Falmouth, being too large to get into the docks, while her skipper had travelled overnight to London after being summoned to the Admiralty. They demanded explanations for the puzzling and alarming signals he had sent them the previous day from the pride of the fleet.

They had sent Carrington, their best man in Naval Intelligence, down to Cornwall to see what was going on. The Captain of HMS *Bosun* was one of the most experienced in the Navy. Was he losing his marbles? Or was something more sinister afoot?

It had been noticeable lately that many big Soviet Bloc factory ships bristling with listening devices had also moored off Falmouth, and their crews visited the town and surrounding area in numbers.

Maybe the Eastern Bloc had sent spies from East Germany to mingle amongst Porth Branven's guests at the celebrations planned for later that day.

Jolly Roger, the Mayor, and a small band of helpers were up early and checking everything with last minute precision. The distinctive black, red and gold German flag hung everywhere with the same coloured bunting adorning lamp posts and the main street. German greeting signs were also in abundance. Roger made sure that the copious supplies of German lager and food were OK at The People's Rooms.

It seemed like the good people of Porth Branven had entered into the spirit of the occasion and most had done their bit to give their guests a grand welcome for the twinning ceremony.

Roger told himself he looked good in his lederhosen, and he couldn't wait to see Molly dressed up in German traditional costume with her hair in pigtails and her ample bosoms being half displayed in those halter type dresses that he imagined all German fräuleins wore when they served up large glasses of beer.

Molly had arrived home by taxi not long ago. She'd kept her word and had got home nice and early for the celebrations. She looked like she'd had a damned good night out with her friend in Truro. Roger wondered why there was sand everywhere. She explained that she'd gone for an early morning stroll on the beach before coming into the house. His Molly was a woman that most people liked.

Roger hoped the younger folk of the town would keep the sauerkraut jokes down to a minimum when their guests, who had been staying overnight in Penzance, arrived in their coaches later in the morning.

Some folk had gone a bit overboard by painting kerbstones black, red and gold in honour of their guests. Roger had parked his VW Beetle outside The People's Rooms in a display to make their guests from across the North Sea feel really at home.

Some time later, Bert and his crew reached home, tired, cold and annoyed.

"Bloody Germans," scowled Bert as he passed Roger on the way home. "I hope I never set eyes on them ever again."

"That's not the spirit we should encourage," said Roger. "We are all friends now. This is meant to be a day of celebration."

Bert let forth a stream of obscenities. Roger looked down towards the harbour to where *The Two Inbred Sisters* was usually moored.

"So where's the boat?"

Bert was livid.

"Why don't you ask Adolf, you self-important, fat, useless article?"

Bert was almost as fat as Roger but didn't see the irony in his statement. Roger wondered what the hell Bert was on about.

"So we won't be having any mackerel for our tea today then?"

Bert continued to walk home and ignored the remark. A puzzled Roger returned to his civic duties, rubbing his big brass bell.

Out at sea, the Chief Engineer thought he had almost fixed the problem and reported that they could be underway before too long. Leutnant Franz Spiegel was a bit concerned.

54

"Mein Kapitan, come look at this."

The Kapitan joined the Leutnant on the conning tower. They looked out together over a calm sea and a beautiful evolving morning.

"Look up to the sky and look at those two strange aircraft, Herr Kapitan."

Von Diesel looked as requested with the binoculars and scanned the blue sky, where he could see two large vapour trails crossing each other. The Kapitanleutnant was concerned as well.

"Franz, what are those aircraft? They leave trails in the sky and I hear no propeller sounds. These aircraft must be propelled by some kind of propulsion rocket system. They must be some top secret planes the British have developed, which have not been known to our intelligence. They look like big bombers to me. I am beginning to have my doubts as to whether we can win this war, Franz. Where are the minefields, hostile ships and coastal defences? There is little evidence of them so far. Those aircraft are moving away from us, which is good, so we are in no immediate danger of attack."

The Kapitan scanned the sky carefully and then the waters all around.

"Keep a close watch out for merchant vessels, Franz."

"Jawohl, Herr Kapitan."

The Commander was about to go below and check on the Chief Engineer's progress, but before he went, he pointed to the land.

"Look at the coastline, Leutnant. There is something here that does not add up. I know this stretch of the coast well, but there are what appear to be large communication masts on the cliff tops, and new sporadic building development also. And take a look through the glasses at the lighthouse in the distance. It too has changed from my last visit. It has a new coat of paint and coloured stripes added to it also. Somehow this place has changed in such a short time and I am wondering how this can be."

He paused for thought.

"Those aerials must be their detection systems or, as you say, communications systems, Herr Kapitan. The British would seem to have far superior and much more advanced weaponry than us. So why do they not attack us?"

The Kapitan didn't have the answer.

Porth Branven police station was open for business. On duty were a Sergeant and two Constables, with two more specials expected later to assist when the celebrations commenced. The Sergeant expected a busy but hopefully trouble free day.

He was not to be disappointed on the first count. One of the two young Constables took off his helmet and sat down in the Sergeant's office. The older man looked harassed.

"This place is falling apart, Constable Harris. We've got these German visitors due to arrive soon, and what do you make of this? Big Bert has reported that his boat was seized yesterday and sunk by a bunch of pirates dressed up as German sailors. Says he, Arthur Pengelly and young John Thomas were taken prisoner at gun point and kept prisoner on board a U-boat. Don't know how Bert's going to claim insurance on *The Two Inbred Sisters* with that story. He asked me to contact the coastguard and the Navy. I've reported the loss of his boat to the RNLI and the coastguard, reporting roughly where she was lost, but I left out the bit about the Germans and their U-boat. I'm a Camborne man myself, Constable Harris, but this place is something else."

"Maybe Bert and his crew had been smoking a strong illegal substance, Sarge."

"More likely the drink they took was far too strong," replied the Sergeant. "Strong German lager, probably brought in by their boat. And here's the good bit. He's reported the theft of four wooden boxes of fresh fish."

"So no mackerel today then, Sarge? And are we going to interview the German visitors as suspects when they arrive?"

The Sergeant shook his head and buried himself in some paper work. He looked up after a moment.

"How could they be involved when they've spent the night at The Queen's Hotel in Penzance?"

Whatever did they teach these new police officers these days? His phone rang for the umpteenth time that morning.

"OK, sir. Slow down. Where did you say this happened?"

The Sergeant took down the details and the call ended soon after.

"Oh, I forgot to tell you, Sarge. Major Beere from The Bluebells Residential Home wants a word with you. Something about seeing Germans and a U-boat as well. Says he has a witness too."

"Don't tell me," said the Sergeant, sighing deeply. "That old bat, the Russian Countess?"

"Why, yes, Sarge, but how did you know that before I even told you?"

"That's why I am a Sergeant and you have a long way to go to become one, son. That old bird is as mad as a hatter in Luton on a wet Tuesday."

He paused to sip some of his stone cold tea.

"The phone call I just received was from this fellow who runs The World of Asbestos theme park place over near Hayle. Says he flew his plane along the coast here yesterday and had the banner being towed behind it shot to bits by gunfire from somewhere. He said when the plane had landed the banner was just a torn mass of rags full of holes and rips."

The Constable looked confused.

"You know," said the Sergeant. "The banner they tow behind the plane to advertise the amusement park. You must have seen it flying around."

"Maybe the Germans tried to shoot it down," said the Constable helpfully.

The duty Sergeant had another explanation, which involved strong drink being involved again. If someone was importing strong alcohol illegally and such sudden anti-German feelings were surfacing, he feared trouble brewing, and on this of all days, when two coach loads of German dignitaries and visitors were arriving as the town's guests in a gesture of twinning and friendship.

His phone rang yet again. It was the Inspector, his superior, in Penzance.

"Yes, sir. I couldn't explain what I was trying to explain."

There was a knock on the office door. Outside stood Major Beere and Countess Olga Trovanovich.

No-one was having a lie in that morning in the normally sleepy fishing outpost of Porth Branven. Even the dogs of the small town had seemed to be howling for no reason since first light. Grown adults wandered around all dressed up as if they had escaped from a night out at a bier keller.

57

Music started to be played through a public address system down by the harbour to test it out for later in the morning. A traditional German oompa band from Liskeard had been hired for the day, and some of their jolly members had already been on the juice to lubricate their vocal capacity.

Jolly Roger, Porth Branven's self-appointed German Ambassador, was really getting into the swing of things and practised his welcome speech to an imaginary audience.

Molly and Jake exchanged knowing looks as they passed each other and then, for the sake of harmony, made a conscious mental decision to avoid each other if at all possible for the rest of the day. Their final words were spoken as they brushed past each other in the main street.

"Jake, I left my knickers down on the beach!"

"You old romantic," whispered Jake, remembering earlier that day.

In the background they could hear Roger "oyez"-ing with his big brass bell.

It seemed that most of the townsfolk were getting involved in some way with the madness of the occasion.

It was Saturday and the coaches with the German guests arrived to a grand reception from the equally self-appointed welcoming committee, AKA the town council, AKA the Porth Branven Improvements Committee, AKA Friends of Porth Branven, AKA busybodies with more time on their hands than most folk, and people who would interfere with the delicate workings of a Swiss watch because they felt it was their duty to do so.

There was to be an official welcoming breakfast and speeches and yet more speeches and even more speeches.

"It is better to jaw-jaw than war-war," said one old Porth Branven self-appointee, which was true, though the turn of phrase could have been more diplomatic in the circumstances.

The German guests had loads of money and expensive Swiss cameras, and looked far richer and better off than their Cornish hosts, but they didn't seem to notice the reference being made.

The guests were led by a jolly round woman called Frau Hertzmann, who exchanged gifts and plaques of the twinned towns with Roger, who represented Porth Branven, and who didn't speak a word of German, as was the case with most of the Cornish delegation. As for the Germans, most of them spoke English in their distinctive sort of way, and one had even learned a smattering of Cornish for the occasion.

Most of Porth Branven had accepted their guests from across the North Sea with a warm welcome, but there were notable exceptions.

The vicar of St Legest Church ordered the bells to be rung to mark the occasion. This caused some consternation amongst some of the older residents, and especially the confused and less lucid ones who resided at The Bluebells Residential Home, some of whom were escorted out for the big occasion.

"The bells! The bells! They are ringing, Matron! Are we being invaded? Are the Germans coming?" asked a worried Myrna, hearing a firework going off suddenly, despite the law, and then another and another for good measure.

"Yes, dear. They are, in a manner of speaking," said Matron in a condescending manner.

Poor Myrna had been in Plymouth during the height of the blitz in 1940 and 1941.

"Matron, this war has been going on for a very long time," said Myrna, shaking her fist at The World of Asbestos aircraft, which suddenly flew over the town, sporting a brand new 'Come to the World of Asbestos Grand Firework Display, 2PM' banner behind it.

Myrna, who was ancient even by residential home standards, shook her frail gnarled fist up at the pilot, who she imagined she could see swooping low over Lockyer Street in Plymouth.

"Matron, we have to take cover! We have to get to the shelter!"

Myrna's confusion was mixed with anger as she continued to shake her fist at the Luftwaffe flying over Porth Branven, or Plymouth.

"Yes, dear," said Matron, still in a condescending manner.

Another rocket was fired up into the sky, just missing the plane and almost setting fire to the brand new banner it towed in the blue sky. Irony!

A fast car had brought Carrington from British Naval Intelligence to Cornwall. He had passed the skipper of HMS *Bosun* going the other way to London. Commander Andrews had a few butterflies at the thought of facing his superiors at the Admiralty. It worried him more to face the stiffs there than all the years he had spent in the Navy.

Carrington's brief was to sniff about, listen to the gossip, and find out what was going on in West Cornwall. These Germans on a twinning visit might have Eastern Bloc spies amongst them.

How Carrington hated Cornwall, a God-forsaken place and the land that time never forgot but didn't wish to know in the first place. The thought of going back there as an adult brought back to him painful memories of childhood.

He recalled spending two weeks at Polzeath where he had been stung twice by wasps, had had his thumb mashed with a wooden mallet and his head cut open by his little sister wielding a red metal beach spade. And the dreadful place they had stayed had had an infestation of bed bugs that bit him constantly. If that was not enough, it had rained for the whole two weeks. The best day spent there was the last, with the train back to civilization from Padstow.

Maybe today it would be different, he told himself. The skies looked promising further to the west.

The Admiralty top brass didn't usually work on a Saturday, golf or shooting in the country being their thing, but these hastily sent signals from their largest warship had stirred the cobwebs in Whitehall. It was an unheard of occurrence for a skipper on the pride of the fleet to report that he had been fired at with torpedoes, and off the coast of Cornwall of all places.

The Navy was aware of the large flotilla of Eastern Bloc factory ships sitting out off Falmouth at exactly the same time as the visit of HMS *Bosun*, the fleet's flagship, which was there on a courtesy visit after conducting exercises in the Irish Sea.

The First Sea Lord, sitting sternly behind the large teak panelled desk, bade the Commander of HMS *Bosun* in and took his salute. He got to the point.

"Now, Timothy, we have known each other for a few years, and have a good working relationship stretching back to our days at Dartmouth, and Eton before that. I am sure you can appreciate our problem.

"We have half the Soviet Bloc's factory ships just off Falmouth with two Soviet warships in the channel admiring your ship even as we speak. And our intelligence suggests the possibility of Eastern

Bloc spies being amongst these German chappies and their fräuleins extending the bratwurst on the west coast of Cornwall.

"I have transcripts of your signals here. You say you were attacked by two torpedoes, which you and your officers saw, but you never managed to detect the boat that allegedly fired them. There was no damage to your ship despite your saying you saw the torpedoes clearly just below the surface of the sea and heading straight at you. You acknowledge the large draught of your vessel so, if you are to be believed, HMS *Bosun* would have been struck twice and would not be in Falmouth today."

The three high ranking naval officers sat in stony silence and awaited answers. The most senior of them got up and walked around the plush room, with Lord Nelson looking down from a painting.

HMS *Bosun's* Commander felt as if he was attending his own court martial. All of this business was too stupid for words, he could imagine his three senior officers thinking, as the two quiet ones sat and studied him. He knew he had seen those two torpedoes aimed at his ship. Maybe they were practice dummy fish, but, even if they were, the big ship would have felt the impact.

The experienced Commander knew that no friendly submarine would have fired on the flagship without notifying her beforehand; for example, in a pre-planned naval exercise. Surely it had to be a hostile submarine in Cornish waters, using a new type of weapon that could mimic the actions of firing torpedoes. Real ones would have struck the ship for sure.

"I don't like this business any more than you do, Timothy. Could it be that you actually saw two dolphins heading for the ship? You know how they can look like a missile in the water. The sea, of course, does play tricks on the mind at times, old man. You say your junior officer corroborated your statement, but we have to expect a plausible explanation. Have you got one?"

"No, sir."

The First Sea Lord went over to the large window and looked out at London. He had his hands behind his back and was in deep thought.

"If we do have a hostile submarine in our home waters without our knowledge, then the fact that it couldn't be located is deeply worrying. The Soviets must have developed a far superior defence system for their boats. By Gad, sir, this business is serious!

"When the first signal was received yesterday from the flagship, we all thought war had broken out, and the PM was about to issue the special codes to our nuclear ballistic missile subs ready for retaliation in the event that things escalated. I want this business sorted out," said the First Sea Lord, turning around to face HMS *Bosun's* Commander.

"Are you going to relieve me of my command, sir?" said the Commander, preparing for life in charge of the concrete land ship, HMS *Oban*, up in the wilds of Scotland.

He waited long seconds for the First Sea Lord's response.

"No, Commander," he said, smiling. "Your skills are too valuable to be wasted at HMS *Oban*. Much as I am worried by this business, we can't afford to lose the skills of one of our best ship commanders.

"Here's what we have decided. A senior operative from Naval Intelligence is already in place in West Cornwall, and will report directly to me about any suspicious activity or persons encountered down there. There is, apparently, a German town twinning event taking place as we speak. There's the possibility that a Soviet agent is travelling with this West German party."

The Senior Naval Officer went over to a large operations map on the wall.

"I have briefly spoken to the Russian Naval Attaché at their embassy and he assures me his nation has no hostile intentions that could have a bearing on this business. Mind you, he is bound to say that.

"We haven't informed the Americans about this, you understand. You can imagine the repercussions there might be, and how they might view our lapse in security, shall we say. Our friends over the pond are already deeply jealous of our flagship; it being far superior to any of theirs. What if it were to become common knowledge that the world's most advanced warship couldn't defend itself against attack and then worse, couldn't find its attacker?"

The Senior Naval Officer paused.

"No, Commander. You are to return to Falmouth immediately after this briefing, and after we have all eaten. I will arrange for a staff car to take you back down to Falmouth and your ship. When the courtesy visit is finished, you will be issued with new orders to sail to the Western Approaches.

"Once there, you will conduct fresh sea defence trials. I want every rivet re-tested on HMS *Bosun*, and, in particular, I want her anti-submarine defence systems re-checked and tested. One of our diesel attack submarines will assist with this.

"I have ordered HMS *Foxglove* to have a presence in those waters until these matters are resolved to our satisfaction. Her Majesty's submarine, *Barracuda*, is also off the coast of Cornwall to back up *HMS Foxglove* and assist with testing your ship's defences.

"Now, gentlemen, let's retire to my club to eat. Transport is at our disposal outside. Follow me."

The Captain of HMS *Bosun* saluted his superior officer and the salute was returned.

"Maybe I'll get a round of golf in this afternoon," said the First Sea Lord, checking his watch.

Chapter Six

Matron at The Bluebells had to take Myrna back to the home on account of the older lady getting a bit upset at the bangs from the occasional firework being let off, and by the obvious German mood sweeping the small town.

That was a bit of a shit, the Matron thought, because she wanted to be involved in the celebrations herself and her dog was going be taking part in the canine show to be held later. Matron couldn't see any logical reason why the presence of a few Germans and the odd firework going off should upset Myrna.

Matron took her resident reluctantly back to the home. She turned up her nose as she heard Myrna let forth a big ripper of a fart, which must surely have been powerful enough to snap the elastic in the big white knickers that the old girl always wore under the flowery summer dress that had served three now deceased residents before Myrna. The woman also had a permanent old lady smell of lavender and piddle.

They passed the Major and Countess Olga, who were on their way into town, having got back from the police station, where no one believed the story about the Germans from a rambling old man and his ageing Russian companion, who they believed had bats missing from the belfry.

"Off out to the celebrations, are we, Major? And you too, Countess?"

The Major laughed with a hint of indignation.

"Celebrating the arrival of the Germans again, Matron? Why, no; the Countess and I are off to keep our own counsel."

"Well, there's talk of us joining the Common Market. We are all good friends now and the past is best forgotten. The West Germans are our European allies now. I expect we will be seeing a lot more of them over the next few years."

"We've seen enough Germans in the past few hours to last us both a lifetime, Matron."

The woman laughed and then sighed. The old soldier was definitely losing his marbles like Myrna and would probably end up "up

Bodmin", as the Cornish said of anybody who was to have likely dealings with Cornwall's St Lawrence's Hospital, which was an old asylum, and now a mental hospital. He and the Countess made a good couple and deserved each other because she was as mad as a bag of ferrets denied their hot buttered toast for breakfast on a cold Tuesday morning.

The two women bade the Major and the Countess a good morning and walked on. Olga walked away on the arm of the Major. Myrna suddenly turned to look at them, stopping Matron in her tracks.

"What's that woman doing with my husband, Mother?"

"Come on," said Matron, having heard it all before, over and over and over again.

Matron could smell piddle even more strongly now as she suspected it had trickled down Myrna's leg. The old lady let off a much bigger ripper, which made the gardener tending the lawns look up. He went back to what he was doing. Everyone got used to Myrna letting off rippers at The Bluebells.

The Countess was a very smart lady who always dressed from head to toe in black, and she wore a Russian brooch depicting a silver bear on her hat, which she said had once belonged to the Tsar. They made an odd couple, the Major and the Countess, but they were happy in each other's company, and were accepted as just two of Porth Branven's many eccentrics. For all her many years, the Countess had a spring in her step and acted like a much younger woman, and she turned mutton dressed as lamb into a fashion statement with some panache. Mentally, she was as sharp as a razor blade; well, sometimes.

"Come on, old girl. I need to get a paper and check up on the cricket results," said the Major, increasing the pace. "Then we can find a nice hostelry where we can imbibe on this rather pleasant Saturday well away from those Germans. Something a bit stronger than Matron's bromide-laden beverages."

"Bromide?" enquired the Countess, quite perplexed.

The Major remembered the night before, and that was not a sight for a lady, except perhaps for the lady indulging in the activity, so this wasn't suitable either. He decided to take the easy route out of the conversation.

"Why, my dear Countess, bromide is something they put in our tea and coffee to keep us quiet and make us conform."

Olga was satisfied and asked no further questions on the subject.

"I need something strong to take my mind off these Bosch," she said, as they could hear music being played from down near the harbour. "Major, did I ever tell you about the night the Bolsheviks came for us? I managed to escape."

"Yes, you did, old girl; many times," said the Major silently to himself.

The Countess Olga was not finished.

"What about how our glorious Red Army drove back the Nazi hordes at the battle of Stalingrad in 1943?"

He had heard that one as well many times.

"Tell me about that again, Countess, if you would be so kind."

He didn't mind hearing the tales of heroism and bravery and sacrifice by the Russian people back then. He thought like most British people outside of the establishment; why were they engaged in a cold war against a brave and proud people who were their allies against Nazi Germany and the might of Hitler's forces?

The Major himself had served in North Africa against Rommel's forces, and had been a prisoner of war. He could forgive, but not forget, like most of the British people, and the Cornish more locally, of which he was one.

The pair wandered into The Anchor Inn. It was the fishermen's local in Porth Branven, where the men usually gathered when not at sea to moan about French trawlers and their skippers and to drink themselves stupid on St Austell Brewery's finest ale, which they called Slug Death, and to tell tall tales about the one that got away.

The Major led the way over to a quiet corner of the lounge, and, whilst the Countess was seated, he went to the bar and ordered the drinks - a half of beer and a tot of Irish whiskey for himself and a generous measure of vodka for the Countess.

A few comments came from the pub's younger clientele, but they were good natured.

"They don't like it up 'em, Captain Mainwaring!" came the usual stock phrase with guffawing from the foot soldiers following.

Major Beere ignored the jibes. He had seen action at Tobruk in Libya while most of these young, long-haired yobs had only seen action in the local disco and the Penzance Winter Gardens. They were only young once, he decided, so let them have their fun as they would soon tire of making the comments. However, Major Beere wished these lads were on parade in his old regiment with their long hair and slovenliness. The regimental barber and Sergeant Major would have had a field day with this lot. These were indeed strange times they lived in, he conceded as he paid for and took the drinks back to the table where the Countess was sitting, looking at the Major's newspaper.

The youngsters chatted away, the fishermen chatted away, and the Major and the Countess chatted away, and nobody really paid any attention to the tall stranger in the cheap grey suit who had just entered the pub. He bought a soft drink, sat on a bar stool and just soaked up the atmosphere and listened to the conversation.

Earlier that morning, things aboard the UB-AF9 hadn't gone exactly to plan.

The Chief Engineer found that he needed more time to fix the electrical problem bedevilling the boat. With communications inexplicably still not working, she was sitting on the surface and vulnerable to attack by the enemy at any moment. In short, she was a sitting duck.

Kapitanleutnant Von Diesel kept calm. If the men under his command could see him conducting himself calmly, then that would spread his confidence throughout the crew.

The men on watch kept their eyes peeled for any signs of enemy activity as the boat sat on the surface just off Porth Branven.

Leutnant Hans Krieger popped into the Kapitan's cabin.

"Herr Kapitan, I have to report that the lobster, Herman, has emerged from his hideaway and is now taking to the eating of the mussels and limpets acquired by this officer on the beach of the deserted cove. He seems to have the acquired taste for the mussels rather than the limpets."

"Good, Hans. If the crew are aware that Herman is well, it will keep up their morale. You did good work, Hans. This lull in the war was making some of the men a bit jumpy. Now sit and have a drink with me, Hans, while things are quiet."

"Thank you, Herr Kapitan," replied Hans.

He watched as Von Diesel went to his personal locker and produced a bottle of some strong German liquor, which could not be obtained generally in Germany at the present time. The Kapitan poured out two small glasses and chinked his with Hans's glass.

"Here's to your good health, Hans."

"Thank you, Herr Kapitan, and so also to yours I drink."

"So, what do you intend to do after the war, Hans? Will you stay in the Kriegsmarine?"

Hans took a sip of the Captain's rye liquor, which had a kick like a mule in Munich with a headache. Hans felt his throat and gullet go all fiery as the sensation warmed all the way down to his engine room and back up again.

"No, Herr Kapitan. I shall leave the Navy and go back to keeping bees and making dolls' houses in Düsseldorf with my beloved wife, Helga, and our two little boys, Willy and Helmut. I also have an Uncle Fritz living on the Heligoland, where he keeps his little boat with blue sails. We will holiday there with Uncle Fritz in the summertime when the sun is warm and the bees flit from flower to flower."

Von Diesel studied Hans. Thank goodness the man wasn't staying in the Kriegsmarine. If he did, he would probably be promoted to Commodore, or even worse, Admiral. Hans was a likeable fellow but needed firing from a torpedo tube at times. In short, he was an idiot who should have remained on dry land in Düsseldorf.

"So, you keep the bees and also you make the dolls' houses, Hans?"

"Ja, Herr Kapitan. In fact of truth, when I am not on watch and not sleeping also, I will be making a grand dolls' house in the engine room out of the old wooden fish crates that were taken from the Cornish fishermen. The Chief Engineer said that the smell from the mackerel will make Herman feel at home amongst all the diesel fumes and noise down there."

The man was incredible, thought Von Diesel. Still, at least while he was occupying himself that way, he couldn't accidentally fire off a torpedo. The Kapitan vowed to himself that if they managed to make it back to the base on the Breton coast, he would try to have a discreet word with the fleet Commodore, and ask politely if Hans could be transferred to the number one dummy torpedo training facility near Hamburg. However, unknown to Von Diesel, Leutnant Hans Krieger was a relative of the Commodore.

"So, what about you, Herr Kapitan? Will you go back to the Fatherland after the war?"

Von Diesel finished off his drink in one go.

"No, Hans, I will leave the Kriegsmarine also. I have heard that Von Ribbentrop, who I had a drink with in St Ives before the war, and who will be the appointed Gauleiter to the Cornish region of the expanded German Fatherland, is planning to take up residence at St Michael's Mount."

Even Hans Krieger knew of St Michael's Mount and its grand castle on the south coast of Cornwall. Hans was impressed. The Kapitan continued with the story.

"Von Ribbentrop will move in, and Lord and Lady St Levan, the current occupiers, will probably be moved to a tiny beach hut at Carbis Bay. I expect to be invited over to St Michael's Mount by Herr Von Ribbentrop for drinks once he is settled in. Maybe that idiot, the Führer, will visit also. I have no wife or sweetheart to worry about, Hans, so I think I will find a less grand house on the cliffs somewhere. They will be much more pleasant times, once the locals realise that it is inevitable that we Germans will win this war."

"You might even go for a drink with Enormous Bert, the Cornish fisherman skipper, Herr Kapitan."

"Maybe, Hans," replied the Kapitan. "Maybe."

Right now, Von Diesel knew that Big Bert, if he was still alive, would be in no mood to drink after the war with the Kapitan of the U-boat that had been responsible for the loss of his precious boat.

Hans saluted the Kapitan and went below to the engine room to check on the progress of the repairs being undertaken. When he got there, Herman arched his claws and hissed, taking up an attack position.

"He doesn't seem to like you very much, Hans," said the Chief Engineer, who had been dowsing the creature regularly with sea water whilst conducting repairs with a rating.

Just then the lights flickered and went out for a few seconds. Hans was terrified and wondered if lobsters could see in the dark. Was he about to be attacked by Herman? To his relief, the lights flickered and came back on again, which was just as well because Herman was a lot closer to Hans now.

"Keep that crustacean under control, Chief. I wouldn't trust him as far as I could throw him."

Hans made himself scarce and went to the other duties on the boat. That Herman was a vicious underwater creature with claws that could do much damage.

In The Anchor Inn, Big Bert sat drinking with Arthur Pengelly, young John Thomas and a few other men who fished out of Porth Branven.

It was hard to believe such an unlikely story, but when did Big Bert ever tell lies? Except to his wife when he occasionally 'went walkies' with Molly to remote places.

The consensus of opinion was that pirates dressed up in German naval uniforms were responsible for this outrage on the high seas.

The idea that a film was being made was discussed, but there was a logical scapegoat - the Germans in the form of the visitors that day. They must have something to do with this business.

Even inside the pub, they could hear the pro-German celebrations taking place down near the harbour with the awful oompa band playing away with great gusto.

Bert and his boys wanted nothing to do with celebrating German culture and were never in favour of this event anyway, even if some of Porth Branven's other residents were.

Carrington sat quietly eating a pub lunch with a soft drink while perusing a newspaper and all the time listening to the words of the fishermen on one side of him and the old boy and the equally old girl on the other side.

The old boy had been ranting on about Germans as well. The landlord threw in his lot with the anti-German sentiment too, but then he would do, seeing as his takings were badly down as a result of the German bier keller Jolly Roger and his clique had organised down by the harbour.

The man who ran The Anchor drove a German BMW, but he conveniently forgot about that as a wave of anti-German feeling pervaded the lounge bar.

"So what's going to happen to your boat, Bert?" asked one of the fishermen.

Bert sipped his pint and felt a mixture of deep thought and anger.

"Well, I informed the coastguard, the RNLI at St Ives and the police here. Fat lot of good they were. Oh, and I phoned the insurers, but they can't do much until Monday anyway. I heard this woman at the end of the line laughing."

"Well, it does sound an incredible story, Bert. You must admit that."

Bert swung into anger mode.

"Well, Arthur and Tommy here were witnesses. For fuck's sake, they were taken prisoner as well. Come on, lads! We are hardly likely to make up such things. Those kraut bastards even thieved our catch. Then there was this mine."

Big Bert needed a bit more drink now that he was in fighting mode.

"Where was The Royal Navy when all this was happening? I'll tell you where they were. Their biggest warship just happened to be passing our coast on its way to Falmouth. The Navy's supposed to protect us fishermen. Fat lot of good *HMS Bosun* was for all her supposed high tech weapons systems. My boat is down there on the bottom at the end of the Carrick Du reef."

The other fishermen rallied around their mate, Bert.

"Well, first thing Monday morning we'll put the wheels in motion to salvage her," said one of them. "We must do that before the bad weather sets in. I have a contact in Falmouth connected with diving and salvage. We'll help you all we can, Bert. I'm taking my own boat, *The Boy Blewett* out this afternoon to pick up some pots. Come out with me and show me the spot where *The Two Inbred Sisters* went down, and we can mark the position with a float."

Bert agreed and was grateful and calmed down a little.

Carrington made mental notes of all he heard and had picked up on the mention of *HMS Bosun*. Maybe her skipper's strange story had not been so far fetched after all.

Major Beere had also been eavesdropping on the fishermen's conversation. He excused himself to the Countess Olga and went over to the men.

"Good morning, gentlemen. Well, it would be if these damned Germans were not everywhere."

"Tell me about it, Major Beere. How are you this morning? And your friend, the eccentric lady?"

"We are fine, young man, except for these Germans. I saw them as well, Bert, and their damned U-boat. I saw them with my very eyes through my telescope. Saw everything that happened to you. The guns, their stealing your fish, everything. Reported the whole sorry business to that useless article, the Matron, and those equally useless articles, the police. Complete and utter waste of my time, old chap. They were not in the slightest bit interested in what I had to say and put it down to the ramblings of an old man who must be losing his marbles."

"You sit here for a minute, Major, and tell us your story. We all believe you. Don't we, boys?"

The chorus came back that they did, which was debatable, it being such a bizarre story, except Bert and his crew knew the truth as well.

Keeping one ear out for the continued discussions about the Germans, Carrington sidled over to the Countess Olga.

"I couldn't help overhearing what you and your gentleman friend were discussing just now. Can I buy you both a drink?"

Before Olga could respond, Carrington spoke again.

"You sound East European, dear lady," he said before the Major returned to the table.

"I am Russian," replied Olga in her distinctive accent. "I escaped the Bolsheviks, do you know? They were coming for me in the middle of the night."

Carrington dismissed the story and thought the old woman was eccentric and confused, but she definitely sounded Russian. On that score, he had no need to doubt her.

"I bet that was an awful experience for you..."

"Countess Olga Trovanovich," she replied. "That is my title."

"Yes, Countess Trovanovich, I expect it was a terrible experience for you," said Carrington, wondering why he had been sent to this place of obvious madness so far west and away from civilization. They probably ate babies in remote parts around here, he told himself with a shiver. The Countess took up the story again.

"And now we are run over by the Bosch."

Carrington allowed himself a smile and produced a notebook and pen from inside his suit jacket pocket.

"You mean overrun?"

"You heard me correct, young man," came her reply.

"How long have you been living in Cornwall?" enquired Carrington, learning that the Countess was partial to vodka, and the Major the odd glass or three of good Irish whiskey.

"I have been over here many, many, many years, young boy. So, why are you asking me all the questions?"

The Major returned to see the Countess had a stranger sitting next to her. He could see that he had bought a round of drinks as well. Curious, Major Beere sat back down a little closer to Olga than before.

"I do apologise, sir and madam, for my non-introduction. I am Paul Sweeney, an investigative journalist for *The Daily News*."

He flashed an identity card to prove it to them. The Countess ignored the showing; the Major scrutinised it carefully before handing it back to the younger man.

"Never read it myself," said the Major a bit scathingly. "Damned scandal sheet, if you ask me. So, thank you for the drink, but what do you want with us, young fellow?"

The bogus reporter breathed a hidden sigh of relief. He was into their confidence and hopefully he might learn more of what had been happening in and around this dreadful place, which seemed to reek of fish everywhere, and had a horrible mixture of British early seventies pop music interspersed with German band offerings, both of which he hated.

"Well," said Carrington. "My paper does report scandal, of course, and this, you must admit, is scandal. But scandal needs to be reported, and is popular to be read. We are doing a public duty by exposing such things. Germans seizing a hard working fisherman's boat, and in Cornish waters. And they have a U-boat as well, and threaten him with guns. How can any of this be true? They must have released him. He doesn't look like he has been harmed in any way. It's very interesting though, and I'm looking to write a feature story on all of this for my paper. I reckon that you two sensible and level-headed people are just the right folk to ask about this strange business."

He knew he had hooked the Major and his apparently daft-as-a-brush companion.

"So, you also claim to have seen these Germans board and scuttle this fishing boat by threat of force. You are a reliable witness as you are an old army officer, sir."

Carrington waited to write it all down in his notebook.

"By Gad, sir! I saw them with my own eyes. And furthermore, the good lady here, the Countess Olga, saw them up to no good early this morning at Spurdog Point cove just to the west of here."

He hesitated. Better not to report on what he had seen Molly and that fellow, Jake Harvey, up to on the sand not a million miles away from the Germans. Bloody Germans were one thing, and guns and U-boats were a dashed inconvenience, but revealing the locals' dalliances could cause real trouble. Jolly Roger could turn nasty with that big brass oyez bell he was so fond of.

The Major returned his attention to the man he believed to be a scandal sheet reporter.

"I am Major Beere, 1st Battalion, the Duke of Cornwall's Light Infantry, retired, you understand. Saw service in the war in North Africa. Taken prisoner by the Germans, in fact, so I have no personal axe to grind with them, you know, young man. Just find it a bit irritating that they have gone back to their old ways, resorting to piracy, it would seem. If they want fresh mackerel then, by Jove, why don't they buy it like everybody else? It's plentiful and cheap enough, and Bert is always reasonable with his mackerel prices. Even gets you the odd lobster if you want one. Dare say the man would have given our friends from across the North Sea some mackerel, if they'd asked politely. I can't see myself the need for all these guns and unpleasantness any more."

Carrington scribbled away and decided that the old soldier was a complete and utter lunatic. The Countess spoke.

"Those Bolsheviks were unpleasant as well and used guns too, young man. They would murder you in your bed, given half a chance. Maybe the Bolsheviks have teamed up with the Germans."

She was even madder than the Major was, Carrington decided as he continued to listen carefully but in utter amazement. Then it suddenly got much more interesting and to the point for him.

"I have been interested in shipping movements for years, young man," said the Countess, quite lucidly, it seemed. "I have been keeping the pictures of ships docking at Falmouth for my scrapbook since I first came to Cornwall many, many years ago. I have a friend called Boras in Falmouth, who gets me the information, and I listen to the radio and look in the local papers as well.

Did you know that HMS *Bosun* from the wonderful Royal Navy is there now? I would love to see her in the steel flesh for myself. She was off this coast only yesterday, en route to Falmouth, but I missed her. How disappointing. Now, that is a fine ship bristling with weapons. I wouldn't be surprised if the Bosch were trying to steal her secrets."

Carrington was suddenly worried. She was Russian and had been here for years. She was a deep cover Russian agent and she had somebody in Falmouth as well. She was only pretending to be doolally. The Admiralty and Naval Intelligence would have to hear about this, and soon.

Carrington had visions of some oik of a new Navy Lieutenant, fresh out of Naval College at Dartmouth, showing a party of Bulgarian fishing klondikers around Britain's newest and largest warship on its courtesy visit to Falmouth.

This German nonsense was an elaborate cover up to conceal Russian plans to glean the secrets of HMS *Bosun*. Not since The Admiralty had run out of bourbon biccies back in 1969 had the Navy and the state faced such a crisis and breach in national security.

There was no possible Eastern Bloc agent amongst the German visitors in Porth Branven. The agent was an apparently silly old bat dressed totally in black and sitting right next to him. And he had bought her and her accomplice drinks. The old man too must be an agent, and him a retired British Army officer.

This business was more serious than previously thought by the Admiralty. Carrington continued to scribble down information under the guise of reporting on the German story.

Chapter Seven

At sea, Kapitanleutnant Von Diesel was getting restless and worried. The problem down in the engine room was still not resolved. They were on the surface and vulnerable to sudden attack. There were still no means of communication with the rest of the German Navy.

The lookouts shouted to the Commander.

"Herr Kapitan! An aircraft approaches from the south west. It is like the one yesterday, and towing another anti-submarine device."

There was no time to lose.

"Man the deck gun, men. Schnell! Schnell!"

The small plane roared overhead at about five hundred feet. Her pilot had recalled being in about the same place yesterday. He couldn't believe that a flock of seagulls could cause so much damage to the expensive banner his plane towed. And then he saw it below.

It was a surfaced submarine. He caught a quick glance and was then past them. He continued on his circled course, sweeping along the coast, and then inland so people on the ground could see the banner advertising his World of Asbestos attraction.

Down below on the deck of UB-AF9, the men were relieved at not being attacked but knew they had been spotted. The Kapitan prayed that the Chief Engineer could fix the problem schnell, but the crew were at battle stations and ready for engagement of the enemy.

The big deck gun fired and ripped the banner asunder from the plane. The Captain had ordered the crew to aim for *it*, rather than the plane itself. It was obvious that the small aircraft wasn't armed.

"I think it might be a reconnaissance aircraft, Herr Kapitan," said one of the deck crew.

The Kapitan had been scanning the oncoming aircraft carefully.

"We have been fooled, men. That is no British RAF plane. It was carrying a message of some kind, probably in code. It said something about asbestos something-or-other. Definitely in code."

A shout came from below.

"Herr Kapitan, the problem with the electrics is now fixed. We can get underway again."

It was the news the Kapitan wanted to hear.

"Then lets get out of there schnell! Dive, dive, dive! Twenty metres, dive!"

There was a scurry of frantic activity on the deck as it was cleared of men hurrying to get below.

Within seconds, the foamy disturbed waters off Porth Branven sloshed around the submarine's deck, and then her conning tower. The grey vessel slipped below the surface.

Before she got to dive depth, Von Diesel scanned all around through her periscope, and, to his horror, there, closing in from about a thousand metres, was a warship, a British vessel. Praying to God Almighty above, the Commander thanked the Chief Engineer and got the boat ready again for battle stations. HMS *Foxglove* had reached the area to check that all was quiet.

On shore, the loud single bang was heard by all. A variety of opinions was offered. Another sonic boom? The Navy firing a one gun salute to the German visitors?

Carrington, who had been pumping his two elderly companions in The Anchor for information, had also heard the bang and was aware that a British warship and an accompanying submarine were in the area. Surely a shot couldn't have been fired by HMS *Foxglove* in anger.

The owner and pilot of the World of Asbestos plane had déjà vu and couldn't believe it. That was no flock of seagulls but a bloody submarine, and it had fired at him! Two banners destroyed in two days. The mayday message to air traffic control had been frantic, and the operator thought the man in the plane had had some kind of seizure, or some other kind of unexplainable flying experience.

He ordered the pilot to make an emergency landing at RAF Penhadn, further up the coast, and then report to the orderly officer there.

The RAF skeleton crew at Penhadn contacted their superiors at RAF St Mawgan, near Newquay, for advice. That was a little further up the coast as well, in fact a bit further still. Then the Royal Naval Air Station at Culdrose, near Helston, was informed.

Before long, the Fleet Commander at Devonport, Plymouth, was informed when he was playing bowls somewhere and pretending to be Drake looking out for the Spanish Amada.

Word got through to HMS *Foxglove*, sitting within distance of the culprit. She was now aware that something was not right, and maybe a hostile submarine was actually operating in these waters. Unlikely, but her crew was put on alert anyway.

Back at Porth Branven the celebrations continued. It was a good excuse for a communal piss-up, and they could forget that Al's garage had put up petrol to the ridiculous price of thirty-five pence a gallon, and in an act of sympathy, the pubs had also put the price of beer up to fifteen pence a pint.

For a few hours, the residents and some visitors could forget their everyday problems and celebrate. The revellers believed the gunshot to be the maroons going up at St Ives to indicate a mariner in distress at sea. The RNLI could deal with that. It was the second time they had apparently gone off today.

Someone was in distress at sea, but not in the usual maritime sense. The Captain of HMS *Foxglove* was alert, as was his crew, to the possibility of this submarine, if it existed, attacking again. The Russians could be testing the British resolve and defences.

Her Majesty's submarine, *Barracuda*, surfaced alongside HMS *Foxglove* in a show of British naval might. The two vessels stayed where they were, some distance away. They couldn't detect the presence of UB-AF9, which remained submerged, but she was very aware of their presence.

Schwartz, on the hydrophones aboard the submarine, listened intently as ever to the sound of the ocean, its inhabitants and those who plied their trade on or under it. They expected attack at any moment.

The Sergeant at Porth Branven's small police station had had enough of crank phone calls on such a busy morning. So far there hadn't been any trouble, but these idiots calling about submarine sightings and even shooting by them at planes was doing his head in. He was seriously considering asking for a transfer to Dawlish Warren or Teignmouth in Devon, where he could still be beside the sea but with no reports of submarines and other such nonsense. Maybe disturbed minerals in the ground from old mining activity around here were having some effect on these people.

He decided to lock up and go out on the beat to join his Constables and check on the celebrations.

Carrington was having tea up at The Bluebells with the Matron. He was a charmer, or an undercover police officer, as he introduced him to her, along with a bogus identity card. Complimenting her on her lovely long legs had also helped to gain him entry over her threshold. Of course, he couldn't divulge too much information for obvious reasons. And could Matron keep a secret? Of course she could. Everybody liked to be in the know with secrets, and only something they were privy to. That was only human nature, and Matron was no different from anyone else. She felt good to be in his confidence.

"So, what do you want me to tell you, Officer Michael?" she said in between sips of her tea.

Carrington got to the point. Time was of the essence. He had to act quickly before that old fool and his Muscovite Madam reappeared, which they could at any time.

"Tell me about the Major and this lady who calls herself The Countess. How long have these two been residents here, Matron?"

Swept away by his charm as he kept looking at her legs, and feeling very important, Matron revealed to him what she knew, and forgot all about client confidentiality.

"He goes out every morning without fail, early, before breakfast, with his telescope."

"Does he now?" replied Carrington, AKA Michael, looking serious and very interested in what she was telling him.

"So, where does he usually go?"

Her reply was quick.

"Out on the cliff tops mostly, to look at the sea."

Carrington soaked it all up.

"And this Countess Olga, does she accompany him?"

"Occasionally. She is living in a fantasy world with the Major."

The Matron laughed after her delivery, and sipped some more tea. Carrington pressed the subject.

"A world that includes U-boats?"

"The very same one," said Matron. "Would you like another biscuit, Officer Michael? Bourbon?"

He accepted two more gratefully.

"So, you don't believe any of this?" asked Carrington.

She didn't and told him so in no uncertain terms. Carrington decided to up the stakes before the old fools returned to the home.

"Would it be OK if I was to take a look around their rooms? With you in attendance, of course."

The Matron thought about it.

"Well, I don't know. I'm not sure about that. They might be a bit mad, but they are harmless. It wouldn't be proper, especially when they are both absent."

"Do you know something, Matron? I do believe I saw your photo some years ago in a magazine; you were modelling? I agree, it's a bit irregular, but these are important police enquiries. None of us wants to go through all the nonsense and fuss of obtaining police search warrants, do we?"

No, she didn't. They might uncover financial irregularities stretching back several years.

"Well, OK then, but be quick. So, are my two residents in trouble of any kind?"

"Why, no, good lady. They are completely innocent. They just happen to be caught up in something not of their making."

His piercing eyes gazed into hers for just that bit too long and swung it for him, along with the veiled threat of a police search warrant.

Matron reached up and bought down a bunch of spare room keys.

"Come on then, Officer Michael. I'll show you to their rooms."

"Success!" thought Carrington.

This was all too easy. These people were so stupid and devious that they made John Dory fish on dope look intelligent.

"I don't think you will find much here," said Matron as Carrington looked around first the Major's room and then the Countess Olga's.

He found nothing of much interest in Major Beere's room, but he had a shock when he put his hand in an old chest of drawers in Olga's room.

"Ow! Shit! Countess Malakoff, or whatever her name is, has booby trapped the place!"

His words echoed through the open door and out into the corridor. Countess Trovanovich had put an anti-trespasser mousetrap in the drawer to catch unsuspecting fingers. It had worked, as Carrington had his fingers subjected to a sharp, sudden, painful snap.

"The cunning old bat," he said, retrieving his fingers from under the sprung steel.

The Matron smiled, and then saw that Myrna was standing in the doorway.

"Have the Germans gone, Matron?" she said in a feeble voice.

She then let off a ripper for the benefit of Carrington, which disturbed him for a few seconds from his search.

Ignoring the intrusion, he continued to look, and then discovered Olga's black plastic backed scrapbooks. Inside them were photographs, black and white and stretching back many years, and all of ships visiting Falmouth, the port of Truro, and ships moored in the River Fal and in the Carrick Roads. There were hundreds of them, and all had the name of the vessel written in neat pen handwriting and a brief note about them underneath.

Myrna interrupted again.

"What are you doing with my husband, Matron?"

Myrna went to grab Carrington's arm, but Matron intervened gently.

"Come along, Myrna. Let's make you a nice cup of tea and settle you down in the lounge."

"Have you seen my husband?" was Myrna's parting shot, accompanied by another ripper as a farewell gesture.

Carrington was left alone for a few brief minutes. He searched quickly and silently, and made a mental note of all he had seen to write up in his notebook later. The only things of real interest to him were the albums containing the photographs of ships, particularly naval ones. The most recent was the RAFA vessel, *Golden Compass*. He could find no reference to Boras of Falmouth.

Matron returned to find him looking carefully at the more recent entries the Countess Olga had collected.

"Surely it's not legal to take photos of ships, Officer?" said Matron, wondering why he was so interested.

"No, of course it isn't, Matron," said Carrington, shutting the album and placing all of them exactly as he had found them.

He then reset the mousetrap and placed that back where it had been situated. Matron smiled.

"She's a game old bird, this Olga," said Carrington, nursing his bruised fingers and wanting to leave this place with its pervading smell of old folk and wandering confused people.

"Matron, when do you finish your shift? Fancy a drink somewhere later?"

He saw that she wore no wedding ring, so took a chance. He was in luck and complimented her on her legs once again.

Out at sea, the two British naval vessels appeared to be just waiting and watching, maybe waiting and watching for UB-AF9, thought Kapitan Von Diesel.

Up at Al's garage, Al and his assistant started to load up the fireworks on to his battered old pick up truck to be taken down to the harbour to get the display under way.

The Major and the Countess were still imbibing in The Anchor Inn.

"I don't trust that reporter chap on reflection," said the Major, stroking his moustache. "If he was a reporter."

"I agree with you," echoed the Countess. "His eyes were too close together and shifty-looking. He could have been one of the Bolsheviks."

The fishermen had dispersed from the pub and Bert and the crew of *The Boy Blewett* had gone down to the harbour. They got there just as Al and his sidekick arrived with the fireworks.

Frau Hertzmann had got a little merry a little too early, and had taken a shine to Roger, changed from lederhosen back into Mayor's regalia with black buckled shoes and his big brass bell.

Molly caught a glimpse of Jake Harvey amongst the revellers in The People's Rooms, and saw the opportunity to allow lust to take over again on this Saturday in summer, when previously she had vowed to resist it. She and Jake slipped away together without anybody noticing.

The Sergeant in charge of policing in Porth Branven could see that all was peaceful in the town, even if the music was a little too loud for his ears. The special liquor licence that had been granted for the day ensured that all - well, most - folk were having a good time and being sensible up until now.

It was time for the dogs to make an appearance and an assortment of canines whose ancestors originated from Germany, or thereabouts, were suddenly brought into the rooms where they were applauded by the German guests and given sausage rolls and even the odd glass of lager, with china ashtrays to drink out of.

There were, of course, the two obligatory Alsatians, Max and Rex, who, upon seeing each other, had to be separated by a couple of brave, or stupid, men. Then there was Carlo the smooth-haired dachshund, the German low dog, or sausage dog, as the kids in Porth Branven affectionately called him. Two boxer dogs joined the canine group. One was Karl, who belonged to the Matron, and who had been palmed off with the promise of money to a teenage girl whilst Matron had other business somewhere with Carrington. The other boxer dog, a handsome brindle called Diesel, belonged to Roger, and wandered around obediently, which was highly unusual for a boxer, and lapped up the attention he received from adoring guests and town folk alike. He also saw off several sausage rolls and an enormous German bratwurst.

A couple of children made paper aeroplanes that resembled Stuka dive bombers, and proceeded to throw them at German guests. They were dismissed with chuckles and the joke laughed off as youthful exuberance. Another child brought a model of a Messerschmitt ME 109 to the party, and made aircraft sounds with it, much to the annoyance of some but the smiles of others, who saw the joke.

Down at the harbour, Al and his mate, Oppo, began to set up the fireworks, smoking cigarettes as they worked. Bert and the others were preparing *The Boy Blewett* for sea. Bert looked at Al with all the fireworks on the quayside. There were enough to blow up the whole town. Maybe the boat would be safer out at sea, away from this mad man and his accomplice, who had forgotten to put the wheel nuts back on Bert's Land Rover when it went into Al's garage for a recent tyre change. The accomplice's hand shook on account of all the drink he'd consumed.

Bert wanted out of here before the fireworks were set off, even if he risked running into some other mad men out there below the waves, who he believed must have escaped form an asylum somewhere.

"This is wunderbar, this show you have put on for us," said a very merry Frau Hertzmann, who was a little unsteady on her feet after yet another drink.

"It is good that we are all friends together now, ja?" Roger agreed and toasted her health with a big glass of German lager as he helped her to sit down before she fell down.

On the bridge of HMS *Foxglove*, her Captain was alert and ready for any submarine intrusion, but there was no evidence of any. He gave the order to leave this immediate vicinity of the Porth Branven stretch of the coastline and patrol further to the north, off Padstow.

What was the Commander of HMS *Bosun* playing at? HMS *Foxglove* and Her Majesty's submarine, *Barracuda*, would have found an intruder with little difficulty. Both British naval vessels steered a course north.

"I can hear two sets of screws, Herr Kapitan," said Seaman Schwartz with relief in his voice. "Definitely two sets. The enemy is leaving."

"We have had a lucky let off," replied Kapitan Von Diesel. "Either that or their detection systems are not working correctly. How strange that we see them no problem, but they appear not to be able to detect us. Their secret future-looking ships look like nothing we have in the German fleet, and yet they are so inept. I think God is smiling on us all this day. We will give the British time to leave the area before we take a course out of here."

The Kapitanleutnant left Leutnant Franz Spiegel in charge of the boat and went down to the wardroom to write up the boat's log. His steward brought him some fresh coffee. The Kapitan committed the words to paper, but could hear his own thoughts at the same time. They were loud and enquiring. Why hadn't the enemy attacked? Why hadn't they managed to detect the U-boat? Why wasn't UB-AF9 able to communicate with other vessels in the German Navy? So many questions and yet no answers.

A sceptical junior RAF officer and a leading aircraftsman examined the small World of Asbestos plane on the runway at RAF Penhadn. Both were bemused at the gibbering wreck of a civilian pilot, who quite clearly seemed to have lost it and wouldn't be flying this crate today or possibly any other day.

A senior officer had already made an initial report based on the mayday signal received from the pilot, and had informed various persons in the chain of command about the pilot's claims of being fired on by the deck gun of a submarine.

The junior officer examined the plane and could see no actual damage to her. The pilot had landed her with no obvious trouble. The banner being towed behind the plane was a different story and was torn asunder. It must have hit a flock of birds, he decided. For Pete's sake, this was 1971. Where had this man obtained his pilot's licence? Monty Python's Flying Circus?

The pilot was taken by another airman to the officer's mess to recuperate and have some strong coffee while the junior officer himself switched on the plane's engines and, after sitting in the cockpit for some time, taxied down the runway and eased the plane down outside a hangar, with instructions for it to be stored in the hangar until further notice.

The official report about this would have to be sent on Monday morning to the Civil Aviation Authority, reporting apparently two similar incidents to this plane.

Up on the Hoe at Plymouth - on a bowling green, to be precise - the Senior Naval Officer of the fleet in Plymouth was losing at bowls to a junior officer. He couldn't concentrate with the nonsense he'd been hearing. He took a short break and spoke discreetly to a colleague.

"Have we heard anything from the Navy's top intelligence man in Cornwall yet?"

"No, sir," came the reply. "He is down there now in West Cornwall, investigating this business, hard at work. If something fishy is taking place with these Russians, then our man will find out about it."

"Well, let's bloody well hope so," replied the senior naval man. "This nonsense is putting me off my game. Drake never had to put up with such idiotic stuff when the Spanish were spotted off the Cornish coast."

"Sir Francis Drake had the good sense to stay away from Cornwall," thought the junior officer.

The small Plymouth Sound island named after him had once belonged to Cornwall, and still did according to a handful of Cornish nationalists down in the far west. Drake should have had a treaty with the Spanish and let them have Cornwall, and then maybe they could play bowls in peace on a lovely Saturday afternoon.

"If you hear anything further, let me know immediately," said the officer, missing yet another shot.

"Yes, sir," replied the junior, wondering if Sir Francis Drake was actually any good at bowls; he must have been better than the senior officer because he was absolutely bloody awful.

Back on the outskirts of Porth Branven, Carrington, AKA Sweeney, AKA Michael, was indeed working hard on the case, in the back of Matron's rusted old 1962 VW Beetle camper wagon, parked out on the cliffs in a quiet spot down a rutted track amongst the gorse bushes. It was a place where nobody normally took a vehicle on account of the high risk of getting a puncture from the fly tipping that had taken place there over the years.

With legs akimbo and her frayed grey knickers down around her ankles, Matron thought she was eighteen again as Carrington, Michael, or whoever, pumped away between her legs for all he was worth. It was frenetic, it was unromantic, it was necessary, for him because he wanted information and for her because she wanted it so badly.

Wrapping her legs around him in an unladylike manner, she screamed as her climax approached, taking over her sense of dignity, privacy and whatever else.

"I'm coming! I'm coming! I'm coming!" she cried passionately as Carrington twisted like a corkscrew and tried to up the pace.

He couldn't keep up with her thrusting back as he vowed to deliver the goods. She raked his bare back with long nails, which made him wince with pain, but it was all in the line of duty, he told himself. She cried out, "Jake! Oh, yes, Jake!" before finally collapsing on the rug on the floor in a trickle of combined spent love juices. She felt sticky, uncomfortable and cold even though it was warm outside, but she was deeply satisfied.

"So, who is Jake?" Carrington enquired after rolling off her and catching his breath. She didn't answer but just purred with contentment.

His next question would be to ask, "Who is Boras in Falmouth?"

Chapter Eight

Down at the harbour, Bert and the boys were about to launch *The Boy Blewett*.

The Major and the Countess had taken a stroll down on the harbour wall to get away from the main celebrations and take in some sea air. They passed Al and his garage mate, Oppo, setting up the fireworks.

"This is a very dangerous place to be right now," said the Countess jumping suddenly and gripping the Major's arm when an unannounced firework from elsewhere whizzed off into the sky. "It sounds like the night the Bolsheviks came."

"Hello," said Bert, seeing the elderly couple looking down on to the boat. "Come for some mackerel, have you, Major?" said Bert cheerily.

"He'll have a job," piped up Bert. "The Germans took the lot yesterday." The Countess joined in the conversation.

"Talking about mackerel, won't that old trout at The Bluebells be missing us?"

"Steady on, old girl. We don't live in a prison where our cells are searched along with our few meagre possessions. We can come and go as we please, within reason."

The Major was aghast at the thought of such caddish behaviour.

"So can prisoners on parole," replied the Countess.

The Major spoke again.

"Forget her, Countess. She has probably got a hot date with a bottle somewhere. Oh, I almost forgot, dear lady. She said something about showing off that dog of hers to our German friends. A German dog to boot."

The words were spoken with a hint of disgust by the Major. The Countess wasn't finished.

"She is a dog. The boxer dog, he is better looking than the Matron, and he is Bosch also. It's impossible to get away from them."

The skipper of *The Boy Blewett* thought he had the perfect solution.

"You could always take a trip out to sea with us. There won't be any Germans out there."

He paused and awaited their answer.

"Hopefully," he added, remembering one of the two reasons why he was taking Bert back out there.

It had suddenly all come flooding back to Big Bert that maybe those pirates were still out there somewhere, skulking and waiting.

No, he decided quickly, they were probably here somewhere, mixed in amongst the visitors from Bremerstunghaven. It was their act of retribution for losing the war.

"Why not? Splendid idea, what?" said the Major. "Haven't been out on the old briny since I've been in that Bluebells place. So what do you say, Countess? How are your sea legs?"

The Countess Olga thought it was a splendid idea as well, if only to piss off Trout Face, who would be lecturing on acting your age when she got to hear about it.

"Wonderful idea, boat seaman," said Olga. "My dear Major, you are such a naughty boy. Why, you will be asking me to be naughty in the bushes at The Bluebells with you next."

Olga flashed a wicked smile at all the fishermen, who admired her pluck, except one of their number, who almost fell overboard at the suggestion.

Big Bert and the boat's skipper assisted the elderly couple down the metal ladder and on to the boat, which bobbed gently, her tyre fenders rubbing against the stone harbour wall.

"You can sit in the stern," said the helpful boat skipper. "I've got a nice thick blanket in the wheel house that you can both drape over your legs. It can get a bit chilly out there, even on a grand day like this one."

"Are you saying we are old, young man?" said the Countess in a false sounding admonishment.

"Why, Countess, I would never suggest such a thing!"

He had to hand it to her. He hoped that, if he ever reached her grand old age, he'd have half of her spirit. She was a lovely old lady, if a bit feisty, and very eccentric. He could imagine her wagging her finger at Adolf Hitler in disgust over the attack on Stalingrad in 1943.

The Boy Blewett made steady progress chugging out of Porth Branven's small harbour, with its occupants pleased to be getting away from Germans, German flags, German music, bratwurst and the imminent danger from Al's garage's impending firework display. Which person with the brain the size of a walnut ever allowed Al to organise a large firework display? It was like allowing a compulsive arsonist to keep a box of matches in a firelighter factory.

Bert wondered whether his fish contained some kind of stupid gene, because Al was a good customer and always had plenty of fish from him, but so too did most of the good folk of Porth Branven. It was a theory without proof, but nevertheless a theory. As far as Bert was concerned, theories, and conspiracy theories in particular, were the gospel and to be believed because the vicar had told him so over a few pints in The Anchor after blessing *The Two Inbred Sisters*.

Everybody around here had suddenly appeared to have gone stir fry crazy. Either that or they were all inbred like the name of his boat lying on the bottom out there off the reef.

The skipper of *The Boy Blewett*, a no-nonsense Yorkshire man from the seafaring town of Halifax, and adopted to these parts some twenty years before, had a similar theory, but with a bit more substance to it. His involved fish and crustaceans as well, plus the waters that washed this coastline with as much frequency as Molly lost her knickers, and he should know because he had found them on more than one occasion after doing little jobs on the side.

His theory was all about CDE *Nancekuke*, or, to give it its proper title, *Chemical Defence Establishment Nancekuke*, which was situated at Portreath, a little further up the coast. This was a Ministry of Defence top secret establishment, so top secret that the clue to its purpose was in the title of said establishment.

They had been mucking around with nerve agents since the early 1950s, storing it, and even dumping the stuff out at sea where Mother Nature, and Ocean, to be more precise, would be a good girl and would wash it back with the tide. The results, of course, had been numerous seals dying minus their eyes through caustic burns, and mutant fish with two heads and strange colours being caught off Portreath around 1969.

But then again, it could just have been that the residents of Porth Branven were incredible thickies with no brain capacity to act any differently. Quite how Roger and his cohorts had actually managed to persuade Bremerstunghaven's finest to twin with it defied logic. Maybe it was some secret government experiment like CDE Nancekuke.

As the boat left the protective arm of the harbour wall, the water got choppier as they met the open sea. The Countess and the Major bobbed up and down, sitting quietly in the stern, enjoying themselves and taking in the sea air. Then a wayward lone seagull, affectionately know to the fishermen as Johnny, suddenly swooped and crapped on Bert's head.

"You bleddy tosser, Johnny!" said Bert, shaking his fist up at the bird. "And after all the rich pickings of the sea I've given you since your mammy orphaned you."

Bert cleaned up the lime smeared mess from his head with a rag thrown to him by the skipper's mate, a young lad who worked part time in the pasty shop next to Al's garage when he wasn't out fishing with Halifax Halibut, as the Yorkshire skipper was known. Johnny the seagull flew away squawking, which was his way of saying thanks to Bert.

The dark olive streaked shadow of the high cliffs to the north of the cove slowly moved behind them on their starboard side, and the big Tooth Rock that was separated from the cliffs by only a short distance came into closer view.

The skipper of *The Boy Blewett* was careful to stick to the narrow channel out of the harbour that protected against the numerous treacherous rocks guarding the entrance to the small port. The channel offered a precious few feet deeper draught for a small boat to manoeuvre its way out to where the Spurdog Cove reef lay.

From the shore, the music drifted out to sea after them and could be heard more loudly than the oompa band, which was taking a break from proceedings.

Outside The People's Rooms, large speakers had been set up and records were now being played. It was the first time The Beatles had played Porth Branven and their feel-good offering from the heady days of the sixties boomed out - *Yellow Submarine*.

"I like the Beatles," said The Countess, reaching for her flask of warm-me-up 'little water'. "I don't like that Yoko Ono. I think she is a troublemaker."

The Major couldn't give a fig for Yoko or The Beatles. His musical tastes were entrenched back much further than the 1960s and those beatniks and their degenerative so-called music.

The Boy Blewett pushed against the current and made steady progress out into the bay, steering a north-westerly course in the general direction of Bert's blue-and-white submarine and Halifax Halibut's pots, which he and his mate were to haul in.

There was always the chance that bad weather might suddenly arrive tomorrow, so they wanted the job done before then.

Aboard UB-AF9, things were quiet. The two British warships were steaming away from the area. The U-boat was prepared to do the same, cautiously. A couple of merchant vessel kills on the way home would compensate for the no-show of the British agent and the non-mission of the patrol so far.

The submarine surfaced to take a last look around. Leutnant Spiegel scanned the surface of the sea as the white water poured off the vessel's hull and drained away from her deck. A large clump of seaweed clung to the surfaced hull. Leutnant Spiegel hollered below.

"Can someone go below, get a couple of buckets and collect some fresh sea water for Herman? Also collect a third bucket full of the seaweed to make him feel at home down there amongst all that oil and diesel fumes! It will keep that idiot, the Düsseldorf Dummkopf, happy. And if he is happy then the Kapitan will be as well."

The Leutnant had said the last few words quietly to himself. He just wanted a quiet life and a safe trip back to the Breton coast. The British hadn't attacked yet, but with that idiot, Krieger, aboard, the British were not the only enemies to be wary of. Anything was possible as long as Leutnant Hans Krieger was aboard this boat.

The nearest rating quickly did as instructed by the officer, collecting the buckets of water and another full of weed for Herman, and he almost fell when he slipped whilst dipping a bucket in the sea.

Thankfully, the man wasn't lost overboard. If he had been lost and presumed drowned, then the boat's log would have been interesting to read.

This war was full of madness, concluded Leutnant Spiegel. When would this idiocy with the needs of Herman end? Even he, Spiegel, normally level-headed, was succumbing to Herman and his takeover of this boat. Still, the lobster would make a better U-boat officer than Krieger, he conceded.

The boat had drifted a little way north on the current, and the little fishing port of Porth Branven was just disappearing around the headland.

The ever efficient Leutnant Franz Spiegel scanned the sea with his binoculars. He could make out the fishing boat heading out to sea and several figures on board. One of them was quite distinguishable. It was the skipper of the boat they had boarded and scuttled. He could quite definitely pick out the larger-than-life frame of the man they called Big Bert.

Leutnant Spiegel was pleased that the adversary had survived and had obviously got back safely to shore where he would surely have notified the military about the U-boat's presence. That would probably account for the unwanted British Navy presence, and maybe that infuriating small plane that had buzzed them.

The Leutnant got a rating to summon the Kapitan from the wardroom. Kapitan Von Diesel appeared alongside Leutnant Spiegel on the conning tower.

"What is it, Franz? Have we a problem?"

"No, Herr Kapitan. Have a look through the glasses. This will interest you."

Kapitanleutnant Von Diesel looked at the small boat heading away from land.

"Ah, Franz. I see it. Big Bert and a different fishing smack."

"Shall we chase after them, Herr Kapitan?"

Von Diesel rubbed his bearded chin. Like the rest of the crew, he smelled, needed a bath, was tired, had stinking breath and had a headache from the diesel fumes inside the submarine.

"No, Franz. She is small fry. Let's not compromise ourselves again in broad daylight for a little fish like that one."

"Well, we did yesterday," thought Leutnant Spiegel. "Ah, well."

The Kapitan was in charge and gave the orders. Franz Spiegel was a little relieved as he wanted to leave this part of the treacherous Cornish coast. They had been here far too long for his liking.

Back on the shore, Al got ready to set off the big ones.

"Stand back and admire, everybody!"

The huge sky rockets were placed in bits of old metal tubes from his garage. The rockets looked very unstable. Al lit the touch paper of the first rocket and waited for it to travel skywards.

"I hope someone's informed the RNLI and the coastguard about this display," came one comment from an onlooker. "We don't want them thinking they are distress rockets fired from a boat."

"Bloody idiots," said Al to Oppo, puffing away on a cigarette, its orange ash defying gravity as it threatened to drop into the box of fireworks. "The sea is out there, that way. Dry land, as far as I know, is here on the harbour wall. I done national service in The Army Catering Corps, so I know all about pyrotechnics."

"Yeah, and I worked as a deckhand on the *Scillonian* ferry," said Al's mate, Oppo, for good measure.

With such a skill mix, how could the spectacular planned firework display possibly go wrong?"

Al leaned over the sky rockets as he prepared them and then leaned back just in time so as not to get injured. The illegally imported heavy duty fireworks from China probably packed more firepower than that boasted by HMS *Bosun*.

The first sky rocket flew up to the heavens with a mighty *whoosh* amidst gasps and cheers from the crowd gathered. When it reached a great height, it exploded with a loud bang, much to the delight of the children present, and especially the younger ones, who marvelled at its delightful coloured stars that fell slowly back to earth.

Jack the Russell, a horrible dog belonging to a tourist, barked and barked and barked before attempting to nip his owner for the fun of it. Jill Russell, his sister, joined in for good measure.

The fireworks had been heard on board the U-boat. Then the music could be heard, combined with the fireworks, the sound drifting out to sea across the bay. Kapitan Von Diesel and Leutnant Spiegel watched through binoculars and listened with interest. Both were puzzled.

"What is going on, Herr Kapitan? It sounds like some kind of attack, and yet no glorious day time Luftwaffe raid. And yet, why would the Luftwaffe attack this place anyway? And furthermore, Herr Kapitan, what is that music we are hearing? It is like nothing I have ever heard before and in the whole of my life so far."

The Leutnant continued to listen carefully along with his Commander.

"Franz, this is no attack, but a celebration of some kind. These Cornish villagers and fishermen are definitely celebrating something or other. They are the Feuerwerke, and big ones also. Grand! Look at that one!"

Al had sent a mega-big rocket into the sky and it reached a height of several hundred feet before exploding violently into a sea of spectacular colours and little stars.

"I have not seen such Feuerwerke since the beer festival in München before the war," said Von Diesel, suddenly feeling homesick and pining for the Fatherland.

Leutnant Spiegel was a little more cautious, believing that they were perhaps being lulled into a trap of some kind. Spiegel seldom relaxed and didn't have much time for fireworks, celebrations or, indeed, fun of any kind. He was an officer in the German Kriegsmarine; a professional with a job to do. These British, and Cornish in particular, were idiots who deserved to be subjugated into a greater German Fatherland.

Despite this, he thought the *Yellow Submarine* song was a bit catchy. He thought that maybe this was some other crazy British secret weapon intended to disarm German naval readiness.

Leutnant Spiegel looked at his Commander and shrugged his shoulders in ignorance. He was cold and wet from the water pouring down the conning tower hatch, despite it being a rather glorious August Thursday morning. Lack of proper sleep had also taken its toll on him.

"What is this? Herr Kapitan, what is this nonsense, *Yellow Submarine*? It is a wunderbar song, but a yellow submarine would be a sitting chicken."

"You mean a sitting duck, Herr Leutnant."

The Kapitan hadn't a clue either.

"I know not what this strange music is, Franz. It sounds good though, ja?"

Franz Spiegel, always Teutonic, did like the strange music but kept his thoughts and expressions in check.

*

More rockets went skywards. The firework display escalated. Al, on the quayside, was in his element, firing off rockets and other assorted fireworks like there was no tomorrow. Porth Branven had never seen such a grand display since the old Trocadero dance hall had gone up in smoke with a fire caused by a petrol tank exploding at Al's garage in 1968.

"Franz, this is some kind of celebration, ja? We must take a closer look at what is going on in this place. Maybe the fifth columnists have seized control of the area in our final victory push."
Franz wasn't so sure.

Out on *The Boy Blewett*, Halifax Halibut was making good progress out to the position where the Germans had scuttled *The Two Inbred Sisters* and stolen her catch.

The Major and his companion were enjoying the trip out to sea, warmed by the thick blanket draping their legs, and fortified by the Countess regularly producing her hip flask of 'little water'. If it ran out, then Major Beere had extra rations in the form of his own flask, which contained brandy purchased at knock-down, ask-no-questions prices through a friend of the Countess.

Yellow Submarine subsided, unlike Al's firework display, which flew into the sky with increasing and frightening intensity. A dazzling array of colours accompanied by loud bangs lit up the beautiful blue sky.

In and outside The People's Rooms, the drink flowed and Roger organised more hot dogs made with German sausage to be cooked. He wondered where Molly had got to. She must be organising something somewhere or other.

His wife was an extremely popular lady in Porth Branven but, for some unknown reason, was not liked much by the women folk. She was missing out on a bit of sausage; German sausage, which was a bit different and spicier than she was used to.

And what about Jake? Jake Harvey was usually Mr Reliable, prepared to get his hands dirty and help out when necessary.

Ah, well. They were the ones missing out, Roger told himself. He, for one, was enjoying himself.

Frau Hertzmann seemed to have recovered a little and got her second wind.

Up on the cliff tops, Carrington and the Matron had dozed off, post-coital, and awoke to find they were still messy and very much dishevelled.

That was the trouble with sex, particularly the outdoor variety; the pleasure was fleeting, the aftermath was messy, and the consequences could be long-lasting and not very pleasurable.

"You naughty man," said Matron, adjusting her clothing and managing to put on her knickers inside out without noticing. "Another pair for the wash. Come on, we can go back to The Bluebells. You can get cleaned up there."

With that, she left Carrington to awkwardly get dressed in the back of the van. Its curtains blocked out the sunlight. He hadn't realised how difficult it could be to get dressed in a vehicle. He was more used to hotel rooms and more comfort. Just for good measure, a wasp had managed to find its way into the vehicle and buzzed on the inside of the window, with the distinct possibility of stinging Carrington at any moment. A bit like the Russians, he thought, trying to remember why he was here in the first place.

Matron had wriggled her way into the driver's seat, and sat touching up her make up and rearranging her hair by use of the rear mirror.

Just then, a familiar car pulled up slowly beside her VW Camper. There was just room for two vehicles to park in the secluded spot amongst the duty gorse bushes, mine spoil and fly-tipped rubbish.

"Why, hello, Jake. What are you doing up there?" asked Matron.

Jake Harvey looked sheepish and guilty as sin as he sat at the wheel of the beat-up old Ford saloon. Looking equally sheepish and guilty as sin, and with her head down, sat Molly in the passenger seat. A thick rug could be seen on the back seat, along with a pillow. Molly looked like she wanted the ground to open up and swallow her.

Carrington lay silent on the floor of the camper van and just listened.

"Well, I have to be off now. I promise not to tell if you don't," said Matron. "I know fly tipping is illegal, but, well, sometimes you just have to when the council doesn't do its job properly."

It was a get-out clause for Jake as well.

"Caught red-handed! I put my hands up. Guilty as charged, Matron. Molly had some rubbish to dump as well, so I thought I would kill two birds with one stone and bring all of ours up here together. It's in the boot."

Molly forced a smile that didn't convince anybody. With that, Matron said farewell and started up the old camper van, which sounded like a Panzer tank that needed a new gear box. She started to reverse out on the track, avoiding a dumped cooker with its door hanging off as she went.

She was deep in thought as she drove. What were those two up to out here? She and Jake had been known to come up here together every so often when needs must, but Molly? Surely not. She dismissed it from her mind; the very thought of Jake and Molly together. Molly and Roger were solid as the turds her boxer dog passed first thing on a morning, Matron tried to convince herself.

The skeleton staff left at The Bluebells Residential Home were as surprised to see Matron return early as they were to see Matron disappear early. They didn't know who the strange man with her was and didn't ask.

Carrington was grateful to take the opportunity to avail himself of the facilities of the staff changing rooms equipped with a shower so he could clean up. He still hadn't learned who Boras in Falmouth was.

Matron got back into normal organising mode before it was time to hit the bottle again. Taking the weekly 'bowel book', she entered the big day room where residents not in their rooms or out somewhere mostly slept, zonked out by medication.

"Time for bowel check!" said Matron quite cheerfully for all to hear, and with little thought for the patients' personal dignity.

Once a week, every resident who came into a certain category was checked to see if they 'had been'. The bowel movements were recorded, with the accuracy of Hansard in The House of Commons, in the little book for the purpose, which was available to all staff to see. If a resident was unfortunate enough to have 'not been', then they were taken into a bathroom, having been given a jollop of something the night before to 'help them go', and sat on a commode 'to perform'. In extreme cases, enemas were administered.

When the senior carer was satisfied that there had been a bowel motion of correct proportions, then it was a case of, "Next please!"

Just then, old Myrna appeared beside Matron.

"Matron, have you seen my husband?"

Matron was in a good mood.

"No, dear, but come with me. Have you been recently?"

Myrna couldn't remember if she had been or not and went with Matron into the bathroom. She had the dubious honour of being the first resident for the bowel book.

The Matron would have loved to collar the Major and the Countess, but those two, wherever they were, had constitutions that defied the laws of nature and elderly folk.

Carrington had finished cleaning himself up.

"Can you see the sea from up here?" he asked.

"Well, you can if you are a contortionist and can lean out of the upstairs landing window," said Matron from behind the bathroom door.

"Do you think the Major would mind if I took a quick look through his telescope?"

"Suppose not, if you are quick," said Matron. "Talking of the Major, where have those two got to today? He's been acting a bit funny lately. I'll have to check on his bowels later."

Carrington managed to achieve a view out to sea, just, by doing as suggested with some difficulty and strange looks from a care assistant.

He focused the unwieldy brass telescope out of the sash window and balanced as best he could, which felt precarious with the wooden stairs only a couple of feet away, should he slip backwards.

He couldn't see the distinctive shape of the U-boat sitting out there on the surface, hidden by The Tooth Rock, but he was immediately attracted to the bobbing shape of *The Boy Blewett*, a bit further out and near to the end of the reef off Spurdog Point, more westerly.

Carrington trained the telescope on to the fishing boat and its dubious occupants. It was strange that he was looking at the Major through the Major's own telescope. He could pick out his distinctive figure quite clearly along with his friend, the Countess, that Russian woman.

This was a stroke of luck because they wouldn't be able to suddenly return to disturb him. This old pair was not out there fishing. So what exactly were they up to?

Carrington observed the boat and the actions of the skipper, his mate and Bert, who was so vociferous in the pub. These people must be spies, he decided. There could be no doubts about it.

Down at the harbour yet again, Al's fireworks were going off like October the 29th and November the 2nd, 3rd and 4th. So far, they had gone off without incident, but they were getting progressively bigger and louder.

Porth Branven had gone German and celebration crazy. Al and Oppo had even been on the sauce themselves. Al's daughter, Lulu Demelza, had discreetly taken the keys away from the ignition of her dad's vehicle so he wouldn't do anything stupid like driving it later.

Frau Hertzmann and Roger were getting on really well and playing footsie under the table as the good German lady, or Frau, proceeded to tell Roger all about life in dear old Bremerstunghaven in West Germany, and how the Germans were better at football than the English, which Roger wholly agreed with, he being a good old Cornish boy through and through so the English cap didn't fit.

And then they discussed who had the better character, the British bulldog or the German boxer, and which breed was uglier. They begged to differ on that particular issue.

Then Frau Hertzmann asked about Frau Roger. Roger said he didn't know where she was, and with the drink flowing, he burst into laughter.

"So, where is Herr Hertzmann?" he asked, looking at her closely.

He now noticed how attractive she was, even though she had worry lines and had lived the years. Frau Hertzmann took a swig of lager from her stein and looked closely at Roger. There was an obvious attraction between them.

"He, how you say, has another, younger fräulein he trades me in for."

"I'm so sorry," said Roger, not a bit sorry at all.

"And then he caught the bus."

"Caught the bus?" asked Roger, mystified. "What, he buggered off with the fräulein on the bus? Different, I suppose."

Frau Hertzmann laughed.

"He caught the bus in Bremerstunghaven when he never looked crossing the road. So tragic. The bus was running on time and he was running late. Only one winner - the bus!"

Roger wasn't sure how to respond so took his cue from Frau Hertzmann. He didn't wish to appear unsympathetic. The German woman put him at ease.

"I am over him now, just like the bus was."

They both burst into spontaneous laughter and chinked their glasses together. The other guests, both local and German, looked on in surprise, but they just faded away from the thoughts and immediate vision of the two new friends.

Away from the main celebrations, an impromptu football match had broken out between a mixture of the younger German boys and girls and some of the Porth Branven locals. For the time being, any anti-German feelings melted away as they all entered into the swing of things.

Out on the harbour wall, some of the town's older residents who had fought in the last war kept their own counsel, smoked their pipes and cigarettes, and passed the time in their own company.

Some just couldn't forget and the raw wounds were just too recent to make friends. A couple of them had soldier sons serving with the British Army of the Rhine, which had fifty-six thousand troops serving in West Germany at that time.

For some, it was a bad decision to hold such a twinning ceremony just twenty-six years after hostilities with the Germans had ended.

Al's fireworks were going down a storm when they really should have been going up a storm. One rocket slipped and decided to fire sideways and headed straight for Constable Harris, striking his helmet and knocking it off with some considerable force, leaving it smoking on the harbour wall. He only just managed to save it from bouncing down onto some steps and into the green water below. PC Harris looked at his cousin, Al, with some disgust.

"Sorry," said Al, thinking it was a danged good aim as his cousin in serge examined his helmet for damage.

He quickly composed himself and walked on out to the end of the harbour wall, where old Trevor, who should have been in a home but wasn't, played his ukulele for the benefit of any passing seagulls who wanted to listen.

I'm Leaning on a Lamp Post etc, with words of his own, drifted out across the harbour entrance, with the gulls that were around showing complete indifference.

Al, meanwhile, vowed to be more careful with the fireworks. Oppo, however, undertook no such vow.

Chapter Nine

Aboard UB-AF9, the Commander was about to give the order to dive and leave their position, when he heard a very familiar collection of sounds.

Music continued to drift out to sea from the Porth Branven celebrations, but it was music with a difference from *Yellow Submarine* and such nonsense.

"Listen, Franz, and tell me what you hear."

Franz listened.

"Why, mein Kapitan, I hear *The Blue Danube* waltz by Johan Strauss."

All thoughts of war drifted away briefly for the two officers and the other seamen, who could hear the strains of Strauss played as if for them personally across the waves. They remained vigilant but listened and felt closer to their homeland, and thought of better times.

"We shall leave after this is finished," ordered the Kapitan.

The crew of the U-boat had enjoyed *The Blue Danube* waltz and, as the two officers scanned the shore, they were very surprised to hear what came next. Franz almost dropped his binoculars.

"Mein Kapitan, *Das Lied Der Deutschen.* They are playing our national anthem. Why would they, our enemy, be doing this?"

The Kapitan listened to the celebrations of the people on the shore, who he could just make out.

"Herr Leutnant, my good friend and fellow officer, these people are, I believe, celebrating the end of the war. They must be. I can think of no other rational explanation for this. They are celebrating a glorious German victory. They have surrendered to our superior forces. The war is surely over."

"Herr Kapitan, we were at war only the other day when we left the Breton coast, and now it's all over. With no means of communications, we couldn't have been informed. What should we do, Herr Kapitan?"

Von Diesel gave the situation some thought and then spoke clearly and precisely.

"Herr Leutnant, we are going ashore. We shall seek out the appointed Bürgermeister and await instructions through the nearest German military unit."

"Herr Kapitan, this would explain why The Royal Navy did not attack us. Technically, Herr Kapitan, we violated The Geneva Convention after the hostilities ended."

"Do not trouble yourself, Franz. We were not informed that the ceasefire had taken place. How could we know? Prepare to move in closer to land and we will go ashore, but proceed with caution until we are absolutely sure that hostilities have ceased for good."

Up at The Bluebells, Carrington was getting cramp and could not see the U-boat, which was masked from his view by The Tooth Rock, which lay a little way off the entrance to Porth Branven harbour. He continued to focus on the activity taking place aboard *The Boy Blewett*, out off Spurdog Point. Her skipper appeared to be placing a marker buoy.

"This is the spot where she went down, Halibut," said Big Bert with some disgust. "Those bastard Germans! I know it was here because I cross-referenced it from The Point and I know these waters well enough without the need for any chart."

"She'll be rect wet down there," replied Halifax Halibut, stating the obvious. "Come Monday, we can go over to Falmouth and have a word with my mate about bringing her back up. She might not be a problem to salvage, if the weather doesn't get too bad."

Big Bert wondered what the insurance company would make of this business. Probably filed under loony claims, he decided.

Carrington didn't quite know what to make of it either. Then he made an instant decision based on all his years of living on the edge and making instant decisions. They were spies and that was a drop-off for a hostile Navy to pick up, say, plans for HMS *Bosun*, or maybe the secrets belonging to CDE *Nancekuke*. This was serious and he had to report quickly to Naval Intelligence at The Admiralty.

From the surface, and just a few feet past The Tooth Rock, the U-boat was close enough to hear the music clearly and to see German flags flying on Porth Branven's west side, along with the Union Flag and the black-and-white cross of St Piran, the national flag of Cornwall. The Commander and his Leutnant were puzzled that no swastikas appeared on any flag, because the red, black and gold of the German flag was unmistakable.

"I wonder if Von Ribbentrop is in residence at St Michael's Mount," said Von Diesel to Leutnant Spiegel.

"I wouldn't have thought so, Herr Kapitan. This war can only just have ended. He would have to hire John Julian of Cornwall to take his furniture over the causeway to the Mount."

The Kapitan was mystified.

"Herr Leutnant Franz, how do you know of these Cornish removers, John Julian?"

"That is simple, Herr Kapitan. I looked them up in a smuggled copy of a local publication called Kelly's Directory. I also did my homework on Cornwall before the war and stayed a little while with my Aunt Gertrude, who used to live at the small cottage near to Lamorna Cove on the other coastal side to this one. John Julian Cornwall, Herr Kapitan; Newquay, Wadebridge, Truro and Falmouth."

"Ah, yes," replied the Kapitan. "John Julian Estate Agents. I remember their distinctive blue lorries on the road when I was in these parts before the war."

Kapitan Von Diesel breathed in the fresh sea air. His headache had eased, and he rotated his crew so they could benefit from the fresh air as well. He pondered over events since they had sailed, and still couldn't remember the time from leaving Brittany to arriving off the Cornish coast.

Franz Spiegel had no memory of it either. It was as if UB-AF9 and her crew had entered a sleep phase and had awakened when hostilities ended.

Kapitanleutnant Von Diesel had a dilemma. The boat had to be crewed and he wanted to go ashore, but who to take with him to Porth Branven and who to leave behind?

The decision was made for him. He wanted that idiot, Leutnant Krieger, alongside him so he would need to hand pick men who he could trust to be with him and give him cover.

Krieger was daft enough to want to go and play the slot machines in the tiny amusement arcade that he knew existed in the port.

The boat would be safe in the capable hands of Leutnant Franz Spiegel and the Chief Engineer. That way, if anything was to go wrong, they could get the boat underway and out of trouble.

So the Kapitan decided that two boats would go ashore - one rubber boat and the wooden skiff - and the men would be fully armed in case of unforeseen trouble. He didn't expect any, but he was cautious anyway. It had been agreed that the flare pistol he was to take with him would be fired once, which would signal the U-boat to leave the area immediately. The men got the boats ready.

"Make sure you look after Herman, Herr Engineer," said the Kapitan through his crew.

It turned out that Herman was well down in the engine room and, while the boat was on the surface, was able to be given fresh water supplies to keep him going. Herman, their lucky mascot, much preferred being down in the safety of the engine room to being put in a pot in the galley.

Leutnant Spiegel kept watch as the party set off to row the short distance to the harbour. He wondered what use a yellow submarine would be.

He wanted this war to end but exercised more cautious thoughts than the Kapitan. This could be some kind of trap. He was happier to stay aboard UB-AF9 than to go ashore.

The Leutnant watched as the boats left the mother submarine and made their way across the shallow neck of water.

The Kapitan was vigilant as his men rowed across, and he kept his finger poised near the trigger of his Mauser pistol.

Schwartz, his most trusted seaman, was equally vigilant and was his unofficial number two on account of Leutnant Hans Krieger being an imbecile who he wouldn't trust with commanding a pedalo on a child's boating lake. Krieger felt important so the Kapitan let him get on with it.

Schwartz, he could depend on, along with Siegfried, Horst and the others. He felt a little safer with these men alongside him.

Von Diesel knew this place and had done his homework here before the war. He thought about The Atlantic Tea Rooms And Gift Shop and Molly. Yes, dear Molly; a sweet fräulein, even if she was on the wrong side. He wondered how she was getting on.

Von Diesel had no sweetheart back in the Fatherland. He thought about Hans Krieger, whose wife and two young children were back in Düsseldorf. Yes, he made fun of the Leutnant, but how he wished the man could go back home to his family in Deutschland.

He snapped back to the present. They were sailors of the German Kriegsmarine, and he had a job to do. The harbour wall drew closer.

"What is that idiot doing up there?" asked Erhard Schwartz, seeing old Trevor and hearing some awful out-of-tune song he played on his ukulele; the man must be a distant cousin of the Düsseldorf Dummkopf, he thought.

Old Trevor completely ignored the two boats as they rowed past him and into the narrow neck of the harbour.

"He is playing a special tune of welcome for us, Herr Kapitan," said Hans Krieger, thinking that the man played a mean ukulele, just like George Formby.

The Boy Blewett made her way out along the edge of the reef to pull up Halifax Halibut's pots, and Carrington, from the window of The Bluebells, had seen enough through the Major's telescope, which he returned to the old man's room, being careful to replace it exactly as he had found it.

Carrington couldn't have seen the arrival of the Germans, as they were tucked away under the high cliffs, their U-boat being hidden from view behind The Tooth Rock.

"Well, you know where to find me," said Matron, giving Carrington a knowing smile, adjusting her knickers through her uniform.

She was in need of her usual drink and he was in need of information.

"Did you see anything exciting out to sea then?" asked Matron, not in the least bit interested.

"No. Only a load of old sea birds depositing lime and fighting with each other in mid air," came the response. "Look, I have to be going now. Today was great. Maybe we can do it again some time."

It sounded like a business arrangement, and, in a way, it was. Both supplier and customer were satisfied.

"I have to report back," said Carrington. "I wouldn't worry about your two elderly residents, the Major and the Countess. They are harmless enough. There is a just one thing more though. The Countess mentioned somebody called Boras, in Falmouth. Do you know of anybody connected with her of that name?"

"I've no idea who Boras is," said the Matron. "The Countess goes to Falmouth regularly to take tea with someone there, I believe. And then she always returns with material for her scrapbooks. She normally goes and returns by taxi. Apart from that, I have no idea who Boras is."

"Thank you," said Carrington, who was now even more convinced that the Russians had a team of deep sleepers in Cornwall spying on Royal Navy movements.

The Matron spoke again.

"Can't see what the attraction is in ships myself. Have you seen her scrapbooks?"

He had and said so.

"Harmless bit of fun, I suppose," continued Matron. "Got to have a hobby of some kind."

"Yes, and we know what your two are," said Carrington to himself.

Carrington hadn't got an address, but he buggered off in haste anyway to Falmouth. It had been a good day's work with an unexpected bonus. Now though, he was pleased to be leaving this town of insanity. There were more idiots here per square foot than anywhere else, he decided.

Matron retreated to her office with the instructions not to be disturbed as she was doing important paper work for a couple of hours.

She left her deputy in charge and was thankful that there were no relatives around. The residents were quiet, even old Myrna, who had been given The Bluebells Residential Home purge. If the bowels were opened on a regular basis, then the home ran smoothly, according to Matron.

Halifax Halibut had a few crabs and a couple of decent sized lobsters, and an angry looking conger eel that had managed to somehow get inside one of the pots through its narrow neck and couldn't get back out again. It still had time to completely devour the fish head bait inside the pot and frighten two crabs and a small lobster half to death.

After some difficulty, the conger, which they called Eric, was released back to the depths to live another day. Its crustacean companions were not so fortunate.

All of the pots had orange coloured floats, except for a couple of green ones. When the boat reached the first green float, the skipper shouted to Big Bert and his mate.

"I'll need a hand with this one!"

The pot they were prepared to pull up looked very heavy. The Major and his companion sat quietly watching events. The men hauled up a specially adapted blue plastic barrel that had been weighted down. Bert opened it up to reveal its contents.

"My dear boy, it's booze!" said the Countess as the men emptied and stowed the bottles of French brandy out of sight in false-bottomed wooden fish boxes.

"You two good people haven't seen anything," said Bert.

A look from the skipper endorsed his opinion.

"There are a couple of bottles in it for you two, if you turn a blind eye, no questions asked."

"I saw nothing. Did you, dear lady?" said the Major.

There was a short pause.

"Only the crabs and the lobsters for the table," said the Countess. "Not forgetting, of course, that unpleasant looking long fish, Eric, with the teeth."

The boat moved off to pick up the other pots scattered out along and just beyond the reef.

Another barrel would contain some more illicit booze and the rest of the pots would hopefully yield a few more crabs and lobsters, which fetched good money and were always in demand in restaurants.

As they gathered in their harvest from the sea, Bert thought about the big lobster that he had caught, and which the Germans had confiscated. That had been a handsome specimen; the biggest lobster he had ever caught.

"I hope the bastards choke on it," he thought as he scanned the surface of the sea, thinking that a German U-boat was about to surface at any time with history about to repeat itself.

"I wonder if the Halibut has some vodka in the other pots under the water," the Countess said quietly to Major Beere.

The Major was an honest, upright individual who wouldn't normally approve of smuggling on a general scale. However, when it was on a more personal level, and booze was on offer, he was prepared to make an exception and turn a blind eye. His ancestors were wreckers. It was in his blood. The Treasury wouldn't miss a few bottles of booze, he convinced himself.

The boats containing the German sailors entered the main harbour without anyone really noticing.

Most of the residents and visitors seemed to be too inebriated and wrapped up in the celebration.

Old Trevor was in a world of his own, playing his ukulele for anyone who would listen. Two gulls appeared mildly interested, but probably because he had taken a short break from playing to take a bite from a ham sandwich he carried with him in an old haversack.

The old guys on the pier were playing a game of dominoes in a rickety senior persons' shelter and never noticed the Germans either. One of them had a good set and chuckled to himself.

"Those Germans would never have invaded this coast, boys. We would have been ready for them on the beaches and in the pill boxes, ready with cold steel."

"Here, here!" came a chorus of replies.

Al and Oppo continued to pretend to be Guido Fawkes and Catesby, setting off fireworks to their hearts' content and with little regard to public safety. Most of the rockets ended up over the rocky beach on the other side of the harbour, where a few people had gathered to watch, even though it didn't appear to be a very safe spot.

The fireworks, rather than being a spectacle in their own right, were a backdrop to the main celebrations taking place mostly inside and outside of The People's Rooms, which, for the day, resembled a German bier keller.

The police Sergeant responsible for law and order in the town had gone back to his office to write up some reports. He was in radio contact with his two Constables out on the beat. All seemed quiet enough, barring Al's firework display, which made the 4th of July in America seem like a sparkler fest.

Al and Oppo never really took much notice of the Germans either. They did see them, but so what? There were loads of them around anyway, all dressed up funnily. Maybe it was in poor taste that they wore World War Two uniforms, but they seemed harmless enough and didn't interfere with the fireworks.

And so the Germans, armed with their Mauser pistols, tied their boats up at the steps leading up to the top of the harbour wall.

A couple of small boys were up at the top, watching them closely and sniggering.

Leutnant Hans Krieger was unfortunate to be the first German sailor to ascend the steps, and raised his head first above the harbour wall.

Toosh! The smaller of the two boys fired at Krieger and got him smack in the side of the face. It stung the Leutnant, who cursed and pointed his gun at the child.

"You little dummkopf! I have a good mind to fire at you with this."

The Captain smirked and placed a restraining hand on the Leutnant's arm to make him lower his weapon.

"That is a peashooter, Hans," said the Captain, secretly congratulating the boy for being such a good shot and hitting this idiot of an officer.

Well, Hans wanted to know what a peashooter was, and now he knew, and had found out the painful way. His cheek still stung.

"I must get two of those, Herr Kapitan. One for my little Helmut, and the other for my little Willy."

"You can buy them in the paper shop, mister," said the small boy, thinking better of trying to have another shot at anybody.

"Where is your local law enforcement officer?" said Leutnant Krieger to the two confused boys.

"Do you mean the coppers?" said the bigger boy.

"Coppers? What is this boy going on about?" queried Krieger.

The Kapitan intervened.

"Leave this to me, Hans. I know these people well. They have many differing colloquialisms for things, unlike us in Germany, who call a shovel a shovel. They call the police things like rozzers, the filth and coppers, like their coins, which are really called pennies."

Hans Krieger was totally confused. The Kapitan went on. He addressed the boys politely but with authority in his voice.

"The Leutnant meant the coppers, ja."

The boys understood.

"I saw the stupid one with his helmet on fire a few minutes ago over by the fireworks," one of the boys informed him. "I don't know where he is now. You should have seen his helmet smoking from the firework."

"Thank you," replied Kapitan Von Diesel, bringing some money out of his uniform pocket. "Here is some money. So go to the shop and buy you and your friend here some sweeties. I think the rationing must be over by now."

"Thanks, Mister," said the older boy, grabbing the money and then realising he had been given German currency. "Hey, this is funny money. The shop won't take this."

"Yes, they will," said his mate. "Everything's German today, remember? And if they don't, we can always shoplift."

"Did that boy say that Helmut was on fire?" asked Krieger, a bit worried.

"He meant the policeman's helmet, as opposed to your little boy's name, Hans," said the Kapitan, beginning to wonder if it was such a good idea to bring along Leutnant Krieger with the shore party.

"This language is so difficult to master," said Krieger, shaking his head.

Hans Krieger also produced some coins and gave them to the boys.

"When you go to the shop that sells the sweeties, please also return with two glorious shooters of the peas, plus the ammunition, whatever that is that they fire."

"That looks like a real gun you are carrying, Mister. Why would you want a peashooter?"

"I want them for my two little boys, like you two, back in Germany. I need them for my little Willy and Helmut. When you return, you will find the Kapitan, myself and the crew at the apartment of the Bürgermeister, where all the celebrations seem to be taking place."

The two boys were about to disappear when Kapitanleutnant Von Diesel shouted after them.

"Hey, little boy! Tell me something. What are these celebrations concerning?"

The older boy smiled.

112

"Well, you should know, mister. It's a German theme day to welcome you lot over here."

With that, the two boys ran off, leaving the German sailors standing alone on the quayside.

"I was right, Hans," said the Kapitan, smiling. "The war has indeed ended and we are victorious. They have surrendered to our forces, and now they honour our presence. We must show some humility in our victory. Everyone has suffered far too much in this war. Let us find the Bürgermeister and cast an eye over these celebrations. Isn't it wunderbar to see our glorious flag fluttering in the warm summer breeze, and without that awful swastika to spoil it?"

Not all agreed with him, but he was the Kapitan, so no dissent was shown over his non-love for the swastika.

"After I have reported to the Bürgermeister, I will pay a visit to an old friend of mine at The Atlantic Tea Rooms."

One of the men drew The Kapitan's attention to a dog that was barking at Al's fireworks.

"Herr Kapitan, it wags its stumpy docked tail. It is the hund from the Fatherland. A glorious German specimen of a hund - a boxer hund."

The boxer dog belonging to Matron was friendly and had broken away from its handler. It nuzzled against Leutnant Krieger.

"I will see what his name is," said the Leutnant, examining a disc on the dog's studded collar.

"The hund is called Diesel," said Krieger, smiling. "He is a good German dog with a good German name like the Kapitan's."

Von Diesel was amused and patted the dog as well.

Al continued to fire off his pyrotechnics, sending money up to the sky in smoke. Porth Branven had not seen nor heard such an awesome display of noise since marauding Spanish pirates had sacked the place in 1520.

"Herr Kapitan, here is another," said Hans Krieger, stroking Matron's boxer dog and thinking of home.

"Another what?" asked the Kapitan.

"A hund, Herr Kapitan. A dachshund."

The sausage dog came sniffing around first the boxer and then the Germans. It too was friendly. The Kapitan checked its collar to see if it had a name.

"Hans," said the Kapitan. "Another fine specimen of Teutonic German doghood, but so far no British bulldogs to see."

Seaman Schwartz alerted the Kapitan to some vehicles paraded in the street leading up to The People's Rooms.

"Look, Herr Kapitan. There are some German people's cars the ever reliable Volkswagen Beetle."

The dogs were not the only ones who had been drawn to the German's arrival.

The boys returned from the shop with their sweets and two peashooters. The older boy handed the peashooters over to a grateful Leutnant Krieger, who thanked him.

"Come on, Leutnant Krieger. We have other matters to attend to of greater importance," said the Kapitan, ushering the men along from the harbour wall.

"Why are those German sailors carrying weapons?" asked a woman pushing a pram, with a toddler in attendance as well. "And they have old uniforms on depicting the swastika. That's not allowed any more in public. That is the height of bad taste, if you ask me, and not in keeping with the spirit of these celebrations."

A woman with her agreed, and suggested maybe they should inform the Constable, who was just down the street. Another monster Al firework zoomed off into the sky, making the women jump and the baby in the pram cry.

Meanwhile, the music continued to boom out, assaulting the ear drums of young and old alike.

Although they carried their arms, the German U-boat crew kept them at their sides so as not to appear provocative and rub in their conqueror status. After all, the good folk of this fishing town had gone to a lot of trouble with the celebrations in their honour, to make them welcome and to mark the end of hostilities between people who should never have gone to war in the first place.

Chapter Ten

Out at sea the Major and the Countess were living a life on the ocean waves, aided and abetted by a generous measure of illicit alcohol delivered to the Cornish coast by suppliers unknown. The recipients were older, wiser and knew better, but had succumbed to the lure of their ancestors' activities, and to the fact that no duty was to be paid on the drink, making it cheap and available.

"I love the briny, dear Countess," said the Major, feeling a little under the influence. "Do you think that Matron would know what to do if a man ever paid her any attention? I reckon she's tighter than a well worn screw head."

The Countess was equally inebriated.

"Bert, did you know that I escaped the Bolsheviks?"

Bert smiled.

"Yes, Countess Olga. I think you might have mentioned it to me before."

Bert looked at Halifax Halibut, who was steering the boat and who also raised a smile as he kept a close eye out for any other vessel that might be near and who might see his activities.

"You know something, Halibut?" said the Countess. "You are an ever so lucky boy in that you have no Bolsheviks in Halifax."

Well, if there were, Halibut hadn't come across any. He had fitted in well in Porth Branven but still couldn't come to terms with how many strange people there were living there, and not all of them Cornish. He only had one more pot to gather in.

"When are we going to go back to dry land?" asked the Major, not really wanting to mix with the Germans.

"No hurry, sir," replied Halibut, lighting up a German cigarette as he steered a course towards the final marker float. "We can take our time getting back. Hopefully all of this German nonsense will be over by then. I hear you saw service in the last war, Major."

"I did, young man," replied the Major, remembering the North African campaign and Rommel. "It was a long time ago and best forgotten about. War is a terrible thing and I hope your generation and those to come never have to go through it again, Captain Doncaster."

The Major was a grand old man, thought Halibut, even if his Yorkshire geography was a little out of sync. The fisherman mentally calculated how much he could get for his catch.

The woman who had seen UB-AF9's crew found PC Harris checking on vehicle tyres in the main street. She was out of breath.

"Officer, come quickly! You must come quickly! There are some Germans down on the quayside."

The Constable sighed and then forced a small smile.

"I know that, madam. There are loads of them about. They are all over town. It is, after all, a German twinning ceremony."

"These Germans are different, officer," said the woman, blurting out the words and still trying to catch her breath. "They are wearing uniforms and carrying guns."

"Are you sure?" asked PC Harris, feeling that his trusty truncheon and handcuffs were in place. "Well, I had better take a look for myself. I don't like the sound of this and don't want any trouble. Al nearly took my head off earlier with a firework. He's by far the most dangerous thing around here today. We can't have people walking around carrying firearms."

You were right to report this, madam. I think you had better sit down over there on that public bench. Now, where are these Germans? The ones with uniforms and guns."

The German seamen had reached The People's Rooms, and the crowd outside partying gradually quietened down when they realised they were present. Slowly the music faded and people started whispering but not moving when they noticed the guns the men carried.

Kapitanleutnant Von Diesel surveyed the people present. He could see many men dressed in lederhosen and the women dressed in German traditional costumes.

"Carry on with the celebrations, please. Do not stop on our account. It is good that you people have even taken to our customs so quickly.

Now, can we have some more music please? I would like to hear the glorious Johann Strauss waltz."

The man playing the music quickly obliged, seeing the weapon the Captain was holding.

"What's he on about?" whispered one man in the gathering. "Why are they dressed like that? And why are they carrying machine pistols? They must think they are still fighting the war."

Another looked at one of the German guests, who was equally perplexed and who looked embarrassed by the presence of her fellow countrymen.

"Are they with you lot?" asked the Cornish councillor, and one of the event's organisers, to a German equivalent.

"They are not with us, Herr Councillor," replied the woman. "I have never seen any of them in my whole life. Whoever they are, this is a poor joke and in poor taste also and in equal measures."

"Maybe they are students from the University of Cornwall in Hayle," chipped in somebody else.

"Or they could be the Free Cornish Republican Army on manoeuvres," said one man, half pissed on strong German lager.

"They are friggin' Navy, you cretin," said his friend, who was pissed too but not quite as badly. "Have they got a unit in Germany now?"

An elderly woman turned up her nose.

"My dear life, they don't half smell."

"I heard that!" said Kapitanleutnant Von Diesel, turning quickly to confront the woman. "There is no need to be offensive. My men have been at sea. You would smell also, if you had been cooped up in the Unterseeboot like us."

"He means a submarine," said the not-so-pissed man. "My God, this lager is strong."

His mate could see Von Diesel in triplicate with blurring around the edges.

Seeing that the visitors had weapons that looked real enough, one person celebrating suggested that perhaps it would be a good idea to offer them a drink.

Maybe the white vans were already on their way down the A30 from Bodmin to collect these strange people who had obviously escaped from somewhere.

"My men do not normally drink on duty," said Kapitanleutnant Von Diesel, "but seeing as this is a special occasion and you are so kind, I accept and will allow this."

Someone made sure the German sailors were given glasses of lager, which they gratefully slurped whilst still holding their guns. The Kapitan ordered his men to raise their glasses in a toast to the hosts.

"This is wunderbar. Beer all the way from the Fatherland. This is good and I toast your good health, all of you. Now, can we have some more music please? I would like to hear the *Yellow Submarine* tune when the waltz is finished, ja?"

The mystified revellers started drinking and gossiping amongst themselves again, not really knowing how they should conduct themselves with these very strange and potentially dangerous men in their midst.

The man playing the music obliged with Strauss, and then The Beatles floated out over the harbour and out to sea.

"Seen any Germans carrying weapons, have you, Al?" asked PC Harris to Guido Fawkes and Catesby down on the harbour wall.

"I saw some earlier, I think," said Al, lighting yet another enormous firework.

"Those guns weren't for real, Officer Harris," chipped in Oppo, who was smoking and who dropped a lighted cigarette end down in the box of fireworks he had just opened.

"Dunno where they're to," said Al, shrugging his shoulders.

Constable Harris held on to his helmet, remembering what had happened down here earlier. He answered his radio.

"Yes, Sarge. OK, Sarge. Everything's all quiet, Sarge. Out."

Another rocket headed skywards from Al and Oppo's early November the 5th celebrations.

"Herr Kapitan, there is something I do not understand."

"So, what troubles you, Hans? These people look a bit uneasy, I think, but they have welcomed us with the flags, the music and the beer. It is even a beautiful day."

"Mein Kapitan, all what you say is completely true, and not to be disputed, and I have the wunderbar peashooters to take home to the

Fatherland for my little Willy and Helmut, but these British, why do they not wear the bowler hats? And where are the famous red buses? Can you not see any either, Herr Kapitan?"

The Kapitan was astounded but kept his personal thoughts to himself. However did this idiot ever become an officer in the elite German Kriegsmarine?

"Hans, my superb fellow officer, what you talk about is what they do in Londres. The English act accordingly like that. They say things like, 'How are you, old bean?' and they also say, 'Jolly bad weather we have been having lately, old chap'. Remember, this is Cornwall, Hans. These Cornish people are different from the English. They smell of fish, and are playing football with the strange shaped ball."

Hans was none the wiser and left that particular discussion at that.

"This is fine good beer, Herr Kapitan," he said.

"I agree," came the reply. "That is because the beer is imported from the Fatherland, Hans. Us Germans know how to make the quality beer."

The Captain finished off his drink.

"I have to make the contact with the local Bürgermeister, Hans."

The U-boat's skipper wondered why there was no evidence of any German military activity but put their absence down to the fact that Porth Branven was so isolated. The German Army would have established military commands in Hayle and Penzance, and there being no obvious resistance here on the coast would explain why there was no visible German Army presence in this small fishing town.

Kapitanleutnant Von Diesel spoke discreetly to Seaman Schwartz before seeking out the local Bürgermeister.

"Erhard, you are my most dependable rating. I want you to keep an eye out over things out here and especially over Leutnant Krieger. Make sure that the Leutnant keeps out of trouble, ja?"

"Jawohl, Herr Kapitan," replied Schwartz, clicking his heels in obedience.

Schwartz remained alert and kept a wary eye out on the celebrations taking place and the people doing the celebrating. He could sense that the people gathered here were somehow uneasy despite their obvious celebrations. He thought this was to be expected on occupied territory, but, even so, he remained alert and kept his weapon handy.

Kapitanleutnant Von Diesel made his way with two accompanying sailors inside The People's Rooms, where the merriment and celebrations took place with equal enthusiasm to those outside the building. Everyone seemed to be having a splendid time, he observed, looking around at the revellers, most of whom appeared to be three sheets to the wind and not aware of his and his men's presence.

At last they were noticed, and some comments were voiced.

"I see somebody's come in fancy dress. It's in extremely poor taste."

Frau Hertzmann came over to the Kapitan, and Roger followed. The German lady was herself well oiled and swayed a little on her feet.

The Kapitan believed her to be the Bürgermeister's wife. He spoke.

"Guten Morgen, meine Dame. Sind Sie die Frau der Bürgermeisters?"

"Nein. Ich bin die Leiterin der Delegation aus Deutschland. Meine Leute und ich besuchen Cornwall wegen der Feierlichkeiten."

The Kapitan looked at Roger holding his big brass bell.

"Also müssen Sie der Bürgermeister sein?"

The Kapitan clicked his heels to attention and acknowledged Roger with a short bow of his head. Roger never gave him the Nazi salute, which pleased the Kapitan.

"This is a civic celebration," said Roger, eying the Kapitan and his men up and down. "You are representing The West German Navy? But, I understand that the swastika insignia was banned."

Both men were confused, but for differing reasons. Roger because the men wore old World War Two sailors' uniforms with Nazi sewn badges, and the Kapitan because of what the man, obviously not German, had said to him. Frau Hertzmann just looked on in a haze of her own making.

"Ah, I know what has happened here," thought Von Diesel. "This small town is still not under complete German military command, even though there has been an obvious surrender to German forces at some point recently."

The comment about the swastika did not upset Von Diesel because neither he nor most of his men were Nazis, just proud sailors of the German Kriegsmarine. The Kapitan spoke to Roger in English.

"So you are not the German appointed Bürgermeister for this area?"

"I am the town Mayor, sir, the Mayor of Porth Branven, and this lovely lady is Frau Hertzmann from Bremerstunghaven."

The Kapitan's eyes lit up and went moist.

"Ah, the wunderbar seaside port of Bremerstunghaven. I know it well. It's a bit like this place."

"That's why it's twinned with Porth Branven, er, Kapitan. I presume you are a Kapitan in the West German Navy?"

Roger, fuelled by alcohol, wasn't too sure, but the man looked to be a Captain in the Navy.

"Ja, I am the Kapitan of Unterseeboot AF9, and I need to speak at once to whoever is in charge here. And tell me something, Herr Mayor. Has Von Ribbentrop moved into the castle at St Michael's Mount yet? And where is the nearest German military unit?"

Roger was mystified and sozzled in equal measures.

"Kapitan, what is your name?"

"I am Kapitanleutnant Otto Von Diesel of the German Kriegsmarine, commanding UB-AF9."

Roger wondered if there had been some kind of mix up over what guests had been invited from Bremerstunghaven. Maybe some of the German military forces had been invited, unbeknownst to him. He had left most of the twinning arrangements to Mrs Pascoe of the WI, who did have lapses of memory from time to time.

"Well, Kapitan Von Diesel, I know that the German Navy frigate, the *Vonstaggenhoffein*, visited Falmouth on a courtesy visit from Bremerhaven last Thursday. The Countess Olga is the person to ask about shipping movements, but I haven't seen much of her today."

Roger went on.

"There are two Panzers and a Tiger tank in a barn at George Laity's farm just outside town, and surprisingly enough, they are in excellent working order. And I think some German soldiers were yesterday doing a joint beach assault exercise with our Royal Marine Commandoes on Perranporth beach, but other than that-"

The Kapitan interrupted.

"Panzers and a Tiger guarding the outside of town? That is wunderbar. Maybe my men and I will stay here until the town is under complete military command and the new German Bürgermeister has been appointed."

Roger needed a drink to add to the ten he'd already had. What was this man going on about? Maybe the Germans had brought some film stars with them and they were getting into character. Roger had seen somebody outside with a camera filming events earlier.

He rubbed his eyes and wondered what had happened to his wife, Molly. She had been missing all day.

"Your men can relax," said Roger with slurred speech, and still lovingly fingering his beloved brass bell. "Have another drink. I need to make an announcement outside. The war is over, Herr Kapitan."

"I thank you, Herr Mayor," replied the Kapitan. "We can celebrate now that we are all good friends, ja?"

The Kapitan wondered why Roger had referred to The West German Navy as opposed to The German Navy. He decided that it must have been just a geographical description by a civilian and attached no great importance to the comment as he sipped his wunderbar lager. He and his men followed Roger outside and joined up with the rest of the crew.

"It is OK, men. Relax and enjoy yourselves, but remember you are professional sailors of the German Kriegsmarine, and so I expect all of you to conduct yourselves in a manner accordingly, ja?"

"Jawohl, Herr Kapitan!" said Seaman Schwartz, snapping to attention.

Roger got ready to make his announcement. He swung his bell for all it was worth, the clanging ringing out and attracting everyone's attention.

"Oycz! Oyez! Now hear this, good people of Porth Branven and Bremerstunghaven! This is to be a joyous occasion when our two peoples meet together and celebrate our friendship after difficult years that are now a memory. I officially welcome Frau Hertzmann and her good citizens of Bremerstunghaven, and Kapitan Otto Von Diesel and his crew from The West German Navy. Please feel free to celebrate and enjoy yourselves. Thank you."

Roger finished off with a short announcement that he read in a failed attempt at German from a card in his pocket.

"Ich ist der Mayor von Porth Branven. Ich herzlich wilkommen die wunderbaren Burger von Bremerstunghaven in unserer Stadt in Frieden und Freundschaft."

"They like us, Herr Kapitan," said Hans Krieger, getting carried away with the festivities. "With the Kapitan's permission, I would like to look around this place a little."

"OK, Leutnant," replied the Kapitan, "but take two of the men with you just in case of any trouble. Things are quiet, but we must take precautions. Not everyone must have warmed to our visit. They may be skulking in the shadows somewhere. I also need to take a little trip somewhere, Hans. Rendezvous back here when you are done."

"Ja, mein Kapitan," replied Hans.

Hans Krieger saw the small amusement arcade in the main street not far from The People's Rooms and ventured inside, past a glass display case that contained an Edwardian laughing sailor dummy.

"What is this person?" he asked one of the seamen accompanying him.

"I have no idea, Herr Leutnant. He looks very much like the gormless sailor from the Idiot Navy. I think I have seen his brother, a similar creation from the same Navy, at Blackpool before the war."

"You have been to Blackpool?" said the Leutnant, intrigued. "What was it like? I have heard it is good."

"It was, Herr Leutnant. It had a tower not unlike the one in Paris, now in the hands of the glorious German Army. The Blackpool Tower is made of iron also, and from the top it is possible to see five countries, it is said, except this is untrue as there is always bad weather up there so no-one can even see the iron floor below them. Blackpool did have many lights on its seafront before the war."

"It sounds like a good place, Horst," said the Leutnant. "But surely these lights would have been switched off so as not to alert the glorious Luftwaffe?"

"I believe so," replied the seaman.

"I have never been to Blackpool, Horst, but I have been to West Hartlepool."

"West Hartlepool?" said Horst, not seeing the immediate connection.

"During the first war, our Zeppelins bombed the town of Old Hartlepool and the docks in West Hartlepool. Old Hartlepool was where the first shots of the First World War were fired, Horst. The big battleships of the glorious German Navy came out of the fog and fired on the town. The Zeppelin also dropped a bomb on the local football club, Hartlepools United."

"I bet they were annoyed, Herr Leutnant," said Horst, wondering where this conversation was leading.

123

"They were, Horst. In fact, the football club had its main wooden spectator stand destroyed by the Zeppelin bomb, and after the war the football club officials wrote to the German government, demanding compensation."

"Did they get the compensation they asked for, Herr Leutnant?"

"Nein, Horst. In fact, the glorious German Luftwaffe bombed the town of Hartlepool only this year, and the football club again. So no compensation, I am afraid. It was just retribution for Hartlepools United beating our glorious football team, Werder Bremen, 2-0 in Germany in 1909. They were only the second English team to play in Germany."

"Tell me, Herr Leutnant. When you went to the Hartlepools, what was it like? Was it like Blackpool?"

Leutnant Krieger laughed.

"Nein, Horst. It is smaller than Blackpool but has the better, longer beaches with the golden sands called Seaton Carew. And the pubs are rough, along with the women. It is not a place to be messed with. And the men there, and the women, they drink copious amounts of the local beer. And there are many iron works and shipyards, and our glorious German Navy sink their vessels on the Atlantic convoys. But anyway, enough about the town of Hartlepool. Let us have a look in this small amusement arcade and see if we can amuse ourselves, ja?"

Just then, a small boy pushed past Leutnant Krieger and placed a coin in the jolly sailor, which immediately "Ho, ho, ho!"-ed inanely as it rocked from side to side. Leutnant Krieger was taken aback by the sudden outbursts of laughter.

"This idiot gormless sailor with the lipstick in a glass case looking like a grinning Popeye The Sailor Man is laughing and mocking me. I will put an immediate end to his insolence once and for all!"

Hans Krieger showed a mean streak for once in his life and levelled his personal weapon at the jolly sailor and prepared to fire to end its inane laughing burst.

"No, Herr Leutnant! The idiot sailor is not laughing at you, an officer of The German Navy. He is automatic, a child's toy worked by inserting a coin into the slot to make him laugh."

The seaman had saved the glass case and grinning music hall mariner from disappearing under a hail of German machine pistol fire. Heaving a sigh of relief, the ordinary seaman almost blurted out that the real idiot sailor was the Leutnant, who threatened the dummy in the glass cage.

Leutnant Krieger studied the laughing sailor as it "ho-ho-ho"-ed so hard that its sides should have split, and then walked on into the arcade, which contained a few slot machines, a horse racing game in a glass cage, and a few other things equally unfamiliar to him.

Two small boys, including the one who had inserted the coin into the jolly sailor, played the slot machines and were oblivious to the German naval presence.

The arcade operator was a rather large man, who sat with his feet up on the counter of the glass booth where he was supposed to dish out change and keep an eye on the patrons of the arcade. He seemed to want to do neither, and sat reading a newspaper and eating a huge pork pie. He was more interested in these activities than serving punters with change, what few punters there actually were in here.

Leutnant Krieger noticed that there was also a big glass box where you inserted a coin and an extended metal arm attempted to grab a prize from a host of cheap tat inside. It was something that Hans Krieger would love to have a go on, but first he wanted to try his hand at the slot machines, and then the horse racing game.

"How do these things work, Horst?"

"It is relatively simple," answered Horst, thinking, "like you" to himself. "But first we need to obtain some British money. I don't think these machines have been yet adapted to take our glorious German coinage. I will ask the fat attendant eating the pork pie and reading the newspaper to give us some suitable change, ja?"

"Thank you, Horst," said the Leutnant, eager to pit his skills against the slot machines in the arcade.

The ordinary seaman went to get some change from the disinterested attendant. Horst handed over some German currency to him. Horst was polite.

"May I have some suitable coins to insert in these machines please, Herr Attendant?"

The man continued to read his paper and eat his pork pie, and gave a load of change to the German sailor with no questions asked. He did look briefly at the strange notes handed over, but it was, after all, a German theme day. It was currency and could be exchanged in the bank on Monday morning.

Leutnant Hans Krieger, on being shown how to work the machines, was not very successful.

"Herr Leutnant, you have lost six times in a row. Why not try your hand at something different, ja?"

The Leutnant agreed and expressed the wish to have a go on the horse racing game. He backed the ten to one outsider and came last, while Horst, the ordinary seaman, backed the favourite at two to one and won.

"I don't seem to be very successful at anything in this arcade, Horst. I reckon that these machines are rigged so as not to win. Maybe on the next one I will be luckier."

The Leutnant was referring to the grab-a-prize machine. Horst had to show him how to use that one as well. Hans Krieger was more successful this time and managed to win a yellow fluffy duck.

"Look, Horst, I am a winner. That is why I am an officer and you are just an ordinary seaman."

Horst bit his tongue and said nothing. This so-called officer of the German Navy had all the intelligence of a lizard in the radiator of a Panzer tank. His view that the man was a complete and utter lentil brain had just been reinforced. At least he appeared happy in his stupidity.

While Leutnant Krieger amused himself in the arcade, Kapitan Von Diesel had his own mission to attend to. He had a quiet word with Roger amongst the musical racket of the celebrations.

"Herr Mayor, I require confirmation that there still exists The Atlantic Tea Rooms Und Gift Shop in Porth Branven."

"Why, yes, Captain. It does, but how do you know of its existence?"

"That is simple, Herr Mayor. I came here before the war started. I had pleasant times there before the hostilities started. I knew the owner, who had a nice lady daughter going by the name of Molly."

"Is that so, Kapitan?"

Roger sobered up slightly.

"Why, Kapitan, Molly now owns and runs The Tea Rooms, but I haven't seen her all day. You see, I married Molly some years ago, but I have nothing to do with The Tea Rooms as they are her concern solely."

The Kapitan's face did its best to contain a mixture of sadness that this jolly oaf of a man had married his beloved Molly and happiness that his only true sweetheart was still around, and only a matter of metres up the road from here.

"Thank you, Herr Mayor, and congratulations on your marriage to this lady."

The Kapitan made Roger feel guilty as he was extremely close to Frau Hertzmann and it was noticeable to the Kapitan.

Frau Hertzmann couldn't give a fig about Roger's wife, if she couldn't even be bothered to make an appearance at the twinning ceremony.

"I should like to go and see this place for myself again," said Otto Von Diesel, clicking his heels and acknowledging Roger.

Roger wondered what was going on. Something strange was afoot here. The Mayor thought that maybe he was dreaming. The Mauser pistol that the German Commander carried, though, seemed quite real and menacing. But how had this German naval officer known his Molly from back then?

He looked at Von Diesel. He was a man maybe in his thirties, but there was something strange about him, something that Roger couldn't quite put his finger on. He decided he needed another drink and helped himself to the enormous quantity of free ale that had been provided for the occasion.

The Kapitan could see that his men had relaxed and joined in with the festivities, and a couple of them had made friends with the local fräuleins.

Everyone had drunk so much that nobody seemed to notice any more that they, the German sailors, wore military uniforms and carried arms.

Someone was filming events with two cameras, and others believed a film about the war was being made.

All of the men were relaxed except for Schwartz, who was, as ever, vigilant and alert.

Von Diesel gave further orders to his men.

"OK, mein colleagues and fellow sailors of UB-AF9. I have some business to attend to, so amuse yourselves, but remember you are professional sailors in the German Kriegsmarine, so I expect you to conduct yourselves accordingly. Now go and enjoy yourselves, and not too much alcohol. If you need me, then I will be in The Atlantic Tea Rooms in the main street."

"Yeah, they are definitely making a film," said one man walking past the Kapitan as he passed the tiny cluster of shops that were the heart of Porth Branven.

Down by the harbour, the man's wife agreed, having seen the cameras outside The People's Rooms earlier.

The rest of the Germans, barring two who had teamed up with local girls and who had headed off to the rocks skirting the beach, had made their way into the amusement arcade to join Leutnant Krieger and his two accompanying sailors. The dummy sailor was still "ho-ho-ho"-ing as they entered, much to their amusement.

"Look. It is our idiot officer," said one, and they all laughed at the suggestion.

Leutnant Krieger, the butt of the joke, was still trying to win on the slot machines, with little success.

The attendant had finished his pork pie and had started on a pile of sandwiches, with buns for afters. He continued to read his paper and give out change automatically without even bothering to look up and see who he was serving.

The Deutschmarks were piling up more quickly than English currency, but he couldn't care less. Before today, the attendant hadn't even seen German currency, and had no idea what a Deutschmark should look like. Some Germans from Bremerstunghaven had been into the arcade briefly and their money was slightly different, but they had given him Marks of some description, so he was happy to take them.

Leutnant Krieger noticed that a jukebox was playing pop music, having been fed money by a few teenagers who had just arrived inside the arcade. They sniggered at the German sailors, but then got on with the business in hand, which was to play the slot machines. The Leutnant glanced at them and shook his head in disgust at Horst playing the machine alongside him.

"Look at these strange people, Horst. They are longhaired degenerates with the strange clothes and the way they conduct themselves. Look how long their hair is. It is almost impossible to tell the difference between the boys and the girls, ja?"

"I agree, Herr Leutnant," replied Horst. "But look at that musical box that plays the songs for money. Like some of their weapons, that is more advanced than anything us Germans have."

Leutnant Krieger looked all stern for a brief moment.

"That maybe true also, Horst, but I will have no more talk of this treasonable nature, you understand?"

"Jawohl, Herr Leutnant!" snapped Horst, coming to attention and saluting the officer firmly.

Krieger smiled again.

"Relax, Horst. I know what you mean, but this is just past our war time and we must be careful what we say. Now go and ask those degenerates if they have that song called *Yellow Submarine* on that musical box's inventory of tunes."

Horst did as ordered.

Chapter Eleven

The police Sergeant in command at Porth Branven had received notice that the promised extra manpower would not now be available, due to them being drafted into another Cornish town, which had a feast day.

At least up until now it had been quiet enough, thought the Sergeant as he ploughed through a mountain of paperwork on his desk in the cramped office. A picture of George Dixon of Dock Green stared down at him from the opposite wall, bearing the immortal words, "Evening, all."

PC Harris was out on the street and had good, reliable civilian back up in the form of his cousin Al from the garage, and Oppo, who, although a little dim and short upstairs, was Porth Branven's champion lobster pot thrower, so was useful to have around if trouble brewed, unless, of course, he had caused it. And the other Constable, PC Toogoode, was equally reliable and could always be counted upon to perform well in his uniform.

In the quiet back stock room of The Atlantic Tea Rooms And Gift Shop, PC Toogoode wore only his helmet, at the request of Molly underneath him on a towel-covered row of stock boxes. He was technically in uniform, he told himself as he thrust away with Molly naked, and his police radio was at hand.

Molly equally thrust away and gave as good as she received as their furtive lovemaking got louder and more frantic as it reached a climax that threatened to wake the dead in St Legest's churchyard and shake the foundations of the old building. Its thick stone walls, however, masked the cries of ecstasy from prying ears, including those of the two young assistants out in the front of the premises, who were blissfully unaware of events taking place in the stock room. They served customers to make money whilst being grateful to even have a low-paid job when very few existed in Porth Branven itself.

"A policeman's lot is a very happy one," said PC Toogoode, finishing off the job he had started. "Mmm... That was good."

Molly thought the same and lay there for a moment in soaking bliss.

The Constable got up and started to get dressed. He heard a message on his radio. He answered.

"Yes, Sarge. All quiet here. Just checking out a report of a tourist's vicious Chihuahua dog. Dealing with it right now. Out."

PC Toogoode, once dressed, leaned over and placed a hand on one of Molly's heaving breasts and kissed her.

"Thank you, Molly. Until next Saturday afternoon..."

Molly smiled, blew him a kiss and discreetly let him out of the back entrance into a deserted alleyway before cleaning herself up and getting dressed.

Once out in the alleyway, PC Toogoode walked out to the main street and headed down towards The People's Rooms, where he met up with his colleague, PC Harris, amongst the celebrators. They exchanged pleasantries, talking about the weather, the rugby, and what a tosser the Sergeant was. They were offered drink by the celebrators but declined politely on account of being on duty. They both accepted, however, the offer of several sausage rolls.

Roger came over to talk to the two Constables.

"Hey, fellas. Has either of you two seen my Molly today? She was supposed to be making a welcome speech, but I haven't clapped eyes on her since early this morning."

PC Harris said he hadn't seen Molly. He was probably the only man in the town who hadn't in some capacity. His colleague displayed a small measure of guilt, which wasn't picked up by the other two men.

"No, Roger. I haven't seen Molly either. I expect she might be having a lie down somewhere. Maybe all these celebrations are just too much for her."

"Yeah, maybe you are right," said Roger, leaving it at that.

"She's probably at home right now. You'll see."

Roger wasn't really too concerned. He preferred her out of the way anyway, and to know where she was, because he had made a new friend in Frau Hertzmann, who came up beside him as the Constables were about to go back out on the beat. She grabbed Roger by the arm.

"Just a minute, Frau Hertzmann. Officer! Officer!" Roger shouted after the two men.

They both turned, one completely innocent and the other completely guilty. PC Toogoode looked a bit sheepish until he heard what Roger had to say.

"Thought you'd like to know that there are some German guests here walking around in old military uniforms with swastika insignias on display. I thought that was against the law. Oh, and they are carrying guns as well. They could be in a film about the war, I suppose, because someone's out there with a camera, but best to keep an eye out for them. As far as I am aware, they are not with the official guest party from West Germany."

"That's right, Herr Officer," said Frau Hertzmann, endorsing what Roger had told them. "They are definitely not from Bremerstunghaven. The wearing of Nazi insignia and the carrying of guns is, of course, illegal there."

"Now, that's a coincidence," said PC Harris, rubbing his chin. "I had a report a little while back about armed German sailors. Took a look down by the harbour and spoke to Cousin Al, whose fireworks nearly took my damn head off. He said he'd seen them but wasn't too perturbed. Still, they aren't around here now, as far as I can see. Anyway, we'll keep our eyes open just the same. Let us know if they show up again or if you are worried any way, Roger."

PC Toogoode had heard the call on his radio when he was otherwise engaged with Molly, but his colleague, PC Harris, was well equipped to deal with some armed German hooligans. He was a first class officer and had boxed for the force.

The two officers set off to patrol the mean streets of Porth Branven. One day, something major might happen here, they told themselves.

On board UB-AF9, the Chief Engineer took a break and lay out on the hot metal deck, sunbathing. Planes occasionally passed overhead, but they didn't seem threatening so he never ordered any evasive actions. Hostilities must indeed have ended.

A Royal Navy rescue helicopter from RNAS Culdrose flew along the coast, but the Chief ignored that as well. Such a strange flying machine he had never before encountered, but that too seemed not to be hostile.

He got up from his allotted rest time and gave orders for the acting Commander, Leutnant Franz Spiegel, to be called from his sleep in his bunk. Spiegel wouldn't approve of such activities as sunbathing as he was a disciplinarian.

The Chief decided to go below and check up on Herman. Maybe The Kapitan should have taken him with him on some shore leave. A change of scenery might do the creature good, thought The Chief.

Herman was, in fact, OK and quite at home in the bowels of the boat, as long as he had fresh sea water thrown over him every so often. He still had food left from Leutnant Krieger's foray ashore. Leutnant Spiegel thought all this look-after-the-lobster nonsense to be just that, nonsense, and if he had his way, Herman would be a different colour and on the table. However, the Kapitan had left strict instructions that the crustacean was not to be harmed. So Herman was safe whilst Leutnant Spiegel was in charge.

The Boy Blewett was making her way back home. Leutnant Spiegel watched her through his binoculars. When she got closer to the harbour, she would surely see the submarine.

Spiegel calmly gave the order to dive down into the gully under the deep water directly behind the Tooth Rock. Although hostilities had probably ended, the Kapitan having not sent a distress signal, and he saw no signs of attack, the Leutnant exercised caution.

The boat sat at periscope level and he maintained all around vision so he could see whether the Kapitan and his shore party were returning at any time with their boats.

The Boy Blewett passed only a short distance away from where the U-boat lurked as she chugged towards the narrow harbour neck.

The Major looked out to port and rubbed his eyes before taking a swig from his hip flask.

"By Jove, it can't be! I must be dreaming."

"What is it, dear boy?" asked the Countess, who was aware that he had seen something.

She was well oiled as well as the Major but had some faculties remaining.

"I thought I saw the periscope of a submarine over there!"

The Major dismissed it as a single kelp frond sticking up from below the surface, and put it down to the effects of alcohol, of which he had consumed more than he normally would have so far that day.

"Better get the mints ready for when we get back, Olga. It wouldn't be proper for a gentleman and his lady to smell of intoxication."

"Well, the Matron does all the time," thought the Countess.

When *The Boy Blewett* eased into the harbour and cruised up to where her mooring was, they saw the boats the Germans had left alongside the berth by the stone steps. It was Bert's turn to think he was seeing things. He wasn't. He could recognise those boats anywhere. They belonged to the Germans, and were from the U-boat that had scuttled his boat and stolen his catch.

"Bleddy Germans!" said Bert, itching to get ashore.

"Did you say U-boat and Germans, Bert?" The Major said, becoming more sober, or so he thought. "Germans here in Porth Branven? Where's my steel helmet? I knew I saw a periscope. The blighters! Better call out the Army and the Home Guard."

Halifax Halibut forced a smile as he made the boat secure with his first mate.

"We don't have any Army units around here, Major. And the Home Guard was disbanded years ago."

"The Major pulled himself together a little.

"By Gad, you're right, man. Who shall we call? The coastguard? The RNLI?"

Bert didn't wish to call anyone. He just wanted to find these Germans and take issue with them. What the fuck was going on here?

Bert, getting off the boat and climbing the couple of feet up the metal ladder and onto the quayside, saw the two boys nearby with their peashooters. They thought better of aiming at Bert or any of the other occupants of *The Boy Blewett*.

"Hey, you two. Come here a minute. Did you see who moored these two boats?"

"Yes, Mr Bert. Some German sailors. One was a stupid officer who gave us money to buy peashooters for him. They gave us some money to buy sweets and also to look after the boats for them."

"Did they?" said Bert with some menace in his voice.

He looked around and saw Al a few yards further down the quayside with Oppo. The two had just set off the last firework and stood up to admire their handiwork. They saw Bert coming towards them.

"Bert."

"Hallo, Al, Oppo. Have you two seen any Germans?"

"Loads of 'em, mate. They're all over town."

"Did any of them have uniforms on and did they carry guns by any chance?"

Al lit up a German cigarette.

"'Ess, I saw 'em a while back, heading into town. Dunno where they're to now, partner. My cousin, Officer Dibble, was looking for 'em as well. They can't have gone too far."

Halifax Halibut finished securing *The Boy Blewett* and made sure that the bootleg booze was stowed away securely for moving elsewhere when it was quieter and darker.

It was time to see that two of Porth Branven's more elderly citizens got home safely after their impromptu boat trip. They'd had enough excitement for one day.

With their own bottles of keep-quiet booze, the Yorkshire boat skipper offered to take them both home in his vehicle parked on the quay, full of pots, ropes and other fishing gear. The two were grateful to accept and shared it with a couple of boxes of that day's catch, others of the liquid variety being still aboard and down below on *The Boy Blewett*. It was extremely doubtful that the elderly couple could have actually made it back to The Bluebells under their own steam.

When they did return home, The Major did his best to settle the Countess back to her room with the minimum of fuss. At least there was no Matron to worry about. She was doing her 'do not disturb' important paperwork exercise in her back room.

One of the carers on duty spoke to Major Beere as he slipped in quietly with the Countess on his arm.

"Had a good time at the celebrations, Major Beere?"

The woman, in her late teens, was chirpy and nice enough.

"Yes, thank you, young Lucy, but we've both had rather enough, I feel, for one day, and one can have too much of a good thing, you know? Just going to show the Countess to her room and then I'm off to my own pit to lie down for a while."

The Major attempted to stop the four illicit booze bottles in the bag provided by Halifax from chinking but without success.

The carer smiled and went about her other business with a fond shake of her head. The old rascal. She was wise to his tricks, except today was a bit early for him.

After seeing the Countess to her room, The Major went back to his own room. He was normally a creature of habit and a stickler for tidiness and order and he knew something was up straight away when he picked up his telescope. It had been handled by someone else.

"Well, I'll be Monty's batman! Some bounder has been at the jolly old spyglass."

Nobody at The Bluebells ever touched the Major's possessions because all knew he was very independent and usually left him to his own devices, like the Countess. Even mad Myrna didn't go into his room alone.

The Major, in mild disgust, went back and knocked gently on the door of Olga's room.

"Come in," was the quietly gentle reply.

The Countess was sitting on her bed, holding a mousetrap in her hand. She had a twinkle in her eye.

"You naughty boy, Major. It didn't take you too long to come back to my room. Come sit with me on my bed."

The Major sat down.

"So, you have had intruders as well, Countess," he said, looking at her holding her anti-trespasser device. "My telescope has been interfered with, and your shipping albums? Have they gone missing, dear lady?"

"No, they have not gone missing, Major, but we have snoopers around the place, and they are interested in our affairs. But never mind them. We can discuss what to do after we have rested. I am personally, how you say, beat of the dead?"

"Dead beat," said the Major, correcting her.

The Countess replaced the mousetrap as before and lay back on her bed. The Major sat beside her on its edge.

"I know my latest album has been looked at because I have the seal, that only I know, broken on it, dear boy, and, of course, the trapping of the mouse device was put back cleverly, but not so cleverly as to deceive this button bright old lady."

"Bright as a button lady," corrected the Major again.

"We have both been personally violated, Major. This is an outrage, but right now I need to do something rather badly."

"I need this also," said the Major, feeling a little worse for wear again, and quite woozy.

The Countess was gone off to sleep almost immediately, and the Major followed her, lying down beside her on the top of her bed.

A few minutes later, the young carer gently checked on the two after knocking first, and after finding the Major's room empty, knew where to find the elderly eccentric couple.

Sure enough, there they were, lying on the Countess Olga's bed. She looked at them with a cocked head. How sweet they looked together.

"Aww..."

The woman knew that Matron wouldn't approve, but she was in the land of Bobo Baggins herself, and wouldn't be around for several hours more. The woman gently closed the door and left them to it.

Otto sat quietly in The Atlantic Tea Rooms And Gift Shop. There was a small huddle of patrons, but most ignored him completely. A middle-aged couple looked at him in disgust occasionally in between sips of their drinks. He ignored them. This was only to be expected in occupied Great Britain, and it would take time before all the population accepted the German occupation of their territory, if they ever did.

The place was different from how he remembered it from his last visit before the war. Then, it had looked so simple, with a few tables and chairs, and the place sold tea and Cornish cream teas, along with a small selection of postcards and assorted gifts from Porth Branven, Cornwall. He particularly remembered the blue-and-white striped pottery items that had been there, but he could not see any now.

There were lots of items he did not recognise, and all the colours were less austere, and much brighter and vulgar in many respects. How could things have changed so much in such a short time? And why did these people dress so differently? Their clothes were so unusual and the colours so bright. Everything was so different. Even their hair was of strange styles he hadn't seen before. The furniture and fittings were different as well. How strange.

He sat quietly in the corner, sipping wunderbar tea from a real china cup and saucer. Such luxury after war time austerity and German naval regulation issue items.

The two girls serving had offered to give him his tea on the house, but he had insisted on paying in full and had done so with German Reichsmarks, which they thought was a bit odd.

They hoped that the owner, their boss, Molly, would soon turn up. The man had a gun in his possession, which stopped them from calling the police. He hadn't threatened them with it and had behaved impeccably so far. He was also incredibly polite. A gentleman, apart from the fact that he wore a uniform, carried a gun and smelled a fair bit as if he hadn't had a bath or shower in ages.

He had asked personally for Molly by name, as if he knew her from somewhere. How odd he was. There was something they couldn't put a finger on, but he was somehow very distant as he sat there quietly minding his own business and looking out of the window of the establishment to the main road.

Molly had used her private bathroom, which adjoined the stock room, and had cleaned herself up and changed into fresh clothes already conveniently in place for her regular Saturday afternoon tryst with her Constable visitor.

She came out the back way, went down the alley and breezed into the front of the premises, which made a little unseen bell tinkle, and went up to the counter. She hadn't really noticed Otto sitting quietly on his own.

"Is everything OK? Any problems?"

The two girls looked at each other and then indicated by pointing over to the Kapitan by the window. He continued to sip his tea. The senior girl spoke.

"The gentleman over there on his own by the window asked for you personally. It's as if he knows you from somewhere. He wouldn't state his business, but he was ever so polite. He is German. We thought about calling the police because he has a gun of some sort with him and he's wearing a strange uniform like you see in the war films. The gun made us think twice about calling the police. We didn't know what to do. We said you were out and didn't know when you would be back. He said that was OK and he would wait. He paid for his drink in old style German money. He is ever so strange. And he smells as well, like a tramp."

Molly looked over in complete mystery.

"OK, you two. Thanks. Leave this to me. I'll deal with it."

She went over to the stranger and he turned to face her slowly. They looked at each other for a few long seconds.

There were flickers of recognition on his face and his sparkling blue eyes were piercing and alert, but so cold and vacant at the same time. It was as if he wasn't sure she was really there.

"Molly? Is that really you? You look somehow older. Despite this, I can still see that it is you, my sweetheart. The war separated us and ended our brief happiness."

The Kapitan couldn't understand how the woman appeared noticeably older than he remembered her.

Molly said nothing for a brief while and then put her hand over her mouth.

"Otto?"

Molly had to sit down beside him. The girls at the counter watched from a distance but were then distracted by a customer who wanted to order. They didn't see the Kapitan stretch his left hand across the table to reach Molly's.

She felt his touch to be ever so cold and somehow distant, even though he was sat only a couple of feet away from her. She found her voice.

"My dear Otto, is it you? And after all these years. You left so suddenly."

She released her hand from his.

"Why the gun, Otto? And the uniform as well?

Otto Von Diesel laughed but not at her.

"Why, my dearest Molly, I am an officer in the German Kriegsmarine. This is my uniform and this is my personal weapon, which I carry not for offensive purposes now, but for my own safety, you understand? We have been at war, but now it has ended, ja?"

Molly was bewildered. What was going on here?

She ushered the Kapitan from his seat and spoke quietly to him as he followed her out onto the street, around a corner and up the deserted back lane to the rear of the property.

"Come inside quickly, Otto. We need to talk."

They went inside, where only minutes earlier she had done the dirty deed with a police officer. Now she was with another man in uniform, only this one stank to high heaven, and he had entered her life again after more than thirty years.

She remembered that he looked like one of the shadowy figures on the moonlit beach in the early hours of the morning when she and Jake Harvey had been disturbed in the throes of passion.

He put his gun down on the floor and sat down on a large box.

"I apologise for my personal hygiene, or lack of it, Molly. I have been at sea in a U-boat and there are no facilities to keep the body as clean as I normally would. Please excuse me for this."

Molly didn't know what to say. She checked that she had locked the door to the room from the shop out front. Eventually, she found her voice.

"Otto, it really is you under that beard. I can see that now more clearly. I can offer you a bath, if you wish. I have a small bathroom for my own personal use through there."

She nodded towards another door.

"I will run you a bath. When you are smelling a little better, we must talk. There is much I don't understand."

Chapter Twelve

The German sailors playing the machines in the arcade were running out of money.

The Leutnant had won a couple of prizes on the grab machine, so he would have something to take back home for his little Helmut and Willy.

Trusted Seaman Schwartz was keeping a careful eye on things as he had promised his Kapitan.

The German sailors were beginning to attract unwanted attention, with comments being made by other customers who had entered the place. Comments were all that were made, however, because of the men being armed.

One person managed to slip out of the arcade unnoticed and thought the police should be informed that men were in Porth Branven amusement arcade with guns. They had an unfair advantage on other punters playing the slot machines.

"Can we hear that strange song, *Yellow Submarine*, just one more time?" said Leutnant Krieger, holding his fluffy yellow duck and two cheap teddy bears he had won from the grab machine.

One of the civilians present saw the guns and duly obliged on the jukebox with the song, which pleased the Leutnant.

"After this, we must go, ja?" the Leutnant said to Schwartz.

"Jawohl, Herr Leutnant," replied Schwartz, clicking his heels in obedience.

Schwartz looked around at the various people playing the machines, and took particular notice of how long the men's hair was and how they all dressed.

"It is no wonder, Herr Leutnant, how these people lost the war."

Leutnant Krieger nodded his approval.

"Now be quiet, Schwartz, and listen to the words of this song, ja? Now that the war is over, do you think that the German Admiralty would allow us to paint our glorious Unterseeboot AF9 in bright yellow like in the song? It would be much more cheerful than the awful, drab battleship grey. That colour is so unappealing."

Schwartz didn't answer, and continued to listen to what he believed to be an idiot song, and wondered, like his Kapitanleutnant, how this man ever managed to become an officer in the German Kriegsmarine.

Down on the beach, which wasn't really a beach as such, but more of a tiny cove bordered by rocks on each side, some children had gathered, having heard all of the fireworks and having eaten all of the copious amounts of free ice cream on offer.

They gathered at the water's edge. Something was washed in with the tide that interested them greatly.

The black metal ball was rusted and looked like an old round metal boiler or something similar. Whatever it was, it had been in the sea for years. This thing provided a great object for the kids to throw stones at.

The kids threw stones, sat on it, tried to roll it back in the water and even hit it with a beach windbreak mallet. One child even produced a proper hammer from somewhere and proceeded to smack the object over and over again, producing a wonderful reverberating clanging sound that echoed across the sand.

A man walking along the sand stopped to watch what the children were doing.

The two German sailors who had disappeared along with two local girls were behind the rocks in a hidden place to the right of the cove by the harbour wall. They looked deeply satisfied as they adjusted their uniforms and looked up. The two girls did the same with their clothes a few seconds later.

"Hey, Dieter. Those children seem to be having a good time with something washed up on the beach. They are having a good time like we have just had, ja?"

The sailor's mate smiled with equal satisfaction. One of the girls giggled and then her mate giggled as well as they both smoothed down their feather-cut hair styles and made sure all the buttons were done up on their cheese cloth shirts. They ensured they both looked respectable once more.

The man walking on the beach looked more closely at the object washed up and could see metal struts sticking out of it.

"You've got to stop hitting that thing at once!" he shouted. "Understand?"

The kids carried on having fun, throwing even bigger pebbles at it to make more noise.

"We're only having fun, Mister," said one of the boys, lobbing a big pebble, which bounced off the object with a loud clang.

"I can see that," said the man, "but it's a bloody wartime mine, and if it goes off, you won't be seeing another summer holiday, and bits of you will be attending school in Hayle, St Ives and Camborne!"

"Spoilsport!" said the boy, not appreciating the danger to all concerned, and continuing to lob big pebbles at the object.

The man had warned them, and, realising the seriousness of the situation, decided that he had to find a Constable, and quickly. He made his way swiftly off the small beach.

By now, other adults had come to take a closer look at the object, and even watched their children join the others in the fun of striking the object with anything at hand.

The man shook his head as he hurried away. Only a mad man would try to set off a one ton mine. Where was the Navy when you needed them? The Salvation Army? The Pope? Woolworths?

The man found the two Constables chatting near the bulk of the revellers outside The People's Rooms. Despite all the drinking and partying taking place, it was all good natured. The man was out of breath as he approached the policemen.

"Officer! Officer! I don't wish to cause a hullabaloo, but there appears to be a wartime mine washed up on the beach."

PC Toogoode looked at this colleague and then at the man.

"Calm down, sir. Was it ticking?"

"Well, I didn't hear it ticking, Officer, but there is a bunch of kids down there hitting it with hammers and stones."

"OK, sir. Thank you. We will deal with it. Better stay back here, well out of the way. I'll inform the Sergeant. He'll know what to do."

PC Toogoode got on his radio.

"Better get down to the beach and clear the kids away," said PC Harris.

In the arcade, one of the German sailors produced some more money and gave it to the Leutnant. He exchanged it for English currency with the switched-off, disinterested attendant.

"Go on, Herr Leutnant. Have a last few goes to see if you can win," said the seaman to the officer.

The Sergeant had received PC Toogoode's radio message, locked up his office and decided to come down and check for himself. The last time that somebody reported a mine washed up on the shore line, it turned out to be an old ship's boiler. He had to be sure before he notified his superior over in Penzance, and the bomb disposal squad in Plymouth, and so on.

"What does it look like?" asked the Sergeant over the radio.

"Well, Sarge, it looks like a mine to us."

"Yeah, OK," said the Sergeant, "but there are different shaped mines. What shape is this one? The last so-called mine reported was a fuckin' old ship's boiler off some tramp steamer that sank donkey's years ago out off the reef."

The Sergeant walked right past the entrance to the arcade and didn't see the Germans inside.

Leutnant Krieger had lost the last few games, much to the delight of his men. He was annoyed.

"These machines, Schwartz, they are fixed if you ask me. Do you think I could demand my money back? Maybe we should have instead landed on the beach at Seaton Carew, West Hartlepool, instead of this place, the beyond of back."

The Leutnant kicked the machine in deep frustration and swore at it. These actions attracted the attention of the arcade attendant, who proceeded to leave his kiosk and come to confront Krieger.

Schwartz could see trouble looming and remembered the Kapitan's words about conducting themselves as German sailors. This idiot, Krieger, could spark off another war all on his own.

Krieger looked at the machine in disgust and kicked it again.

"This idiot machine takes the money but never pays out!" said the Leutnant. "It is a justice of travesty!"

"Oi, you!" said the attendant, looking menacing. "You don't go kicking my machines. It's a game of chance and you lost, my 'ansum. I've a good mind to take your head and..."

The man backed off when Seaman Schwartz levelled his gun at him. The man became more conciliatory.

"I'll tell you what, mate. To show there's no hard feelings, I will give you half of your money back and also give you one of those large teddy bears on display over there. What do you say?"

The man looked nervously at the gun and those of the other sailors, who held them a bit more menacingly now, expecting trouble.

"OK, Herr Attendant Person. That seems reasonable in the circumstances. I accept. The big teddy bear can go home also with my other prizes. I shall give the big teddy bear to my beloved Helga in Düsseldorf."

"Thank you, Herr Proprietor," said Schwartz, lowering his weapon. "We didn't want to cause you any trouble. The Leutnant was just a bit upset at losing, you understand? We will be leaving the premises after you give us the money and the Leutnant the big yellow teddy bear."

The man did as he promised and heaved a big sigh of relief. Bullet holes in the ceiling and through the machines would take some explaining to the owner when he and his wife returned home from holidaying in Spain.

The Germans, satisfied that honour for the Leutnant had been restored, left the building. As they passed the grinning dummy sailor at the entrance, which had stopped "ho-ho-ho"-ing, Leutnant Krieger spoke with some disgust.

"I would like to shoot him. He is by far the most stupid sailor there has ever been."

That was debatable, thought Schwartz, pleased that they were leaving this place and were out in the fresh air again.

They made their way back towards where the main revellers were still going at it for all they were worth and were seemingly oblivious to what was happening down on the beach.

The policemen had reached the crowd down at the water's edge. Al and Oppo were also there to see what all the fuss was about. The old men who had been playing dominos in the shelter on the harbour wall had had enough, and they too went to see what was going on.

The Major, the Countess and the Matron were all in the land of Mahoojanonie, and old Myrna was keeping regular and drinking plenty, and wondering when rationing would eventually end.

Roger and Frau Hertzmann had found a quiet deserted office away from the main party and the German lady locked the door after them. Roger was a bit nervous as he removed his clothing and placed his bell down. It was the first time it had been out of his hand all day. Molly always accused him of going to bed and sleeping with his hand on his bell.

"I have never been unfaithful to Molly before, you know?"

Frau Hertzmann smiled and gave Roger the glad-eye come-on look.

"Do not do the worrying, big man, Herr Roger. I think she will forgive you just this once. I mean, what is your favourite meal?"

"Beans on toast," came the reply.

"Well, you don't eat beans on toast every day of your life, nein? You eat some differing things, ja? A variety? Well, now you can try some variety, ja?"

With that, the two of them began ripping off each other's clothes in a frenzy of lust. Soon they were grunting and squealing with delight like two well fed porky pigs. They were oblivious to the other guests in the main part of the building, and the revellers were oblivious to them.

Cornish-German relationships were being cemented there on the floor of the duty office, which hadn't seen action like this since it just escaped a German bomb in 1940.

The two German sailors who had been with the local girls picked up their personal weapons and took a greater interest in what was going on over on the beach. The girls kissed their men and drifted away to join the crowd there. The Germans wondered what was happening. One of them, Dieter, looked concerned.

"Sebastian, something happens over there. We should return to the others. We have had our fun, ja?"

His mate agreed and the two replaced their caps and proceeded to leave the rocks.

Soon they joined up again with the others of their party by The People's Rooms.

"You two look like you have had a good time," said Leutnant Krieger, clutching his prizes. "I bet you two have not had half so much fun as we have had in the small arcade of amusements."

"No, probably not, Herr Leutnant," smirked Sebastian.

Dieter looked at his officer and thought what a dummkopf the man looked standing there holding children's toys, including the ludicrous big yellow teddy bear.

The sailor had been experiencing some much wanted fun with a girl who called herself Lulu D, along with her friend, Loveday, and this dick from Düsseldorf was there parading a teddy bear and claiming he had had more fun than Dieter and Sebastian had down behind the rocks with the two local girls who were more than willing. Dieter had never expected this trip to be so exciting.

Schwartz looked around and then at the officer in charge of the party, Leutnant Krieger.

"Herr Leutnant, we are all here except for our Commander. Do you think he will be all right?"

The Leutnant, daft though he was, realised that he was attracting unwanted attention from the gathering. He was being made fun of.

He saw the solution to his problem; a couple of young children were with their parents nearby.

"Here, little girl and little boy. Please take these cuddly toys with my compliments, ja? It will be scant consolation for losing the war and being occupied but consolation, ja?"

The gifts were received with thanks, and the parents of the children were deeply confused. What was this guy going on about? He must be one of these people involved in the film that was being made and that people were going on about.

"Herr Leutnant, this is a noble thing that you do, to give these gifts to these children of the occupied locals, but what about Herr Kapitanleutnant?"

The Leutnant gave some thought to his Commander, who he had clean forgotten about, such was his interest in playing the slot machines in the arcade. Leutnant Krieger spoke.

"He said something about going to the Café of Atlantica and the giving of gifts and tea, or something like that. I am sure he will be OK and will be here with us when he is ready and good. We shall stay here until he returns."

That satisfied the men, who got themselves some beer. All the action seemed to be taking place down at the beach.

Carrington had reached Falmouth that afternoon and summoned a man messing around on a boat moored against The Prince of Wales Pier.

A sign indicated that for fifty pence he would take people on a boat trip out to see HMS *Bosun* in The Carrick Roads. Having to wait twenty minutes, Carrington was impatient to get out to the flagship.

The skipper of the twenty-six-foot boat, a Cornishman, took his time and headed the boat out past the starboard side of The Black Rock as Carrington sat quietly but impatiently in the stern.

These people were all stupid, he thought to himself. Russian spies were in their midst everywhere, and all they were interested in was eating pasties, angling off the end of the pier for garfish and generally sitting around looking gormless.

Carrington had to get aboard HMS *Bosun* to get a secure signal sent back to The Admiralty. The Russians were here in force, and had been for years. This was a serious business.

Once he had contacted The Admiralty, he would find Boras.

Back over in West Cornwall, Porth Branven to be precise, the sky turned suddenly from a beautiful rich blue to an interesting dull grey with clouds gathering, menacing and not fluffy and white in any way. They became uglier and dumped big buckets of rain over all outside. The proverbial heavens had opened with a watery vengeance.

Revellers outside had few choices - vacate the beach and seek shelter in The People's Rooms, frequent the arcade, or stay on the beach getting soaking wet and having the mine for company.

Most fled for shelter, while the more hardy and foolish stayed to keep Cornwall's latest tourist attraction, the mine, company.

"Welcome to Cornwall," said PC Harris sarcastically to his colleague.

"Back to normal," replied PC Toogoode.

"I thought it was too good to last," barbed PC Harris, who thought the joke was funny while PC Toogoode didn't.

"If I hear that fucking joke once more... Come on. The Sarge needs a hand to clear these people back."

The rain did most of the clearance needed.

The Sergeant was on his radio to his Inspector in Penzance, relaying information about the mine through his superior and on to the bomb disposal unit in Plymouth.

PC Toogoode looked at PC Harris.

"Let's hope it doesn't go off bang. One bang is enough."

PC Harris didn't have a clue what his colleague was on about. PC Toogoode was a good copper but a bit strange at times. Then Toogoode listened carefully and placed a hand on Harris's arm.

"Hey, listen. Can you hear it?"

The sound was unmistakable and PC Harris looked at Toogoode with horror.

"I can hear it all right. It's ticking. The fucking thing's ticking! Let's get the fuck out of here!"

The two Constables told the Sergeant, who was on the radio again, and they helped the last remaining onlookers away with a sense of more urgency than before.

PC Harris turned to look at the menacing thing there a few feet away as if that was somehow going to make it safe.

"Looks a bit like a conker when it's in its horse chestnut shell," he said, remembering playing conkers as a child with some fondness.

"I never saw a conker as big as that one," added Toogoode.

Most of the crowd now didn't need any encouragement to leave the scene because it was raining heavily, and the thing could go off at any minute, or so they believed, having seen mines in war films. Maybe Porth Branven was about to be blown off the ordnance survey map.

Oppo, who was with the beach leavers, turned to Al.

"Hey, Al. We should have had that in our firework display."

Al shook his head. That Oppo could be some stupid at times. How the hell would the mine fit in a firework box, for heaven's sake?

The rain continued to cascade down like a hundred million wet and torn-up losing bingo tickets on a Saturday night, fluttering in what was, after all, an August afternoon.

The children who had been responsible for the panic decided to move off and cause mischief elsewhere.

Chapter Thirteen

Plymouth was a hive of activity. The shoppers shopped, the bomb disposal team went through their familiar call-out drill, and prepared to leave for West Cornwall.

The Admiral had lost at bowls, trying to emulate Drake, and had retired to the officers' mess. A steward summoned him, much to his annoyance. It was the Admiralty on a secure line wanting an update from Cornwall. The Admiral hadn't a clue. He was waiting for Carrington to report.

Carrington stood up impatiently in the boat as it approached the imposing HMS *Bosun* at anchor in The Carrick Roads. Not far away, and also at anchor, were several large Eastern Bloc factory ships and a fleet of trawlers accompanying them.

The skipper of the pleasure boat was about to guide his small vessel out around the big warship so his passengers could get an all-round view of her.

Carrington went up to the skipper at the wheel in the covered area of the deck.

"Skipper, I need you to take me up to her to go on board. I have to go on board."

The skipper, his head turning slightly from following his course ahead, said, "Sorry, mate, but this is only a trip out around the warship. If you wish to go aboard, you'll have to wait until Monday when she's open to the public in the afternoon."

Carrington was insistent.

"I have to go aboard, skipper. This is an urgent matter. I am an officer in The Royal Navy. Here, have a look at my identity card."

The skipper looked at it closely and relented.

"Well, if you insist, Commander. I'll get you alongside, but whether they let you board her is another matter."

The skipper manoeuvred his boat around to HMS *Bosun*'s port side, to where a landing stage with a metal ladder way had been put down her side. Moored against it was the Commander's launch.

Two sailors from the warship came down the ladder way as the boat approached the warship. One of them shouted out to the pleasure boat.

"Sorry, mate. You can't come aboard today. Official visiting isn't until Monday afternoon. The details are on a poster on the pier."

The boat came alongside. Carrington flashed his identity card.

"I'm a serving officer in The Royal Navy. It's imperative I come aboard and speak to your Commander."

The sailors looked puzzled as they hadn't been informed of any official visit in the port, and certainly not from a Royal Navy officer on board a pleasure craft. They helped him over onto the landing stage anyway.

The pleasure boat eased away from the warship that dwarfed her using her reversing engines, and was well adrift of HMS *Bosun* as Carrington stood there talking to the two sailors.

They both examined his identity card and then brought themselves to attention and gave him their salute.

"Welcome aboard, sir, but we need to know what this is about. We were not informed about any official visitors, especially aboard a pleasure craft."

"It's OK, lad. At ease, you two. I need to speak to your Commander at once."

The leading seaman responded.

"Sorry, sir, but The Commander was called away on Navy business. The Deputy Commander is in charge of the vessel."

"Then take me to speak to him at once," said Carrington.

The three men made their way up to the deck high above. Soon Carrington, over coffee, had briefly explained a version of events to the Deputy Commander of HMS *Bosun*.

"So, you see, not only have you got a nest of Soviet and other Eastern European spies moored just out there who are working under the cover of fishing, there are sleeping Russian agents ashore, and here in Falmouth, and they have been here for several years. I need you to authorise the sending of two top secret, UK eyes only signals."

It was not what the officer in charge had expected on a pleasant afternoon on a courtesy visit to Falmouth. A life on the ocean waves was never dull. It was well known that Eastern Bloc spies at sea monitored British naval warship and submarine movements, but this sounded a bit more serious, so he authorised the sending of the signals to Plymouth and The Admiralty.

Earlier, Kapitan Otto Von Diesel of the Unterseeboot AF9 had met up with Molly, the wife of Roger the town Mayor, the girl he had met in Porth Branven, Cornwall, in the summer of 1937 whilst on a fact-finding holiday on behalf of German Naval Intelligence.

They both stared at each other, him wondering why she had aged and he hadn't, and her confused as to why he hadn't and was still in a World War Two German naval uniform and carrying a weapon. It was as if he was still fighting the war.

Molly had been seventeen in 1937, and had met this handsome German tourist with the money and flash clothes and camera. He'd seduced her and they'd had a glorious fling during his visit, which both had managed to keep quiet. He had left a deep impression on her.

Otto seemed calm, very calm. Something very strange was happening here.

Molly was in a mild state of shock. She decided it was time to break the deadlock.

"Otto, where have you been all of this time? And you look so young."

Otto Von Diesel smiled.

"Well, my dear Molly, this war has broken up many a relationship, and scarred us all. Very sadly, many have died on both sides, but I am so pleased it is now finally at an end. My beard probably covers up my own scars of war. I don't intend for my rudeness to intrude on you, but you somehow look older."

Otto hadn't intended to be so blunt, but it was plainly obvious to him. She had aged, and he hadn't appeared to. He placed a hand on her cheek in affection and she lovingly held it with her own hand. His felt so deathly cold and distant.

She looked into those piercing blue eyes she remembered. They ate into hers, knowing but somehow vacant.

After his bath he smelled better; his uniform, although neat, smelled of damp.

"Otto, what date is it today?" she asked, pushing the conversation on.

The Kapitan thought it was a joke question.

"Why, my dear Molly, it is Thursday, August 7th, 1941. Why do you ask? Do you not know what day and date it is? Maybe you have been indulging in the celebrations a little too much, ja? I have a question for you also. When did this war end? It must have been very recently, and since we sailed from Brittany. I feel so confused. It is as if I fell asleep after we sailed on this failed mission. I find myself, and my crew also, waking up here with the glorious victory celebrations taking place. This is all so strange and unexplainable."

"Otto, it is not Thursday, 7th August, 1941. It is Saturday, 7th August, 1971. The war ended over twenty-six years ago. I don't know where you have been all this time. I don't understand any of this either."

Otto laughed.

"My dearest Molly, how can this be? It is Thursday, 7th August, 1941. Why do you joke about this? We have won this war. The people outside, your people and also some of my own countrymen and women, they celebrate our victory."

He looked at her with pleading eyes.

"Otto, I don't know how to tell you this, but you didn't win the war. The war ended with a massive defeat for Germany in May, 1945. Adolf Hitler shot himself in his bunker in April, 1945, just as The Red Army was about to encircle and capture him and his last few followers."

Otto was dumbfounded.

"This cannot be true, Molly. The Führer dead? Germany defeated? Saturday, August 7th, 1971? This is all too much for me to understand."

Otto sat quietly and thought about things. Suddenly he remembered that people here acted differently and wore their hair and clothes so differently from in 1937. And he hadn't actually seen any evidence of the German Army of Occupation.

"If this is true, then I would be a man the age of fifty-three, but I look and feel like I am still a young man. How can this be?"

"Otto, look at the calendar up there on the wall."

He did as requested.

"Read out today's date please, Otto," asked Molly, looking at him closely. "I have put a ring around today's date in red pen because it's a reminder to order certain stock on Monday morning next."

"It reads Saturday, August 7th, 1971."

Otto looked at her in complete surprise.

"You realise what this means, Molly?"

She shivered and met his steely gaze.

"You are older to fit in with 1971, and I am not. I cannot remember how I got from the Breton coast to this Cornish coast. It can only mean that I am dead. I could not have survived the war. I never told you I was a German Naval Officer, sent here to relay information to German Naval Intelligence, under the guise of being on a vacation. My crew, who also seem so well, must not have survived the war either."

Otto put his head in his hands and looked to be in a state of total shock. He needed a couple of minutes to consider his situation. He composed himself and then spoke to her softly.

"Please forgive me, Molly. This is a big bombshell that I don't understand also. Can you show me some more proof of this? My men are in town and they are armed, and the Unterseeboot is also armed with torpedoes, machine guns and a deck gun."

Down on the beach, the policemen had cleared the area, or so they thought. The Sergeant, from what he considered a safe distance, stood guard and awaited reinforcements to arrive from out of town, plus the bomb disposal squad, which would arrive a couple of hours later.

They had somehow missed Al and Oppo, who had decided to take matters into their own hands and become heroes of the hour.

"Hey, Oppo. We are supposed to be the pyrotechnical experts around here, so what do you say we see if we can make that big baby safe? They say it's ticking. That must be a good sign. It shows the parts inside aren't seized up. If we can stop it ticking, then surely we can stop it from going off. I've got my tools in the truck. What do you say?"

"OK," replied Oppo, scratching his head. "Make sure you bring a hammer."

Al returned with his tools in a well worn bag, and he and Oppo skirted the beach by the harbour wall and were out to the device before anybody realised, the police being distracted by reports that the armed Germans were inside The People's Rooms, mixing with locals, tourists and their civilian countryfolk from West Germany.

"So, where are these new Germans?" asked the Sergeant. "Harris, you go up to The People's Rooms and see what's happening. Toogoode, you had better accompany him, just in case of trouble. I'll hold the fort here and keep people away from the beach as best I can. Armed Germans and U-boats? Some tricksters are having a good laugh here. I've got a couple of spare officers coming over to help us before too long and the bomb disposal squad will be here later. Until then, we are on our own, boys."

Al and Oppo made their way quietly over to where the mine had pushed in a few feet with the tide.

When they reached it, Al placed his two hands on the sphere and put his right ear to it.

"It's ticking all right, Oppo. Pass me a hammer."

He did and Al smacked it to make a loud clang, which could be heard way back off the beach.

The Sergeant heard the noise along with most of the onlookers. He strained his eyes to see.

"What are those two halfwits doing out there with the mine? Al's my cousin and should have more sense."

The Sergeant wasn't sure what to do. He didn't fancy making the trip out to the mine again, not when it was ticking. That must mean that the bloody thing was about to go off, with bits of Al and Oppo likely to be scattered all over West Cornwall.

"Al! Oppo! Don't be bloody idiots!? Get back here where it's safe!"

Al heard the shout and waved an acknowledgement to his cousin.

"My cousin's waving to wish us good luck," said Al, getting back to what he was doing.

"Hey, Al. The ticking must be coming from one of the conker spikes. If we can find which spike is making the ticking noise..."

"Yeah, we can concentrate on hitting that spike."

"Al, how many spikes can you count on this thing?"

They both counted.

"Well, I made it ten," said Oppo.

Al made it nine.

"Better check them again," said Al, "just to be on the safe side."

The first time checking, they had missed out one spike at the back of the sphere.

When they checked again, they found a wind-up alarm clock with two bells attached to the spike with heavy black tape. Al removed it and showed it to Oppo.

"What a coincidence," said Oppo. "It's ticking as well as the mine. So, who put it there and why?"

They listened to the clock ticking together for a few seconds and then the alarm went off suddenly, causing them to both panic. Al dropped the clock and put his fingers in his ears, and Oppo shut his eyes. Despite being dropped, the clock still continued to ring. Al gained his composure and picked it up again.

"How the hell do you switch this damned thing off?"

Oppo didn't know either, so he put it on the sand and hit it with the hammer. It ceased to function.

"Now we can listen to the mine," said Al, putting his ear back to it again. "Well, I can't hear it ticking now, so it must have been the clock all along. I reckon us hitting the mine has made it safe. Good work, Oppo. Maybe we could claim the casing for scrap or something."

They walked off the beach together and reached the irate Sergeant.

"Cousin, that was a damned foolhardy thing you did there, you and Oppo. You're lucky you weren't both blown to kingdom come. So what's that you got? Looks like a smashed alarm clock."

Al replied, "I think we made the mine safe, cousin. This clock was fixed to the back of the thing and that's what everyone heard ticking."

The Sergeant examined the smashed clock.

"Well, I'll be a bloody duck with a petrol can. Those bloody kids from the top estate; they did this. I heard they were hanging around the mine. So where are they now? Up to no good, I shouldn't wonder. Good work, boys. Better let the bomb disposal lads look it over and deal with it when they get here from Plymouth. Got to be on the safe side."

Roger and Frau Hertzmann were fooling around in the locked room and quite oblivious to the events outside.

While all the celebrations were continuing, the kids from the estate above Porth Branven, who were responsible for the clock prank, had found something else with which to cause mischief.

Up on the back roof of The People's Rooms there still existed a World War Two Carter air raid siren, and it was in working order. It was last used in 1962, when Porth Branven thought it was about to be obliterated in a Soviet first missile strike, after the then vicar panicked and rang the church bells at the height of the Cuban Missile Crisis.

The siren and a few other old artefacts from the war had survived in various places, including an Anderson shelter inside Al's garage, right next to his petrol tanks, and a pillbox down on the beach, which was usually frequented by courting couples and underage drinkers.

While everyone was inebriated, one of the kids, whose mum worked as a clerk at The People's Rooms, found the key to the door leading out to the roof and into the special canopy that protected the siren from the elements.

The alarm clock was funny; this would be even better.

The boy had been present when his dad had maintained this relic only recently and had pumped him for instructions on how it was used. Porth Branven was in for a treat, something it hadn't experienced for years.

"I have to get back to my men, Molly," Otto Von Diesel said in the café. "I do not know what to say. I have the bulk of my crew out there behind the rock that is called Tooth, on the Unterseeboot. I must go to them."

The Kapitanleutnant was a man deep in thought.

"I will come with you, Otto," said Molly. "I have to put in an appearance some time today. Roger will wonder where I am. He will be missing me."

He wasn't. Some sounds were emitting from and reverberating around the room that Roger and Frau Hertzmann had sneaked into for their illicit lovemaking.

"Roger! Oh, ja, Roger! Ich bin coming!"

The two German sailors who had been engaged in pleasurable activities behind the rocks on the beach with the local girls were in a huddle with Leutnant Krieger.

"Herr Leutnant, all this excitement is due to the fact that some kids found a mine down at the beach. Now that we are at peace, can we not do something to help?"

The indecisive Leutnant hadn't a clue.

"Better wait until the Kapitan returns. He has been gone for an age and should be back soon. A mine, you say? I don't like the sound of that," he said, looking suddenly ashen as he recalled that a mine had almost sunk UB-AF9.

Just then, the Kapitan arrived back at The People's Rooms along with Molly.

The German sailors whispered and sniggered amongst themselves.

"That must be the Kapitan's woman from ashore. She looks old enough to be his mother!"

A sheepish and dishevelled Roger and Frau Hertzmann appeared. They managed to straighten up their clothes before re-emerging into the gathering. No-one had missed them. Roger than saw Molly.

"Ah, Molly, where have you been all day?"

Molly thought quickly.

"Roger, you wouldn't believe the day I have had. Loads of problems at The Atlantic. Had to stay and sort out stuff."

Roger was satisfied with the explanation but glowing from the better satisfaction from his encounter with Frau Hertzmann.

"Dear Molly," he thought fondly to himself. "She'd help out anybody, would Molly."

Frau Hertzmann was jealous and wanted to stick pins in Molly.

Molly never noticed how close her husband and the German woman seemed to be.

Frau Hertzmann could feel Roger's civic juices trickling down her leg. It felt damp and cold after the passionate hot encounter of the just recent, but she glowed and was warmed by the experience anyway. The German lady excused herself and went off to the toilets.

PCs Harris and Toogoode saw the German sailors and their guns. So there *were* armed Germans in town. Were they in a film?

Leutnant Krieger spoke to the Kapitan.

"Herr Kapitan, it would seem that there is a problem on the beach with a mine."

The Kapitan took control of the situation.

"Ah, here are the two law enforcement officials. The Constables, as they call them here. They come to ask for our help with the mine, ja?"

PC Harris confronted the Kapitan.

"Sir, I have to ask you why you are dressed in German military uniform, which some feel is in bad taste, but worse, you and your other crew members are carrying illegal firearms."

PC Toogoode came up to support his colleague, saw Molly, and gave her a knowing smile, which was discreetly returned. Kapitan Von Diesel snapped to attention and saluted the two Constables.

"I am Kapitanleutnant Otto Von Diesel, in command of the Unterseeboot AF9. These are some of my men. We carry regulation German Navy weapons with correct authorisation. I was about to offer you both my men's help in this matter, under my command."

The Constables looked at the weapons and wondered what to do. Hendon Police College never covered what to do when you were armed with only a regulation truncheon and confronted with men who carried more hardware than the police, or the army for that matter, in peacetime Cornwall.

Maybe The Sergeant would know what to do. He was commended for bravery years ago for disarming a man with a machete in Hayle, who was annoyed at being overcharged in a chippy.

Kapitanleutnant Von Diesel ordered his men to stay put, and agreed to go to meet The Sergeant who was in command of civil forces in this district. The Kapitan made sure that his personal weapon was at hand. He was also accompanied by his most trusty sailor, Seaman Schwartz.

The Sergeant saw the German issue weapons and realised in a hit-home moment that, fuck, there *were* Germans in Porth Branven and they *were* carrying guns. Why was this happening to him in West Cornwall on a Saturday afternoon?

Usually Porth Branven was a quiet outpost of the Devon and Cornwall Constabulary. There was the odd drunk, a parked car that blocked a shop in the main street or complaints of a dog barking, but today was different.

Bert and Halifax Halibut were in The Anchor Inn, drowning their sorrows and grievances, in the case of Bert, and, in the case of Halibut, he just wanted to get pissed. Both agreed for differing reasons that they wanted nothing to do with Germans.

At one point, Bert wondered if the mushrooms he'd had for breakfast two days previously had had some influence on him. None of this could be real, surely. Usually Pam Trevaskis sold only normal ones in her corner shop in the main street.

The children on the roof of The People's Rooms had a grand view of all going on below them without being seen. They bided their time.

"I accept your offer of help, Captain Von Diesel, but I must insist that you surrender your weapons. The war has been ended some twenty-six years, for goodness' sake. Unless you are in a war film, of course?"

Von Diesel remained on alert, despite the information being relayed to him.

"Do not jest, Herr Officer. I have no proof as yet that the war has ended, at least when you claim it had. Twenty-six years ago? I sailed from the Breton coast two days ago and the war was in full swing and now it is apparently ended, so it must have just occurred with the German forces being triumphant, ja?"

Otto gauged the reaction of the Sergeant.

"The war ended, Kapitan. It was in April, 1945. Today is the 7th of August, 1971. You are now a West German citizen and we are both on the same side with a common enemy, the Soviets."

"You are the second person today to tell me that the war has ended some twenty-six years ago, Herr Sergeant. I am beginning to believe that something is not altogether correct here. I still need to see some proof of this claim, ja?"

Someone produced a newspaper, which he studied carefully. The Kapitan thought to himself quietly for moment.

The strange ships and aircraft he had seen, which seemed to be more advanced than he could remember before, the strange clothes these people wore, their hairstyles, and the British and Japanese cars he had seen; lots of things were different. Maybe the law enforcer was correct after all. However, the Kapitan still had some doubts.

The police wanted to know what further proof they could provide.

The kids in command of the air raid siren decided it was time to crank up the fun.

The unmistakable frightening wail of the old World War Two air raid siren attacked the air waves of Porth Branven after several years of inactivity. It wailed mournfully out across the rainy August afternoon in an act reminiscent of the Cuban Missile Crisis of 1962, some nine years before.

The kids laughed at the mischief and confusion they had caused, both with the mine and now the air raid siren.

Kapitanleutnant Von Diesel held his weapon more closely and looked up to the skies, which were grey and horrible in contrast to earlier that afternoon.

"Ach du meine Güte! Greift die Luftwaffe uns etwa an? Wir stehen doch auf der seiben Seite!"

"What did you say, Kapitan Von Diesel?" asked the police Sergeant.

"I said, 'Oh, my goodness! Is the Luftwaffe attacking us? We're on the same side!'"

"I'm not on your side, Kapitan, and it's not an attack by the Luftwaffe. Maybe it's the Soviets. They could have launched a first missile strike at us!"

"We have to get to the air raid shelters!" said Von Diesel with some urgency in his voice. Roger and the Sergeant shrugged their shoulders.

"We don't have air raid shelters," said Roger. "I suppose we could go to the old pillbox at the end of the beach, but we wouldn't all be able to fit in there."

The wailing from the siren was ear-splitting and could be heard up at The Bluebells.

The Major stirred, looked around and saw the Countess lying beside him. He shook her awake.

"Good lady, you must get up immediately. We must go down to the cellar to shelter. By Jove! Where's my tin hat? The Germans are attacking us!"

The Countess stirred and saw that she was lying on her bed next to the Major.

"It might be the Bolsheviks, Major. They might be coming for us!"

The Major got up and almost fell down.

"It's not the Bolsheviks, Countess. It's Jerry! Can't you hear the air raid siren? These Germans have decided to try for a third time, but our boys on the coastal defence battery will give them a taste of their own medicine."

Gradually the Major, whose head felt fuzzy, started to remember where he was.

"My dear Countess, you could be right about the Bolsheviks. They could be about to attack us. Is nowhere safe? I call this whole business damned unsporting and ungentlemanly. They could have given us a warning first!"

The Major was still half inebriated, the Countess was even more three sheets to the wind and the Matron was even more pissed and went back to sleep in her room. The siren continued to wail across town.

Meanwhile, in The Anchor, Bert and Halifax were slowly getting drunk in an effort to help Bert forget his loss and the Germans.

"Did you hear that, Bert?" said the Yorkshireman, finishing off his pint.

"I heard it all right," replied Bert. "Some imbecile in The White House or The Kremlin has started World War Three. So, what should we do?"

Halifax considered the options available, which were extremely limited.

"I suppose the best thing to do in the circumstances is to get the pints in. My shout. Same again?"

Bert nodded and Halifax went to the bar where the landlord was polishing glasses with a cloth. The man knew what Bert and Halifax drank without even having to ask them.

"I wish somebody would turn that dreadful racket off, Halifax. It's playing havoc with my corns," said the landlord.

On board UB-AF9, Leutnant Spiegel, in temporary command, told his men to be vigilant.

"Our Luftwaffe are about to resume hostilities, it seems. All the celebrations ended with the Feuerwerke. Maybe the war hasn't ended after all. We must hope that the Kapitan and the others are not harmed."

Roger had half sobered up.

"Come on, folks. It's only the old World War Two air raid siren that's gone off. Some damned fool has activated it. This is no attack by the German Luftwaffe or the Soviets."

Frau Hertzmann was confused. Kapitanleutnant Von Diesel was confused. Leutnant Krieger was even more confused.

"Herr Kapitan, maybe the plane with the anti-submarine device will make a sudden reappearance. I am worried that we might be stuck here and I will never set eyes on my little Helmut and Willy in Düsseldorf again."

Everybody looked at each other and then at the skies.

The Sergeant and the rest of the Cornish contingent expected to hear, or maybe see, Soviet intercontinental ballistic missiles arriving in a few short minutes.

Kapitanleutnant Von Diesel expected to see his glorious Luftwaffe bombing the hell out of the enemy People's Rooms and taking him and his men out at the same time.

Only Roger seemed to be thinking straight in the chaos.

Molly had got closer to Otto Von Diesel for protection.

"Come on," said Roger, taking Frau Hertzmann by the hand. "I'm putting a stop to this nonsense right now."

The pair went to sort out whoever had sounded the siren.

164

Al and Oppo were downing strong German lager.

"Hey, Oppo. We've got to service the Mayor's official limousine on Monday morning. Have we got those spark plugs yet?"

Oppo scratched his head.

"Sorry, boss. Completely forgot about them. I'll take a run over to my brother's scrap yard tomorrow. He'll sort a set out for me."

"So, what do you reckon all that noise is about?" said Al.

"Well, isn't it obvious, boss? There's some place on fire somewhere."

Up on the roof, Roger intercepted the would-be air raid wardens.

"Right, you two. You've had your fun. Now scram before I call the Constable."

The two kids smirked and were obviously pleased with their handiwork. They were just about to do as instructed when Frau Hertzmann had a thought.

"You two children! Wait! Do not go anywhere just yet."

The strong, commanding German voice made them stop in their tracks. Frau Hertzmann spoke again.

"Roger, do you know how to turn this thing off?"

"No," said Roger, suddenly feeling foolish.

Frau Hertzmann looked at the children. She didn't have to say anything to them. They understood and knew they would have to turn the wretched thing off. It was now getting on everybody's nerves.

Roger had a thought as well.

"We can't just turn it off. There has to be the all clear siren to follow it."

"That is good thinking, Herr Roger," said the German woman, looking again at the children.

The children agreed to sound the all clear.

Roger heaved a sigh of relief. Whose bright idea was it to keep this museum piece in working order? Then he remembered it was his.

Roger, Frau Hertzmann and the children waited for the all clear to sound for a while and then the thing went back to silence, hopefully never to sound out again. They all went downstairs to join the main party. Roger rang his bell to gain their attention.

"Oyez! Oyez! Crisis over, good folks of Bremerstunghaven and Porth Branven. This was a drill. Please go about your business calmly. God save the Queen!"

Roger thought that would go down well with everybody, especially as her family had German origins.

There were some murmurs of disapproval because not everyone in Porth Branven was a royalist.

Out on the end of the pier, Old Trevor stood to attention for a few seconds and then recommenced playing his ukulele. The birds edged closer to his sandwiches.

Kapitanleutnant Von Diesel raised a hand.

"Listen, you people. By all means, enjoy yourselves, but I, as the senior Military Commander in this town, am now in charge of the situation."

PCs Harris and Toogoode looked at their superior for guidance, but the Sergeant had resigned himself to playing ball with the Germans. He had no other choice. They, The Germans, had guns; he and his men did not.

Another siren was heard coming into town. This time it was an emergency vehicle, a police car, which drew up outside. Its three occupants, an Inspector and two Constables, came into The People's Rooms to be confronted by the armed Germans, the revellers, and their colleagues from The Devon and Cornwall constabulary.

"What's going on here, Sergeant?" asked the Inspector.

"I can explain, sir," replied his colleague.

The Sergeant wondered where he would start. The Inspector exercised caution with these armed men present. Who were these maniacs wearing old German naval uniforms? This was West Cornwall, and Porth Branven, to be exact. Usually the only excitement around here was Bert and Halifax having to be sorted out after too much to drink, weaver fish stings on the beach in summer and complaints about Al and Oppo and the so-called garage they ran.

Kapitan Von Diesel was in command.

"I am also confused, Herr Inspector, as to what is happening in this crazy town, but until I am completely satisfied that the war has ended, then this town is under German command, ja? I give you my word as an officer and a gentleman that no-one will be hurt, if they do not do anything stupid."

The Inspector looked at the guns the Germans carried and agreed to co-operate. Von Diesel spoke with authority and calmness.

"My men will help you to keep the good order, Herr Inspector, and you and your men must ensure that the area around the beach is completely clear and the people of the town keep back to a safe distance, ja?"

The Kapitan delegated his men accordingly and placed Krieger in charge, with Schwartz as his right hand man. Schwartz could be relied upon to keep order and an eye on the Düsseldorf Dummkopf.

Von Diesel summoned Roger and Frau Hertzmann over.

"Herr Mayor, is there somewhere where we can speak a little in private?"

Roger beckoned the German Commander to his office. Von Diesel turned to the others.

"I would like the German lady and Molly to also accompany us, ja?"

He clicked his heels and politely gestured them to follow him and Roger to the office.

When they got there, The Mayor indicated for all to be seated. The Commander removed his cap and relaxed his weapon.

"There is something very strange about this small seaside town. You people claim the war is long over, but here I am in command with my men. So both of us cannot be right. Frau Hertzmann, you are a German. So you and our other countrymen and women folk are here celebrating the end of the war, which I believe had just happened, but it is claimed the conflict ended over twenty-six years ago. Tell me straight, Frau Hertzmann. Is Molly correct over what she says about the Führer, Adolf Hitler, being dead, and the war having ended in May, 1945? And is today Saturday, August 7th, 1971?"

There was a pause of silence.

"I am afraid this information is correct, Herr Kapitan. I cannot explain what has happened to you and your men, but the war did end in May, 1945. Germany is no longer unified and we are now citizens of West Germany. East Germany is under Soviet control. Roger, can't somebody find a history book or something to convince the Kapitan?"

A few minutes later, a young girl fetched a world history book down to The People's Rooms and handed it to Molly. She gave it to Kapitanleutnant Von Diesel to look at. He went silent and thumbed the pages.

Roger spoke as the Kapitan studied the relevant pages of the history book.

"And we have a Queen now, Kapitan, ever since 1952. The King had died."

The German Commander had a serious expression on his face and stood up. He handed over the book to the child and thanked her.

"I am confused, Herr Mayor, by this information presented to me. However, I am a German Naval Officer and a man of honour. I must accept this situation and report at once to the Inspector, the senior civilian Law Enforcement Officer in this town."

At the edge of the beach, The German sailors and the Cornish policemen stood guard in almost silence. Both groups eyed each other suspiciously. The Inspector had told his men to do nothing to antagonise the German sailors. The Sergeant whispered to his superior.

"Sir, what are we supposed to do?"

The Inspector responded.

"Sergeant, I have received several garbled messages about armed men and German military individuals running amok in this small town. I requested an armed response unit to attend the scene. They are in Bodmin and it will be a while before they get here. And I believe the bomb disposal squad have been called to deal with this mine, but they are on their way from Plymouth and will be a bit longer still."

"Couldn't we call out the army or something, sir? How the hell is a four-man armed response team going to deal with guys like these with those weapons?"

The Inspector was mystified.

"Well, I have never had to deal with a situation like this before. There is a Territorial Army unit just outside Camborne, and an army camp at Penhale, Holywell Bay, but they are there for training purposes. We don't have any regular army units in Cornwall and it would have to be the government who could authorise their use anyway. The nearest active military unit is in Plymouth, so they won't be coming to our aid today."

"Well, at least we have the bomb disposal boys from the Navy on their way," said the Sergeant. "Perhaps they are armed."

Both men knew they were powerless and in the hands of invaders who never succeeded back in 1940.

Chapter Fourteen

Carrington had contacted The Admiral of the Fleet in Plymouth and the Admiralty.

The Deputy Commander of HMS *Bosun* wondered what the hell was going on. The vessel's Commander had been suddenly summoned to London on Admiralty business and now Naval Intelligence was sending top secret, UK eyes only signals, and this was supposed to be a cosy courtesy visit to Falmouth?

Carrington received immediate orders back from Naval Intelligence to find Boras; turn Falmouth town upside down if needs be, but find Boras. Two other agents were dispatched to Cornwall to assist him.

Kapitanleutnant Von Diesel came up to the police Inspector.

"Herr Senior Officer, can we speak alone please?"

The Inspector nodded. The two men moved away from the rest of the men. The Kapitan spoke quietly but firmly.

"Herr Inspector, I have come to realise the position of myself and my men. I wish to honourably surrender to you as the head of the appropriate authority. The war is over. I now accept this position and wish to act accordingly. I wish to surrender my men's weapons over to you. I will seek your assurance that my men will be well treated and allowed to return unhindered to our vessel. Once there, I will arrange for the rest of my crew to hand over the weapons they have, and for my boat, the Unterseeboot AF9, to formally surrender to the British authorities."

The Inspector thought he had heard everything. Now he was being asked to accept a formal surrender of German forces twenty-six years after the conflict of World War Two had ended.

"I will accept your surrender, Herr Kapitan, and will give you my assurance as a police officer that you and your men will not be harmed in any way and you will all be allowed free, unrestricted access of passage back to your U-boat. Normally, being in possession of firearms would mean the suspects would have to be held in custody, but, these not being normal circumstances, we can conduct this business at the police station. It will have to be a formal handover. Kapitan, I will instruct my Sergeant to take over here while you organise your men. Is that acceptable to you, sir?"

"Jawohl, Herr Inspector. It is correct and appropriate."

And so there was the curious sight of the German naval presence marching smartly up the main street with their weapons and being escorted as prisoners of war by an unarmed Inspector, a Sergeant and a Constable.

The men reached the tiny police station and entered after the Sergeant had opened up.

Kapitanleutnant Von Diesel ordered his men to make safe their weapons and place them on the floor in the custody of the police officer.

The police Constable checked all the weapons and proceeded to lock them all up securely in a heavy metal cabinet. It would be another thing for the Plymouth bomb disposal squad to deal with, along with the mine.

"I had better make a report of some kind, sir," said the Sergeant to his Inspector, scratching his head after removing his helmet and placing it on the table.

The senior police officer was equally as confused as the Sergeant.

"I'll make a brief handwritten report, sir, and then I suggest you sign it, along with the German Kapitan, and I will sign it as a third person, a witness."

It sounded the best option to the Inspector, who couldn't think of anything else in these bizarre circumstances. The main thing on his mind though was how he was going to explain all of this later on.

The Sergeant drafted an appropriate document, and the three respective parties signed the paper.

"That all seems to be in order, Herr Inspector," said Von Diesel. "Can I now be allowed to march my men back to the boarding boats in the harbour with dignity in surrender, and then back to my vessel?"

"That would be all right by me, Kapitan."

The German Kapitan came to attention and saluted the senior police officer. The salute was returned.

"And now that I have formally surrendered, I must instruct my men accordingly. I wish you success with the diffusion of the mine on the beach, with no injuries or fatalities."

"Thank you, Kapitan. My officers and I will escort you. I am sorry that this has ended the way it has for you and your men. I wish you all well."

"Thank you, Herr Inspector. I also have to check on Herman, to see that he is well."

The Inspector said nothing and thought that maybe Herman was a sick seaman aboard the German vessel.

The German party marched down the street towards the harbour for the last time, escorted by the three police officers and watched by little knots of curious bystanders.

They passed Roger, Molly and Frau Hertzmann outside The People's Rooms. Kapitan Von Diesel paused briefly to acknowledge the three.

"Auf Wiedersehen, Herr Mayor. Auf Wiedersehen, Frau Hertzmann. Und auf Wiedersehen, Molly."

Molly whispered a silent goodbye to Otto. He could see a tear come into her eye. He smiled directly at her and then turned to walk away towards his boats.

Once at the steps of the harbour wall leading down to the moored boats, Von Diesel saluted the senior policeman once again.

"Auf Wiedersehen, Herr Inspector, gentlemen."

"Goodbye, Herr Kapitanleutnant," replied the Inspector, still trying to get his head around what was happening. "And good luck."

The boats, led by the U-boat Commander, pushed slowly out from the harbour wall and into the harbour basin.

The police officers watched the Germans paddle out and then the Inspector turned to his two colleagues.

"Well, men, better get back to it. Don't ask me to explain it either. We have a mine to deal with. Better get back to the beach and see how the other lads are coping. And the bomb disposal team and the armed response unit will be here shortly. At least the issue of Germans running around with loaded guns has been resolved without bloodshed. For that, I am mightily relieved."

Just then a small boy on the pier who had been watching events stumbled and fell into the water. It was obvious from his screams and terror that he couldn't swim. There was no time to lose.

Leutnant Krieger removed his cap and dived into the water. Within short seconds, he had hold of the boy, who continued to struggle and scream.

"Be quiet, little boy. You are safe now. I return you to the stone steps of the harbour wall and advise you to learn to swim so as not to repeat this unfortunate accident, ja?"

An almost breathless Leutnant Krieger swam with the small boy in tow, clinging to him, and landed him safely onto the stone steps.

"Now, go and get yourself dry and warm, ja?"

With that, the German Officer swam back to his boat and was helped aboard by two of his seamen.

"Well done, Hans," said the Kapitan. "You are a hero and saved the young boy's life."

Maybe the man was not such an idiot after all. The Kapitan reserved judgement, but Hans had saved the boy's life, which counted strongly as a redeeming feature.

As the Germans paddled past the end of the pier, they met choppy waters and the frail boats rocked.

Old Trevor was stood out at the end, playing his ukulele as before and pretending to be a poor version of George Formby. He was murdering a classic song and putting his own words to it.

"I'm leaning on a lamp post at the end of the pier, watching certain little Germans go by. Oh, me! Oh, my! Watching certain little Germans go by."

Leutnant Krieger listened with disgust as the man was slowly left behind with his gulls and crows that swooped.

"Herr Kapitan, is that fool taking the Mickey Mouse? Shall I shoot him?"

The Kapitan shook his head in disbelief.

"So, you think he is taking the Mickey? Shall you shoot him? What with? Your peashooter, Leutnant Krieger?"

The Kapitan thought that, although his junior officer had exercised bravery minutes earlier, he was still an imbecile more often than not.

Krieger suddenly remembered he was no longer armed and felt foolish.

The Germans paddled towards the towering Tooth Rock, which guarded the north approaches to the harbour.

"Come on, Leutnant Hans. Let us leave this mad place and these mad people and return to the sanity of the Unterseeboot AF9, where we can be reunited with the others and Herman, that marvellous specimen of a lobster."

173

Von Diesel thought that maybe the Düsseldorf Dummkopf should have remained in Porth Branven. After all, apart from Molly, Frau Hertzmann and maybe the Mayor, they were all strange people much different from those he remembered from 1937.

The boats inched around the jagged features of the rock that reminded Von Diesel somehow of the iceberg that sank the *Titanic*, and the UB-AF9 came into view, sitting on the surface of the choppy waves.

The sun suddenly began to emerge high in the sky.

"Here comes the cavalry," said PC Harris, as the bomb disposal squad rode into town.

The young officer leading the squad got out of the leading vehicle and went over to the Inspector.

"Afternoon, sir. So what have we got here?"

The man looked out over the beach and immediately saw the object washed in on the tide and everybody present keeping their distance.

"Ah, I see her. OK, Inspector. Thank you. My men will take over now."

The Royal Navy Captain spoke with a tone of voice that suggested he was about to deal with a beloved child who had gone astray.

The Inspector heaved a sigh of relief. These lads from Plymouth were welcome to the mine. Then suddenly he remembered.

"Oh, Captain. My cousin, Al, said he heard the thing ticking."

"OK," replied The Royal Navy Officer, suddenly putting on a face that suggested he was suddenly tiring of the child who had gone astray.

It turned out that Devon and Cornwall's armed response unit had been diverted to another, "more serious" incident en route to Porth Branven. The Sergeant got a message through to Divisional HQ, saying they were not needed now anyway. Relief all around.

The celebrations had become a little subdued after the excitement of earlier.

Molly took herself off back to The Atlantic Tea Rooms And Gift Shop, leaving husband Roger to enjoy the company, once again, of the German lady, Frau Hertzmann.

174

Up at The Bluebells Residential Home, Major Beere had a headache and had sobered up enough to realise that neither the Bosch nor the Soviets had attacked Porth Branven, or anywhere else for that matter.

The story of how the air raid siren had been sounded by the kids from the estate had reached the ears of all at The Bluebells, except for Matron and the Countess, who were otherwise engaged for the same reason.

A sympathetic carer had brought the Major some strong tea and two painkillers. The Major was a gentleman to the end.

"God bless you, young lady. You are an angel. 'Tis so kind of you to help an old man in his hour of distress. By Jove, I do think I rather overdid the jolly old celebrations, what?"

The young woman smiled.

"Have your tea and take your tablets, Major. You will soon feel better. And then you had better get back to your own room before Matron, er, returns from town for the afternoon."

They both smiled, knowing full well that the boss of the home was out of it in her back room with Valerie Vodka for a sleeping companion.

"Oh, Major. Let me have the bottles of booze so I can hide them in my locker for you. Better not let the Trout see them, or there will be trouble. They will be safe with me and I will let you have them when you want them, without her knowing."

The woman smiled again. She and the Major had an understanding. He was a lovely old boy who deserved to put one over on the Trout, as the Matron was called behind her back by both staff and residents.

"Better take the bottles belonging to the Countess as well," said the Major.

"Leave it with me, sir," said the woman.

The carer and the Major knew that the Trout would sleep a while longer and then return to duty as if nothing had happened. She wouldn't even suffer a hangover. They both looked at the Countess.

"Well, she's out for the count," said the woman wryly.

Both knew she, too, would wake when she was ready and, again, minus a hangover.

The celebrations stretched on into the evening and the night thereafter, until the last man or woman was standing.

Later, the two coaches arrived to convey the party of Germans from Bremerstunghaven back to their hotel in Penzance for the night, pending their return to West Germany on Monday.

Roger had gone home, ditched his Mayor's regalia, packed a few things and had joined Frau Hertzmann on the coach for Penzance.

Molly was nowhere to be seen, which was normal for a Saturday night anyway. She must have some understanding friends over in Truro, decided Roger, as she was always visiting them and staying over. Now it was his turn to disappear.

Earlier, as the sun had dropped down, the bomb disposal squad had made the device as safe as they could, but it would have to be towed out to sea later and exploded in deeper water on Monday to make it completely safe.

The device hadn't been ticking after all. It had, in fact, been Oppo's expensive deep sea diver's watch, which had, allegedly, once been owned by Jacques Cousteau, and which Oppo had purchased at the Porth Branven Second Hand Emporium along with a jigsaw of St Michael's Mount with the pieces of the castle missing.

The German sailors never returned to Porth Branven harbour.

The Inspector sat in the Sergeant's office, talking to his junior police officer.

"What a day this has been, Sergeant. What do you make of it?"

"Well, sir, I'm like you - totally confused. It must be the case that those Germans must have been playing some strange war game, or maybe it was a stunt for a film."

The Sergeant paused.

"Or, dare I say it, sir?"

He paused again, not wishing to sound stupid.

"Go on, Sergeant. Say what you're thinking."

"Well, sir, could it be that they have been somewhere and didn't actually know the war had ended?"

The comment invited heavy scepticism, as expected.

"So, where have they been all this time, Sergeant? And why haven't they aged? Didn't you notice that they were all relatively young men?"

The Sergeant remembered that they were. The Inspector had been in deep thought.

"I don't know what the truth is here, Sergeant. All I know is this incident will have to be filed away along with UFO sightings and other unexplained strange phenomena. This is almost as bad as when a Yeti was supposedly spotted on Hayle Towans back in 1967."

"I remember it well, sir. There was a load of hippies around. They were stoned out of their minds, smoking illegal substances and waiting for the second coming of something or other. As I recall, the something or other was us, and we nicked the bloody lot of them."

The Inspector got up from his seat.

"Sergeant, I wonder. Give me the key to the metal cabinet if you please."

The Inspector proceeded to open the door of the heavy metal filing cabinet and took a pace backwards.

"So, where are the weapons, Sergeant? Yet another mystery."

The Sergeant was equally gobsmacked. The ammunition was missing as well.

"Sir, we both saw them secured."

"Yes, we did," the senior officer replied. "As I said, this is a mystery we will never solve. It's one for the UFO file, I guess. I reckon we need a Plan B, alternative report, Sergeant. That is unless we wish our police careers to end over this nonsense."

"I quite agree, sir."

The two men sat down together to work out the final details of what was to go into the revised report.

The bomb disposal squad had decided that, because it was unstable, the mine needed to be moved off the beach as soon as possible and towed carefully out into deeper, safer water to be blown up with a controlled explosion on the Monday.

They set about attaching the floats and marker buoys to it, and now needed a boat to tow it out to sea.

Very surprisingly, two volunteers came forward.

"Well, we are the two best equipped men in town to undertake this important mission," said Al to the Navy Captain in charge.

Oppo agreed.

The Captain had reservations but reluctantly agreed, and so Al and Oppo went to the harbour to get their own boat, *Daughter of Titanic*, ready to go around to the beach. There would just be time to tow the mine out to sea and secure it before darkness fell.

Soon they had manoeuvred their thirty-six-foot boat out of the harbour and to a position just off the beach.

The operation wasn't quite as straightforward as they believed it would be, but, after a while, and almost beaching their boat, they managed to get a tow on the mine and pulled it gently out into the waves, making sure it never came close enough to the boat to knock it.

The mine scraped the bottom at first, causing near heart failure for Porth Branven's two would-be heroes, and then disappeared just below the surface of the waves as they made slow but steady progress away from the beach.

"Make sure it doesn't strike The Bear Rock," said Oppo as they got some way off the beach.

The Bear Rock was a single rock in the bay, almost central, which was a favoured mark for the better swimmers to make for to show their prowess. It only occasionally just broke the surface of the water when there was an exceptionally low tide.

Al, steering the boat, had completely forgotten about the rock, and the mine must have missed it by inches. A very worried Oppo looked out over the port side gunwale and went green as the boat passed right over where he knew the rock was.

The two made it out to the suggested spot the Navy had indicated without any mishap, the mine being towed just under the surface. The very nervous pair secured the mine as instructed by the Navy and made sure it was well marked.

"Now, let's get the fuck out of here!" said Al, increasing the boat's power. "I thought we had made it safe, but now I'm not so sure."

The first few feet away from the secured mine was the longest journey of their lives, as the boat churned up the water and headed back to the harbour.

"Say, Oppo, do you reckon they might give us bravery medals for what we've done? We might have saved Porth Branven from being blown off the map today."

Oppo didn't answer and continued to look back over the stern to where the distinctive floats and buoy bobbed on the sea's surface, marking the spot where the deadly device sat some hundred feet or so down on the bottom, waiting to be dealt with by the Navy on Monday.

Sunday morning in Porth Branven was hung over, with silence mostly except for Old Trevor back out on the pier after eating a hearty breakfast, and singing *Jesus Wants Me for a Sunbeam*, or, to be more correct, the hymn, *I'll Be a Sunbeam*. This, of course, had the musical accompaniment of his ukulele.

The older residents of the town made their dutiful way to the Methodist chapel in the main street, or to the C of E grafted-on church of St Legest on the edge of town.

Pam Trevaskis, at her corner shop, had the good sense and forethought to stock up with every type of hangover cure and alleviant available, and had also bought in a large batch of specially baked Cornish pasties for the German celebrations.

Her suffering customers soon drifted in, mostly after church or chapel service, but some before, to purchase the *News of the World* and *The People* newspapers and, of course, the obligatory cigarettes, sugar and milk forgotten the day before.

Pam made a killing. She also sold that morning four fountain pens, twelve balsa wood gliders and plenty of headache pills, and took enquiries as to where people could purchase alarm clocks that sounded like World War Two air raid sirens.

All in all, it was a normal Sunday morning in Porth Branven.

Chapter Fifteen

Roger had left Molly for Frau Hertzmann. A minesweeper, HMS
Morton, patrolled the coast to enforce an exclusion zone around the
mine. Meanwhile, Porth Branven recovered from the biggest
hangover in its long history.

Over in Falmouth, Carrington was a guest on board HMS *Bosun*, as
the ship's compliment, who hadn't gone ashore, awaited her
Commander back from London.

Later, Carrington teamed up with the two agents, a younger man
and woman, brought on board this time by the flagship's launch from
The Prince of Wales Pier. He briefed them later that Sunday in the
plush officers' mess on the huge ship.

Carrington believed that once this business was sorted out he would
be well on his way for a commendation to be knighted. He,
Carrington, who had only ever served briefly as a lieutenant aboard a
minesweeper, was the Navy's - and Britain's - top spy catcher, or so
he would believe.

Carrington thought briefly about the Matron and that awful
residential home for the elderly in Porth Branven. Sex with her had
been good, he had to admit, exciting even, but he was doing a job,
which took priority. Carrington saw himself as the true professional,
and business always came first.

On Monday, he was determined to wrap this business up, make his
report to The Admiralty and hopefully be rewarded with a Far East
posting somewhere much warmer and more civilised than that
dreadful place in West Cornwall, which had a pervading smell of
fish. Falmouth, he could tolerate but Cornwall generally he hated
with a passion.

As Porth Branven's collective hangover eased, the town suddenly
found itself popular again, and on a Sunday of all days.

The media had descended, having heard strange stories regarding German tourists, some of whom had been apparently seen in World War Two naval uniforms.

A genuine reporter from *The Daily News* quickly sought out people to tell their stories. It seemed like everyone had one to tell.

The Anchor Inn did a roaring trade as reporters and other interested parties arrived in their quests for information concerning these alleged stories of rampaging Germans.

It was, perhaps, inevitable that reporters should find their way up to The Bluebells.

Matron sobered up and guarded her words carefully, believing that she was in the confidence of "Officer Michael", an undercover policeman.

The Major indicated to the reporter from *The Daily News* that he had already given a story to another reporter from the same "scandal sheet".

After hearing what he had to say and interviewing the Countess, who had to mention the Bolsheviks for good measure, the newshound went away thinking that the pair was as daft as cuckoos in October. Whoever heard of a German U-boat visiting a Cornish fishing port in 1971?

The reporters went elsewhere for their stories.

Bert and Halifax said it had all been the work of the Bremerstunghaven twinning party and kept quiet about the loss of *The Two Inbred Sisters*, despite being told the Major had said he saw the boat being boarded and scuttled by the Germans.

Bert laughed nervously and looked at Halifax before looking at the reporter. It was generally agreed that the Major liked a drink; more than was good for him.

Their plan was still the same in that they would travel to Falmouth on Monday to see Halifax's mate about organising a salvage operation.

Al and Oppo told the story of how they had saved the port and its people from destruction posed by the mine. Now, that was a half-true story that the Navy on guard out off the coast could verify. The other half of the story was, of course, that the two lentil brains almost blew themselves to bits before deciding to play the heroes.

Molly let them all get on with it and opened up her establishment to cash in as well on the increased trade that had suddenly discovered Porth Branven.

She had a surprise when, out of the blue, her only child, a son called Peter, arrived home from working overseas.

The fit and tanned man gave his mum a big hug and then sensed that something was wrong.

"You had better sit down, Peter. I have something to tell you."

She paused.

"Your father has left me for some German woman called Frau Hurtsmen or something similar."

She awaited his shocked reaction.

"So, big fat Roger has finally done a runner. I didn't know he had it in him."

He studied his mother.

"You don't look too upset about it, ma."

"I'm not!"

Her reply was to the point and definite.

"I suppose I should be, but I couldn't care less. It sounds cold and callous, I know, but it's you I really feel sorry for, Peter."

Peter laughed.

"You've no need to be. That big, fat lump is a joke. He's not my father. He doesn't even look anything like me, ma."

Molly gasped.

"You... you know?"

"Of course I do. I've known for years that he isn't my father."

Peter looked at his mother, who now needed to sit down herself. He put her on the spot immediately.

"So, come on, ma. Spill the beans. Who is he? Who is my real father?"

He looked at her closely with those piercing blue eyes he had inherited from the man.

"I'm thirty-three now, so it's about time I knew the truth. Don't worry. I'm not about to burst into tears or anything like that."

She hesitated before answering.

"OK, son. I guess you do have the right to know the truth. It was just after I first met and went out with Roger. I had a brief fling with this handsome young German tourist over here on holiday in the summer of 1937."

Peter laughed again.

"So my real father is, or was, German? That's a delicious irony, seeing as the man you thought I believed was my real father has suddenly buggered off with a German woman. The revenge of Roger? Did Roger know this other man, the German tourist?"

"No. He always believed that you were his son. I couldn't bring myself to tell him."

"Well," said Peter, whistling quietly. "This is a strange present to come home to after working away in the Middle East. So, do you know what happened to my father?"

Molly paused before answering, making sure she chose her words carefully. Peter just wouldn't be able to get his head around the fact that his deceased father had sat here in this same room only a few hours ago, and all these years after he had been killed in the war. Even Molly had difficulty grasping the concept.

"It was just a brief fling, Peter. He was a handsome, sweet and kind man; a true gentleman. I can see a lot of him in you even though I only knew him briefly. You have his ways and looks. The war came soon after you were born and I never heard from him again after he returned to Germany. If he had stayed here, he would have been interned for the duration of the war. I don't know what happened to him."

It hurt Molly inside to tell her own son further lies, but the truth was just too much for him to be burdened with now; maybe one day, when all this business had settled down.

"So, tell me, ma. What is all this stuff about Germans and Porth Branven? I heard somebody just now saying something about strange goings-on here yesterday. Oh, and is it true that there is a mine that Al and Oppo towed out to sea and that the Navy are due to blow it up tomorrow?"

"Well, the story about the mine is true. Here, let me make you something to eat and then I will tell you all about the mine. As for the Germans, well, there was a bunch of German tourists here, including the one who took off with your supposed father. You know how people around her like to tell tall stories."

He did but was intrigued and interested to hear anyway.

"You must tell me all about it, ma. It all sounds very interesting."

Molly sighed with relief, having given herself a little breathing space and time to get her story straight.

When the newspapers came out on Monday morning, the story of the Porth Branven Germans had made the headlines. There was *THE GHOST OF ADOLF HITLER SEEN ON SATURDAY, MONSTER MINE, GERMAN GUESTS PRETEND TO BE SUBMARINERS*, and even *TITZKRIEG!* Anything, it would seem, concerning Germans appeared to be fair game.

The Daily News, which ran the story on Hitler's ghost, even offered a big cash prize to anyone who could produce an authentic photograph of the mysterious U-boat that had allegedly been spotted by some in Cornish waters.

Monday morning in Falmouth was warm and pleasant and buzzing with tourists from the USA, Germany, Australia, Macclesfield and Spalding.

Carrington had gone ashore nice and early to clear his head for the coming day and to take breakfast in a café overlooking the central Prince of Wales Pier.

His two assistants had made their way over to Porth Branven to get the feel of the place and to seek more information.

Carrington had purchased a newspaper and paused to look at the headlines on the others. All of this German coverage annoyed him. It was all a cover for something far more serious, in his opinion. How could such espionage be happening in Cornwall of all places?

He sat quietly looking out over the sea front from a table outside the café, which afforded a good view of the various knots of people walking out onto the pier and returning. There was a mixture of visitors, locals, pleasure boat operators vying for trade, and some imbecile at the far end of the pier, who, having already caught a garfish, almost hooked some old man's hat when he cast out to try again.

Carrington kept one eye on passers by, tucked into his full English breakfast with extra toast, and stole a glance at his newspaper with his other eye. As soon as he had eaten, he would make tracks to hunt down Boras, who, it would seem, was central to this Soviet spy ring.

When he'd finished his breakfast, Carrington sipped his tea at leisure and read the story of the Germans in Cornwall more closely.

"What a load of lurid nonsense!" he declared. "Lurid, tabloid-reporting nonsense."

It was difficult to distinguish what had been made up by the residents of Porth Branven and what was courtesy of the reporter himself.

Carrington put down the paper with some disgust. Then he had a stroke of luck. He couldn't help talking aloud to himself.

"Well, well, well. What have we got here?"

The small group of people passed, seemingly oblivious to his presence. There was Bert the fisherman and the skipper of the boat on which the two had acted suspiciously. And look who they had with them - the Russian Countess Trovanovich. What a strange but welcome coincidence on Carrington's part that they should all be in Falmouth together that morning, and right under his nose.

Carrington carried a small camera around with him and clicked away, catching the three together. This was evidence. He noted the time he had seen them together.

They ignored him; he could have been just another tourist.

He tried picking up on their conversation as they passed by, heading out on to the pier. He couldn't really make out what they were talking about. He didn't need to. They just looked suspicious, so he knew they were guilty.

The three walked out a bit further on to the pier and stood looking out over the water at the flotilla of assorted small boats and yachts that bobbed at anchor. The water close to the pier was being churned up by the arrival of the St Mawes passenger ferry.

Carrington watched and could see the little group clearly. He finished off his tea and left the café, mingling with other folk who walked up and down the pier. He managed to get a bit closer and pretended to study something in his newspaper.

185

A rough looking unshaven man wearing a woollen hat and a lumberjack style checked shirt came down the pier and walked over to join the three. It was obvious that he knew Bert's mate, the other skipper. They greeted each other like long lost friends, and then Bert was introduced to the newcomer. The two men shook hands before the new arrival acknowledged the Countess in a manner that looked polite and businesslike from a distance.

The three men spoke for a couple of minutes and then they moved off together, after Bert waved a farewell to the Countess, who walked away a few yards to look out over the boats at anchor.

Carrington had seen it all. Another piece to the jigsaw puzzle. He took a couple more photographs and made a mental note of the new man, who looked very dodgy.

Carrington had to make an instant decision. Who to follow? It was tempting to follow the three men and he mentally cursed that the two younger assistant agents sent to help him were not around, because he could have kept tabs on all of these suspicious people.

In the circumstances, Carrington decided that his best bet would be to keep an eye on that old bat of a Russian Countess. She had to be in Falmouth to meet Boras. Of that, he was certain. It might save him doing a lot of spade work, though, in finding this Russian spy link in the port.

The Countess looked at her watch. Carrington looked at the Countess, and then he glanced back to see the three men disappearing off the pier and into the summer crowds that packed the bottom of High Street where it joined Market Street in Falmouth town centre. Just then, Bert stopped.

"Back at the café, that was that reporter guy just now. The one in The Anchor on Saturday."

Bert wondered whether he should go back and say something to the man.

"Did you notice how he was taking photographs of us and the Countess? If I remember rightly, he bought her a drink when Major Beere was talking to us."

The friend of Halifax Halibut was confused.

"You mix with some strange people, H," he said, smiling.

"Do you reckon the Countess will be OK?" said Halifax to Bert, looking a bit concerned.

Bert thought about it for a few seconds.

"She'll be fine. She's a tough old bird, the Countess. She can handle any newspaper reporter. She'll probably bore him to death with tales about the Bolsheviks coming."

They all laughed.

"Yeah, you're right," said Halifax. "Come on. We've got your boat to salvage. Geoff here is your man. Still, if we have a reporter snooping around, we'd better curtail our liquid import business for a while, just to be on the safe side. He can look for a U-boat if he wants, but we don't want him to discover our liquid assets."

Geoff, who knew all about what they were talking about, led them off to his car and then back to the yard further down river, where his own boat was moored.

Carrington forgot about the fishermen and concentrated his efforts on watching the Russian Countess. She was obviously obsessed with boats, ships and all things nautical, as she looked out over the water and in the direction of the docks, a handful of ships were in for refits. He continued to observe her for a few minutes and then she made a move.

Carrington allowed the woman to keep a comfortable distance in front of him and then he followed her. She was quite an elegant lady for her age, he decided. It was also his belief that she was perhaps crazy, but she was also a spy. He continued to follow her into town along the main street. He willed the old lady to lead him to Boras.

The Countess took her time, paused to look in shop windows, and was seemingly oblivious to being followed.

Carrington continued to keep his distance but found himself side-stepping and continually avoiding the hordes of tourists, who had descended upon Falmouth like locusts. They were a bloody nuisance, but they did offer him valuable cover.

After what seemed like an eternity, the woman looked at her watch and paused outside a posh café before entering.

It was obvious to Carrington that the Countess was planning to meet someone at this pre-designated location. Carrington couldn't enter the establishment for fear of being compromised. He had, after all, spoken to and bought a drink for the Countess fewer than forty-eight hours previously, so she was certain to recognise him.

He decided to hover outside, and stole an occasional glance through the window. He mentally hurried her contact to show. He was lucky and didn't have to wait too long.

While he was busy watching the Countess sitting at a table having her order taken by a young waitress, Carrington became aware of the man who had entered the café from the other end of the street. He could see that the stranger was in his late fifties or early sixties, and looked pretty ordinary.

The man joined the Countess at her table and the waitress returned to take his order as well. He and the Countess exchanged greetings and he kissed her hand.

In the couple of minutes it took the waitress to return with two cups of coffee and what appeared to be tea cakes, the man handed over to the Countess a fairly standard buff-coloured file. She opened it up and perused the contents eagerly.

Carrington could make out that the file contained photographs, but he could not tell from outside the window what their subject matter was. He didn't need to see. He knew already. They were photographs of ships. He congratulated himself on being led to the man who he believed to be Boras. The Falmouth-Soviet connection had been established.

Carrington would have liked to have had a photograph of the two meeting, but that would be impossible without compromising himself. He continued to steal glances through the window and acted as if he was waiting impatiently outside the café for someone.

His targets drank their coffee and exchanged conversation, and the Countess studied several photographs before placing them back inside the folder.

He had seen enough to be satisfied he had his man. Across the street, he saw a public bench outside a church entrance, which broke up the uniformity of the shops on the main street. One other person sat on it.

Carrington avoided the slow-moving traffic and joined the middle-aged woman, who looked harassed from shopping on a warm August day. They exchanged a brief smile and he sat down and had a splendid view of the café entrance, so could see exactly when the pair left the place.

Carrington scribbled down some notes in a little black book he carried. He noted down everything that he had witnessed so far that day, making sure he got his timings accurate. He also made sure he didn't miss the Countess and her mystery contact leaving the café.

The Countess emerged first, after about twenty minutes. She was carrying the buff folder now. The man kissed her on both cheeks and on her hand, and then they parted. The Countess wandered back in the direction from which she'd come and the man walked off at a brisker pace in the general direction of the docks.

Carrington got up from the bench, acknowledged the shopping woman and set off in pursuit of Boras. Weaving in and out of the tourists and local shoppers, he kept the man carefully in his sights, knowing how easy it would be to lose him amongst the holiday throng.

As he carefully followed the man, Carrington believed he would be making his way to Falmouth docks. He was wrong. The man reached a car parked about ten minutes' walk away from the town centre.

Carrington had to act quickly. While the man hunted for his car keys, he walked on at a brisker pace and caught up to the man as he opened the car door. The man wore a beard and glasses. Carrington coughed loudly and had to engage him in conversation.

"Excuse me, sir. Can you help me?"

The man turned around and looked at Carrington.

"I'm sorry. Were you talking to me?"

The man sounded a little guarded. Carrington put on a relaxing face.

"I'm not from these parts, sir, and I was wondering if you could help me. I heard that the Navy's new warship was in Falmouth and I was wondering where I might get to see her."

A smile broke out over the man's face. This man spoke ships; he liked that.

"You mean HMS *Bosun*? Are you interested in ships then?"

Carrington knew he had his foot in the door and the man was completely unsuspecting of his motives.

"In a manner of speaking, sir."

The man relaxed and leaned on his opened driver's door and spoke over the roof to Carrington on the pavement.

"Well, you can actually visit her this afternoon. Trips out to see her are being organised from The Prince of Wales Pier back in town. You can find it easily enough."

"I might do that," replied Carrington. "Thank you."

The man spoke again.

"You could, of course, get a good view of her from Pendennis Point. She's out in the bay at anchor. I would have dropped you off there myself, but I'm in a bit of a hurry right now, you understand?"

"No, that's quite all right," said Carrington. "You've been more than helpful. Thank you."

"That's OK," replied the man. "My pleasure."

With that, he waved Carrington farewell and got into his car. Carrington pretended to walk slowly back into town. The car pulled off and Carrington got out his notebook, leaned on a low wall and started to write. He wrote down the time, a description of the man, and noted that he didn't in any way sound Russian, but, in fact, had a broad Cornish accent. Carrington also noted that the car was a green Hillman Super Minx estate, with the registration, ACV 309B. The car was registered in Cornwall in 1964.

He had all the information he needed for now and made his way more briskly back to another part of town where he had parked his own car in a residential street before he had gone aboard the fleet's flagship.

Chapter Sixteen

HMS *Bosun* was all set to welcome visitors aboard in managed parties.

Carrington took his turn with the queues for the boat trips. He wanted to mingle and see for himself if any familiar faces appeared on board.

Some time later, he went on board and met up with the skipper, with whom he shared some information, but not all he knew. Carrington told the man that he was interested in the visitors to the warship. The Naval Intelligence man had the run of the ship and continued to mix with the visitors from ashore as they were escorted around. Carrington half expected Boras to make a reappearance, but the man did not show. However, someone else familiar to him did; the Countess Trovanovich.

The Naval Intelligence man observed her and what she seemed most interested in. Carrington bade his time and then went up to the woman. There was a flicker of recognition. He noticed that she no longer carried the buff file. The cunning old bat had deposited it somewhere. That was suspicious in itself.

"I know you from somewhere, young man. Now, let me see."

Carrington allowed the Countess to work it out for herself.

"Ah, I remember now. You are the reporter from what my friend calls the scandal sheet. You bought us a drink in the Porth Branven public convenience."

"Public house," replied Carrington, smiling.

"Yes, of course; public house. The public convenience is where the Major has to go when his dickey bladder is playing up when the weather is cold."

Carrington laughed again.

"So, where is the good Major today, dear lady?"

The Countess seemed to be a bit forgetful but then composed herself.

"The Major is obviously an old soldier. He doesn't have the same passion about ships as I do, young man."

"So, you like ships, Countess?" said Carrington, reeling the woman in as if he was fishing.

"I love them, dear boy. Ships and boats of all descriptions. Do you know that I have a large collection of photographs of ships that come into Cornwall? Truro and Falmouth, to precisely be."

"Be precise," corrected Carrington, "but I know what you mean."

The Countess was not finished.

"So, why are you on this ship, young man?"

Carrington went into reporter mode.

"My newspaper naturally wishes me to do a feature on this magnificent vessel. I am soaking up her atmosphere like you, dear lady."

The Countess went off on a tangent.

"Do you know, Mr Reporter, there are some very strange people living in Porth Branven?"

"Tell me about it," thought Carrington. "And you, you old black bat, are one of them."

Carrington spoke aloud after getting his thoughts out.

"Who are these people, Countess?"

The old woman got angry and shook her frail fists.

"Mr Scandal Sheet Man, someone has tampered with all my photographic prints, and the Major's brass telescope has also been interfered with. It's a disgrace. If I caught the culprit, I would do him some severe damage, like the brave citizens of Stalingrad inflicted on the Nazi hordes in 1943."

"Yes, I'm sure you would, dear lady. That's awful; a personal intrusion. It's disgraceful that you were both interfered with in this way."

The Countess calmed down.

"So, how did you get to Falmouth today?" asked Carrington politely.

"My good friends, Bert and Hull Herring, gave me a lift in their wonderful pick up truck. I travelled in the back with the wind blowing through my hair, and my legs covered with a thick woollen blanket. It was exhilarating and so exciting!"

Carrington had added another piece to his jigsaw puzzle. It was time to collect yet another.

"So, your friends gave you a lift here? That was kind of them. So, are they not visiting this wonderful warship?"

Carrington had the old lady in his palm. She was a likeable old bird, even if she was an old black bat who he thought should be knitting in some nursing home instead of taking such an interest in one of Her Majesty's warships. And, he told himself, she was, of course, a spy.

"They have other things to do in Falmouth. Some business concerning raising something from the bottom of the sea."

"Yeah, I bet they have," thought Carrington.

They were spies as well. Cornwall was full of them. They were all in this together and it was his mission to root out every last one of them.

"So, who are these strange people in Porth Branven?" asked Carrington, conveying an innocent enquiry in his voice.

"Well, there is the Matron for starters. She likes her gin and her men in more than equal quantities. Only last week she attended the local hospital. Rumour would have it that she was treated for some sort of infection. I am a lady and don't like to speak of these things, but you are a man and you will know what I mean."

The Countess had whispered the last few words. Carrington suddenly found an imaginary itch down below and wondered whether his alfresco pursuit with the Matron had been a good idea after all. He tried to dismiss any unpleasant images from his mind.

"So, tell me, Countess, who else is strange in Porth Branven? You have told me about the Matron. Who else?"

The Countess gushed forth.

"I don't like that town Mayor, Roger, with his big brass bell. Do you know he once went to Germany for a holiday?"

"Did he really?" replied Carrington.

The Countess went on.

"And his wife, dear Molly; well, let me just say she is extremely popular with the men folk of our town. A man who hasn't been shown her favours is as rare as a virgin in a brothel. And let me tell you about Al and Oppo, who manage the automobile establishment."

"Please do."

"Well, one day, a wooden barrel of Irish whiskey got washed up on the beach, and it was claimed by those two. Anyway, to shorten the story and cut it to length, it turned out that it was a special presentation barrel from a top Irish whiskey distillery and worth a lot of money. In fact, the barrel was worth more than the whiskey, and a £1,000 reward was offered to anyone finding it and handing it over intact. So, Al and Oppo had decided to chop the barrel up to drink the whiskey. So, I wouldn't let those two go anywhere near your automobile, Mr Reporter. Although they did make the mine safe to stop us all being blown up, which was good."

Carrington made an excuse to leave and the Countess remembered she was there to look around the ship, so they went their separate ways.

In Porth Branven earlier that day a crowd had gathered to watch the Navy explode the wartime mine.

As people congregated on the shore, at the end of the pier, in the harbour, and out on the cliff tops, the Navy divers went down to place the charges.

A couple of hours later, HMS *Morton*, the minesweeper enforcing the safety exclusion zone, sounded a large single blast on her ship's horn, which echoed for miles.

Seconds later, a huge plume of white sea water rose into the August sky with an accompanying deafening blast as one thousand pounds of explosive lying dormant for thirty-two years was detonated below the surface. It exploded with a loud and spectacular vengeance.

There were cheers and clapping from spectators, which included the two agents sent to assist Carrington. It wasn't every day one experienced seeing a World War Two mine explode.

Such was the power of the explosion and the spectacular visual experience it offered, no-one gave any thought as to what it would have done to its intended target and all the men aboard.

Back in Falmouth, on board HMS *Bosun*, Carrington sought out the ship's Chief medical officer to discuss a possible personal problem he might have developed. After an examination and some reassurance, he was much relieved and decided he'd had enough of the mass of tourists invading the ship like locusts, and he took the next available pleasure boat back to shore.

It wasn't too often that Falmouth police had a guest from Royal Navy Intelligence, and Carrington was offered every available courtesy and co-operation after a senior police officer had checked out his credentials with a superior officer at Divisional Headquarters and had phoned a special MOD number Carrington showed him.

He kept his dealings with the police low key for now. He was interested in the driver of the Green Hillman Super Minx registered in Cornwall in 1964 that he had noted details of earlier. Could the police assist him with his enquiries regarding the identity of the owner or driver of this vehicle?

Carrington waited patiently, and then the information he sought came through police channels. The vehicle was registered to a Mr John Trebannan, resident at 4 Barrangwaneth Row, Falmouth.

Carrington had struck gold of sorts. Another very important piece of the puzzle was fitting into place. He now had the name of the Russian agent in Falmouth supplying the Russian Countess in Porth Branven with the secret information about Britain's naval capability.

There was still some work to do on discovering what information was being passed and the Porth Branven drop-off point operation, but it was fitting together nicely.

At a guess, Carrington believed that whatever information was being passed was finding its way, probably by trawler in the dead of night, from the north Cornish coast to France, and from there on to Moscow.

Despite his mission not being fully completed, Carrington congratulated himself on making such progress in such a short time scale.

For now, he decided that John Trebannan, if that was his real name, could be left alone. The powers that be could strike when the time was right, and, with a bit of luck, a few more fish, maybe even bigger ones, might be caught in the net.

Halifax and Bert had sorted out a deal with Geoff and his diving and salvage crew to attempt to raise *The Two Inbred Sisters* later on in the week when the tides were right, and the Countess had made her own way back to Porth Branven by taxi.

In the early evening, Carrington also found his way back over to Porth Branven, after checking out and photographing the Trebannan property, which afforded a good view of the docks.

Carrington knew from a previous arrangement that his two colleagues would be at The Atlantic Tea Rooms And Gift Shop. He joined them there, it being a convenient place to meet up seeing as the establishment opened late in the evenings during the summer months.

"Well, at least there are no Germans here," said Carrington, sounding pleased. "Although I saw a few in Falmouth today."

The three sat quietly at a corner table and pooled their knowledge and thoughts.

"So, what do you make of this town?" asked Carrington, sipping tea from a china cup.

"Well, so far it looks pretty much like any other Cornish seaside town in summer. Busy kids fishing for crabs in the harbour, fully booked up with no available accommodation left, and a mine being detonated out to sea this morning. I suppose the weirdest person here we have come across today was some old guy out on the pier playing a ukulele. Only the seagulls paid him any attention. Maybe that's what the Cornish do for entertainment," said the male agent.

"I can assure you that he is not the only strange person in this town," replied Carrington, trying to dismiss a mental vision of crabs from his mind. "When you have finished your tea, I will show you where all the lunatics in this particular asylum hang out."

He sipped his own tea.

"So, what have you managed to find out today?"

Carrington said the words knowing that the principal suspects were mostly in Falmouth, of all places, on the day that *HMS Bosun* was open to the public for viewing. How convenient.

The woman agent spoke.

"Well, after watching the mine being detonated, I had a wander up to this Bluebells Residential Home. I spoke to the Matron. I said I was a colleague of yours. She was a bit suspicious this time and intrigued to know what was going on so, as I couldn't divulge anything, I didn't find out much either. She did tell me I could speak to the Major if I wanted. Turned out he was having a nap, but he did wake up. He showed me his telescope, quite proudly as a matter of fact. There was no sign of this Countess Trovanovich. The Matron said she had gone out for the day somewhere. The woman wouldn't allow me to look through her room."

Carrington intervened.

"Well, I can account for her whereabouts. Have one guess."

"Falmouth?" answered the man.

Carrington had no need to reply.

The woman agent went on to say that after the Major had woken from his nap, she had asked him about Germans and what he claimed to have seen Saturday last.

"He got a bit annoyed, and said the police were useless and that he had told them everything and he had nothing further to say on the matter. The Matron, of course, told me he was just an eccentric old soldier who saw the world through his telescope and who was not exactly the most reliable of witnesses. 'Doo-lally at times' was the description she actually used."

Carrington knew much of this to be correct, but he had a sneaking suspicion that Major Beere was in on this and undoubtedly connected, even if he didn't share the Countess's passion for ships. Carrington had observed the man acting suspiciously aboard the fishing boat skippered by the strange Yorkshireman known locally as Halifax Halibut.

Carrington spoke decisively.

"Right, you two. I want you to follow the old man, the Major, tomorrow morning when he goes out on his dawn patrol with his telescope. See if he meets up with anybody, and find out what he looks at. I'll be down here, at the police station or thereabouts. You will locate me easily enough in this mad place. So, what else have you two found out today?"

It was the man's turn to speak. He produced a tatty notebook.

"Well, we had a look at the garage run by those two known as Al and Oppo. It's like something out of a 1940s motor museum. How Al and his thickie mate, Oppo, got to run a garage is beyond me. The place is a complete and utter death trap, and those two are obviously dishing out dodgy MOT certificates. Quite honestly, if brains were dynamite, those two wouldn't have enough to blow their caps off. They told me about the mine and what they claimed to have done to make it safe, but they smelled a rat, I'm sure. Had they seen Germans? Of course they had. Who hadn't? The place had been buzzing with Germans from Bremerstunghaven. Nothing of any use from those two, I'm afraid, but they looked as guilty as sin."

Carrington had been listening carefully.

"Bremerstunghaven, West Germany. It's like Oban. It should have been twinned with there instead. The place was probably meant to have been in East Germany but got forgotten about."

Having had to listen to Carrington extolling the virtues, or otherwise, of Oban and Bremerstunghaven, the man went on.

"It would seem that everybody had seen Germans, and even armed ones wearing naval uniforms. They were definitely seen in that ancient amusement arcade. I was told there was a film being made about the war. That would explain things, particularly the uniforms and weapons. Nobody was hurt, as far as I am aware. With visiting Germans all around, it's easy to see how these stories can develop into Chinese whispers."

Germans? Soviets? Carrington saw spies in both of them. He had some more questions.

"Right, so we know the place went bratwurst crazy, but who is making this film and, more importantly, where is the film crew making it? We need to speak to them and everybody connected with them. The police know nothing about a film being made."

Carrington felt as if something vital was getting away from him here. He now had no need to show them the lunatics, as they had met most of them already.

"Our enquiries would suggest that filming of some sort did take place here on Saturday. It wasn't a professional film crew but a local film society who were recording the twinning ceremony. Apparently though, they had a couple of decent cameras."

The woman awaited Carrington's response.

"So, we find these people and look at their footage first thing tomorrow, after you have reported on the Major and his dawn excursion."

Carrington's mood had changed and he was now more determined and meant business. He gave the other two agents a description of Halibut and Bert, who he said could almost certainly be located at The Anchor Inn at about this time of evening. Those two had met Paul Sweeney, AKA Mr Reporter, AKA Carrington, on Saturday last so he was compromised.

Carrington had a parting shot for the two.

"Go to The Anchor and listen for any conversation between those two. I'm off to Penzance for the night to find accommodation. At least it is one per cent more civilized than here. I'm sure that if you two ask nicely at the local police station, they will put you up for the night. You'll catch the Major at around 6am, going for his telescopic constitutional. See you in the morning. Good night."

"Good night, Commander," came the reply.

After Carrington had gone, they made their way to the pub as ordered.

Carrington couldn't get out of town quickly enough, and drove off to Penzance with indecent haste.

Chapter Seventeen

Carrington had discovered that the German twinning party had stayed at a Penzance hotel during their time in West Cornwall. He reached the hotel and was even lucky enough to book a room for the night.

After checking in and sorting out a few things in his room, he wondered downstairs to the hotel bar. He sought out the bar manager. There were a few guests dotted about, but Carrington learned by friendly enquiries that things had certainly calmed down since the German party had gone back home.

Carrington encouraged the woman to tell him more. She was friendly and informative enough, but she said she had work to do and maybe Carrington should have a word with the young barman on duty, who could tell him what it was like when the Germans had hit the hotel.

For the price of a few drinks, the young barman-come-student told Carrington that they had spent loads, were friendly and polite but very raucous, and that their number had suddenly been swelled by one in the form of a jolly Cornish man known to all as Herr Roger, who had apparently announced to all and sundry that he had been the Mayor of Porth Branven. He had been a real party animal and had been the star of the leaving party, along with a rather loud and equally jolly German lady, Frau Somebody-or-Other. The barman couldn't remember her name.

The young man went on to inform Carrington that the ex-Mayor, Jolly Roger, said he'd had enough of Porth Branven and was off to West Germany with the Bremerstunghaven twinning party and the jolly German lady.

"Was he really?" thought Carrington. "How interesting."

Carrington thanked the man and slipped him some money for his information. The British Naval Intelligence man told himself he deserved a proper drink for all his efforts. He hoped his two assistants back over on the north coast had been as successful in their quest for information.

*

Over at The Anchor Inn, Porth Branven, it had looked promising for the intelligence couple in the pub sniffing for gossip.

Halifax and Bert were indeed resident there as Carrington had indicated and, for a short while, the man and woman pretended to be a couple and paid no attention to them, apart from keeping their ears open. That was until Al and Oppo arrived and, after getting served, went over to the usual tables to join Halifax, Bert and their mates.

It was a couple of minutes before Al noticed that the two 'police officers' who had earlier been snooping around his garage, were present in the lounge bar. Al indicated this to the others, who looked uneasily at the pair sitting a few feet away at the bar.

"Come on," said the male agent. "We need to avoid trouble. It's time to get out of here."

"Pity," replied his colleague. "Just when it was beginning to get interesting."

"Bloody police. We don't want them sniffing around here," said Bert, examining his pint of beer as if somehow it had changed after all the years he had been drinking the stuff.

"Nothing personal against your cousin, Al. He's OK, you understand? Constable Harris is kosher. He knows when to turn a blind eye."

"No offence taken, mate," replied Al. "Yeah, we don't want them around here. They are obviously plain clothes detectives. Came around my garage today and were asking questions about Germans."

The two Naval Intelligence Officers outside the pub decided to call it a night. They were obviously not going to learn anything in The Anchor, and their presence could be counterproductive.

Carrington's suggestion that they enquire for temporary accommodation at the police station was unproductive as well. It was a case of being closed for the night, so no room at the inn.

Eventually they managed to secure a B & B just out of town for a single night. They had an early start next morning so were glad to find somewhere not too far away.

Up at The Bluebells, Major Beere and the Countess Trovanovich were chatting together in the lounge before retiring for the night.

She told the Major all about her visit to Falmouth that day and informed him what a wonderful warship HMS *Bosun* was. She also informed him of how she saw the reporter from the scandal sheet on board. She reminded the Major of how the man had bought them drinks in The Anchor on Saturday last. For once, the Major's memory had temporarily let him down and the Countess was completely lucid.

"Major, my dear man. I sense some dullskuggery afoot in these parts. You would do well to keep your hand well and truly on your precious telescope. Someone, I fear, is taking an unhealthy interest in us and our movements. Trust no-one, Major; only me. I will also do this as well, and likewise for good measure."

The Countess paused.

"Oh, and Major, dear friend. You be making sure of exercising caution on your walk tomorrow."

"I will, dear lady, and thank you for your concern. This is a dashed bad show, if you ask me. A dashed bad show all around. Just you make sure, Countess, that you keep a watchful eye over your extensive photographic record of all things nautical. It would be a crime if they were to be interfered with again or, indeed, stolen."

The Major made a sign with his hand that only the Countess recognised. It was time to adjourn for a night cap in his room before they both turned in for the night.

That night the rain lashed West Cornwall in a band coming from across the Scillies. A summer in Cornwall would just not be the same without a few days and nights of good old rain in delicious, refreshing quantities.

It was around 1am on Tuesday, 10th August, 1971, when Molly woke up with a start and in a strange bed - her own. She was sweating profusely and her heart raced. Gradually she calmed down and sat up, rubbing her eyes as the rain hit the window.

Then she saw him standing there in the corner of the bedroom. It was the unmistakable form of Otto, her dead lover.

Molly spoke softly and wondered if she was dreaming. She felt cold but had no fear.

"Otto? Is it you? Why are you here? You have to go back now and be at peace. Goodbye, Otto."

The handsome German sailor came closer, as if gliding across the floor of the bedroom. He stood at the end of her bed and his eyes stared at her lovingly. He smiled and then his apparition faded before her eyes. At that second, the rain outside seemed to cease and it was a still night with the only noise being that of the sea finding its way in and out of the harbour.

Molly got comfortable and went back to sleep.

In the spare bedroom, Molly's son, Peter, had also woken up suddenly in a cold sweat. Before this, he had slept soundly as he enjoyed the warm comforting company of the woman he had met earlier in town and had hooked up with.

The same woman, lying beside him, purred like a big contented lioness and rolled over as sleep came easily for her. Al's daughter, Lulu Demelza, was some woman, Peter decided, and could sleep through anything. He had sworn her to secrecy and promised to smuggle her out at first light. His mother wouldn't have bothered too much, but if Al found out, he was likely to come looking to do damage to Peter with that big wrench in his garage.

Peter got up to look out of the window. He could see the orange street lights outside twinkling, and he could hear the boats at anchor in the harbour making all their usual nautical tinkling noises. The rain had stopped and it was a glorious night, he noted; or it had been up to now.

As he looked out of the window at the deserted street and adjoining harbour wall, he could hear Lulu D sighing softly back in the bed. Pleasant thoughts of what they had done together earlier began to drift back into his contented mind.

He turned to go back to bed and Lulu D when he suddenly saw him standing there. The man was a German Naval Officer. Peter could make out his distinctive features and uniform in the half light, with the moon slowly shining through the open window.

The spirit spoke. His voice was soft and soothing.

"Peter. Peter, I wish I had known these things earlier. I wish things could have been..."

His words were fading.

"Auf Wiedersehen. I love you."

The spirit of Otto Von Diesel fixed Peter with a father's loving, longing smile, and then he faded.

Peter, too, thought he had been dreaming. He returned to bed in a bit of a daze and sought the warming comfort of Lulu D's gloriously young, sculpted body. He placed an arm around her and cupped her breast gently. She sighed in her sleep and Peter joined her, much more restful than before.

All three, in those two bedrooms, had a glorious night's sleep after the nocturnal disturbance.

At the crack of dawn, the Major was up and, having been made a cup of tea by a drowsy night carer, prepared to go out for his usual walk.

He wrapped up warmly against the cold August morning. It wasn't unusual for August days to be gloriously warm but to start off with an early morning frost.

The two bleary-eyed agents did as ordered and watched the man leave the home from the sanctuary of their parked car on the road outside.

Holding his telescope, he took the route that would take him to the north, passing The Tooth Rock tucked under the cliffs, and on further along the coastal footpath.

They followed him some way at a distance. There was no-one else about so early and they managed to keep him in sight without being spotted.

He stopped suddenly and looked out to sea before setting up his telescope on a tripod.

They kept him under surveillance, thinking this was a complete waste of time. Being professionals, the two stuck to their task anyway. They got a bit closer, having cover of tight scrub, and could see him looking out through the spyglass.

It was a cold morning and the sun was having a lie in before rising in the east to warm up land and sea.

All the agents could see was just that - sea. Then they saw the Major appear to spot something that commanded his attention more fully. The man spoke quietly to himself.

"By Jove. There it is again."

He had seen the U-boat on the sea's grey surface, about half a mile out to sea to the north of the Tooth Rock.

The two agents walked briskly up behind the Major. He heard them coming and turned to face them.

"Ah, the police again. Good morning, you two. You're just in time. Come and see this."

He offered the telescope to the man, who was in front of his colleague. The woman agent looked out to roughly where she thought the telescope was pointed and, yes, she could see it in the cold light of day. It was a submarine conning tower beginning to disappear below the waves.

The man had to adjust the scope to his own vision and, by the time he had it focused on the disappearing boat, he only managed to see part of the periscope slipping below the waves.

"Well, did you see it?"

The Major waited for an answer.

The man wasn't sure what he had just seen. Maybe it was a dolphin, or even a basking shark.

"I couldn't quite make out what it was, sir," said the man. "It could have been a marine animal. What do you think you saw, sir? A German U-boat?"

The man had said the words half mockingly.

"Of course it was a U-boat, young man. Saw it plain as daylight. 'UB-AF9' on its conning tower."

The Major was disappointed that the man hadn't seen it as well.

"What about you, young lady? Did you see it?"

The woman agent thought for a few seconds. There was no doubt she had seen it, and without the aid of a telescope. She wasn't a submarine expert, but that was certainly a submarine of sorts. She told the Major she hadn't seen anything and apologised to him.

With no confirmation forthcoming, the Major resigned himself to not being believed. He started to pack up his telescope.

"I've seen enough for today, you young folks. I'll have a stroll back, take a fresh cup of tea and prepare for a hearty breakfast."

The male agent excused himself and went off into the scrub to have a pee.

The woman felt sorry for the Major and spoke to him quietly.

"Sir, I did see it. I believe you when you say it was a U-boat. That's what we are here to investigate. This is all hush-hush, you understand? You being a military man and one of honour will understand our need to keep this business a bit quiet while our enquiries continue. My colleague is a bit sceptical, shall we say, and a bit wet around the ears. So can we keep this to ourselves? I'll put my findings and your sighting in my report."

The Major was delighted that the woman had confided in him and promised to keep it quiet, placing a finger on his nose for emphasis.

"Thank you," he said to her with a smile as her colleague was returning.

She returned his smile. The male agent seemed suitably relieved.

"I say, young man," said the Major. "Dashed sloppy of me, what? My old eyes must have let me down. I guess I was mistaken. It must have been a dolphin I saw out there. I'm off home now, folks. This sea air has made me peckish. It's a bit cold up here this morning. Care to walk back down to The Bluebells with me?"

They agreed and accompanied him. The male agent carried the man's tripod for good measure.

"So, what do you make of our Matron?" asked the Major, smiling mischievously. "We call her Old Trout."

The pair shared the joke as they walked back towards the town.

"Told you it was a waste of time," whispered the man to his colleague as they walked.

The woman said nothing but thought that, if the Major was anything, he was a harmless, eccentric old man and in no way a spy, unlike what Carrington believed, and even her colleague too.

Later that morning, the two agents met up with a more than happy Carrington, who had rested well overnight in his Penzance hotel.

The three went to the local police station and had tea with the Sergeant on duty.

The police officer was polite and official but wanted these people to go back from whence they had come, and for this small seaside town to get back to normal. He'd had enough of Germans and almost pined for occasional fall-outs with Bert, Al and the crew in The Anchor, or dealing with the occasional wayward tourist. He was coming up to retirement age and sought a peaceful life. Now what did these people who worked for the government in some capacity want?

They wanted the police reports on the incident with the Germans, and Carrington wanted to know something about The World of Asbestos and "Biggles, who ran it," in his own words.

The Sergeant said he could help him with information about the eccentric owner of The World of Asbestos, who loved to fly his aeroplane around the district, towing a banner advertising his attraction, if that was the right word for it.

"Who the fuck wants to visit The World of Asbestos?" enquired Carrington.

The town was definitely full up with conmen, weirdoes, spies and every other undesirable lowlife who had found their way here.

Carrington wondered if the Soviets would really bother if they knew some of the people in these parts.

Carrington was informed that the police files on this matter were with the senior officer in Penzance. The Navy man expressed mild annoyance that he had just driven over here from Penzance. He could, and should, have gone to Penzance police station first. No matter; his plan for the day would still remain the same.

"Right, you two. Briefing later. I'm off to the bloody Asbestos Experience, or whatever it's called. Its pilot is grounded, so I believe. Bloody good thing too, if you ask me. That's the last thing we need. Biggles flying around the skies. He's probably spying on the RAF in that kite of his."

"He's losing the plot big time," thought the woman agent.

The police Sergeant said nothing. This man made Al and Oppo look like geniuses. Well, almost.

"While I head off to Asbestos and then Penzance, you two track down those amateur film makers. I want that footage. Do you understand?"

Carrington was annoyed. The two agents nodded their heads in acknowledgement.

The police Sergeant was happy that this man, Carrington, was about to vacate his office and annoy somebody else. The other two seemed OK, but they would be gone soon as well, which would be good for his health and sanity. He could then get on with some real police work, such as checking on local farmers' shotgun licences and catching up on a mountain of paperwork.

"Oh, I almost forgot, you two," said Carrington. "We, all three of us, are guests of Captain Andrews on HMS *Bosun* tonight for dinner. Meet me in Falmouth on The Prince of Wales Pier at, say, 5pm."

With that, he disappeared.

As he went out on to the street, he muttered to himself, "With a bit of luck, we can get this business wrapped up at this end today, and I can get back to civilization tomorrow."

Carrington dreamed of promotion and the honours list as he got into his car.

His two helpers had some breakfast down at the Harbour Café and then set about making enquiries about the local film club, only to learn that the secretary was on holiday and the club only met on the third Tuesday of every month.

They managed to track down two brothers called Nigel and Eric, who did the filming, and ran a photographic shop in Camborne. These two individuals would have made concrete blocks look interesting.

They were happy to help but not too happy to hand over the film footage they had obtained at the twinning ceremony, which was, in their view, completely understandable. They lived, breathed and dreamed films, so only reluctantly parted with their material after being promised it would be returned after being analysed, and they would be compensated by being bought new film as well. Money talked, it would seem, even in Camborne.

Of course, they did ask a few questions until the woman suggested that maybe the police might be interested in certain other films they were processing at the back of their shop, and not ones for public consumption.

Before they left the shop, the woman agent had a question for Nigel and Eric.

"So, did you actually see any armed German sailors in Porth Branven on Saturday last?"

The two smiled in unison and gave a look that suggested it was a stupid question.

"Of course we saw them. Everybody saw them, even the police. Have a look at the films for yourselves and see. It's all caught on film, folks, and, as they say, the camera never lies."

"Thank you," said the woman sincerely.

The two agents made their way with the precious film out of the small shop and into the bustling Trelowarren Street.

"What a pity nobody captured the U-boat on film," said the woman, pausing on the pavement.

Her colleague sounded mildly irritated.

"There was no U-boat to film. End of story."

The woman placed a hand on his arm.

"I beg to differ. I saw the conning tower of that submarine for myself this morning. The Major is no more a spy than I am. He has seen the U-boat, and so have others in that port."

"Not you as well! It's all rubbish, Becky. Are you going to put that in our report? No-one will believe you. It will be the end of your promising career. And I beg to differ over this as well."

The man was quite adamant. He paused.

"Come on, Becks. Let's go for a cup of coffee and discuss this away from ears. We need to agree on this before we write up our report. Quite clearly, at present, we have differing opinions and I know which one the Commander is going to like and agree with more and it won't be yours."

Molly took a break from The Atlantic Tea Rooms and went down to the harbour to reflect on the night before. She walked out to the end of the pier where, thankfully, Old Trevor was taking a break from entertaining the gulls with his ukulele and had gone for a late breakfast in the café.

The woman looked out to where the restless waters swirled and swept into the harbour mouth and around the Tooth Rock, a little way out to the north.

Molly never noticed the two people who had joined her. She was thinking of the glorious summer of 1937, Otto, Roger and Peter. Her mind was in a whirl.

"Mum? Penny for them?"

Peter tapped her shoulder. She was startled.

"Oh, Peter. You... You shouldn't just creep up on someone like that."

Molly soon calmed down and saw that her son was hand in hand with a woman - Al's daughter. Peter's mother was surprised.

"Hello, Lulu. Are you two…?"

The look on their faces said they were. Lulu wanted to say something to Molly about being sorry that Roger had gone, which was now common knowledge, but she changed her mind and decided to stay quiet.

Peter broke the silence.

"So, what are you doing out here, mum? It's not like you to venture out here on your own."

Molly chose her words carefully.

"I had a restless night. I have things on my mind and I just needed to clear my head a little bit, so what better place than out here to do it?"

Molly breathed in the cool but refreshing sea air and could smell the scent of fresh seaweed on the rocks the other side of the pier.

"Funny you should say that, Ma, because I had a restless night last night as well."

Lulu Demelza dug him in the ribs from behind and tried to suppress a knowing smile.

"I never thought you two would ever get together," said Molly in utter surprise. "Does your dad know about this, Lou?"

Lulu Demelza smiled and gripped Peter as if they had been together for years.

"Don't you worry about dad. I can handle him. He's just a big pussy cat, is my dad."

Molly wasn't convinced and neither was Peter. The couple had yet to run into him when they were out together. Peter thought that maybe he could avoid Al while he was home on leave from his job, and then thought maybe he couldn't; it was extremely unlikely. If Al didn't see them together, then somebody else would, and it would soon get back to him.

"C'mon," said Molly, making a movement sign with her head. "I'll treat you two to coffee and whatever else you want down at the Harbour Café."

Before they accepted and left, Peter stared out over the ever restless waves beyond the harbour entrance. Somewhere out there, and not too far away, he just knew. It was becoming clearer to him now. Peter had missed all these German celebrations but had seen something in the early hours that had its place in the scheme of things. He had plenty of time on his hands and decided that, after taking coffee with his mum and Lulu D, he would make some important enquiries.

Chapter Eighteen

Carrington conducted his business and relaxed in Falmouth to await the arrival of his two junior colleagues. They arrived early.

The three talked away from the crowds as they waited for the Captain's launch, being sent over to collect them at an appointed time.

Some time later, and having worked up an appetite, they had a splendid dinner aboard the ship with the Captain and his officers.

Carrington heaped praise on his two operatives and congratulated them on a job well done.

Rebecca, the woman agent, exchanged glances with her colleague but kept quiet and thought that the film footage of the twinning celebrations would prove interesting to watch.

After dinner, one of HMS *Bosun*'s high security clearance clerks worked to type up Carrington's report to The Admiralty.

The next morning, after being ferried ashore, Carrington was off to London to submit his report to The First Sea Lord at The Admiralty, whilst also submitting a report to the Navy hierarchy in Plymouth on his way.

The two operatives sent west to help him left in their own car after being despatched to another, internal naval assignment.

Back in Porth Branven, things had returned to relative normality.

With Lulu Demelza at work part time at the town's aquarium, Peter had a wander up to The Bluebells Residential Home. He located Major Beere sitting out in the garden reading his newspaper. Peter came up behind the man and coughed to announce his presence.

"Major? Major Beere?"

The elderly man looked up and put down his newspaper onto his lap.

"Good morning, young man. Can I help you? Yes, I am the Major in question, and plead not guilty to all charges."

Peter smiled.

"Would you mind if I pick your brains, Major?"

The elderly man was always pleased to receive and chat to visitors, the precious few he ever had.

"Come sit yourself down, young fellow."

Peter pulled up a nearby chair and sat beside the Major.

"I don't know you, young fellow. Should I?"

Peter laughed.

"No, sir. I work abroad so I'm not around here much. I have a few days home. You might know my mother, Molly, who runs The Atlantic?"

"Ah, yes," said the Major with a look of instant recognition. "Yes, I know the good lady. So, how can I help you? I'll organise some tea for us."

The Major attracted the attention of a carer at the window overlooking the garden. She came out and the Major whispered in her ear. A few minutes later, she came back with a tray of tea and biscuits for the two men.

The Major thanked her. He had a good rapport with the people who worked at The Bluebells and they would do anything for the old man.

The two men had chatted about the weather and various events until the tea had arrived, and when the girl had left them to it, Peter got to the point.

"Major, you are a local man, and your memory of the last war must be good." The Major hesitated before answering.

"Porth Branven through and through, young fellow. Peter, you say your name is? Well, Peter, I didn't see much of the old place as I was serving in North Africa with the Dukes. Taken prisoner of war, you understand. Didn't actually get back to Cornwall until 1947."

"So, tell me if you can, Major Beere. To your knowledge, was there ever a German U-boat sunk off Porth Branven? I've heard of U-boats being sunk further up and down the coast, but what about here?"

The Major thought carefully. Bloody Germans again, and U-boats. Still, the lad was polite enough. Only a few persons apart from the crew of *The Two Inbred Sisters* had believed his tale of seeing the U-boat whose crew wasn't aware that the war had ended. However, this young man looked and sounded so much different from reporters, and much more genuine.

212

"As I said, I wasn't here myself during the war, but let me think... I do believe there was an unidentified U-boat sunk about five miles off Porth Branven. Struck a mine, as I recall. Read something about it after the war, and an old Navy man who I once knew said something about it as well, although he's dead now. All hands lost on this submarine, If I remember correctly."

The Major paused and was deep in thought.

"So, forgive me for asking, young Peter. Why your sudden interest in a lost U-boat?"

The tone of the Major's question was curious but friendly. He had heard rumours of Molly's husband, Roger, buggering off with a German woman after the twinning ceremony, and all things German seemed to be invading Porth Branven life. Maybe the young man was just curious. Whatever; he had his own reasons.

"Sir, can I ask you? When you saw this U-boat, could you see any identification marks on her?"

The Major was now pleased that someone had begun to take such an interest in what he knew he had seen.

"Yes, I identified her all right. Clear as day. UB-AF9. There, crystal clear on her conning tower. I've made some enquiries of my own through my friend, the Countess, who is interested in shipping. This was a small coastal submarine of the First A Flotilla, home base in Bremerhaven and operating out from the Breton coast."

"UB-AF9?"

Peter thought carefully.

"Do you know, Major Beere, that's exactly the same number as Bert and his two crew said was on the U-boat that seized them?"

"Quite," replied the Major. "Bert told me himself, and I told the police, as he did. They never believed either of us."

The Major kept quiet about the woman agent and what she had said to him.

"So, sir, in your opinion, which I value as you are an ex-army officer, could this U-boat that you all saw be the same as the so far unidentified boat you say lies five miles out from here after hitting a mine?"

The Major stared up to the blue sky and then at Peter.

"By Jove, young fellow. Well, Peter, there's a thought. Of course, there's no definite identification so far of this wreck. It will be a war grave, so no-one is allowed to dive to her without permission. That's not to say that other, more unscrupulous divers haven't already. Not sure what's left of her, having struck a mine."

The man went quiet and seemed to be suddenly sad at the men's fate, despite fighting against them in the war. He suddenly spoke.

"Germans or no Germans, nobody deserves such a terrible fate as they suffered, Peter. War is a terrible thing, lad. A terrible thing."

Peter had learned all that he needed to know. When he had stood out at the end of the pier with his mother, looking out to sea, he just knew then that his late father, the father he never knew until briefly the previous night, had perished out there under the cold Atlantic waters.

He finished his tea and chatted some more to the Major. He promised to have a drink with the old soldier before he returned to the Middle East.

As he got up to leave, he had one last question.

"Major Beere, that German U-boat that hit a mine; when did that happen? 1941?"

The Major knew the answer.

"I do believe it was. August of that year. Thirty years ago."

"Yes, thirty years ago," replied Peter. "Could it have happened on Thursday, 7th August, 1941?"

The Major didn't reply. He didn't have to and just gave Peter a knowing look.

Peter thanked the old man and shook his hand before leaving the garden and making his way home.

The Major went back to reading his paper and fell asleep in the warm August morning.

He was suddenly back in North Africa, fighting a war that destroyed so many lives and caused so much heartbreak.

Peter had reached The Atlantic Tea Rooms where his mother was working that day.

"Mum, can you take a break? I need to talk to you. It's important."

"Please don't tell me you've got her pregnant," thought Molly, knowing it would be too soon to know but fearing that she might hear it anyway.

214

On Thursday morning, Geoff, the diver-come-salvager from Falmouth, came over to Porth Branven, and he, Halifax and Bert went out on *The Boy Blewett* to the site where *The Two Inbred Sisters* had gone down.

The idea was that Geoff and his son, both qualified divers, plus another of their crew, would dive the wreck before arranging to raise her.

The weather had been kind and had held out, much to their surprise and relief.

The men made the dive down at the end of the reef, where the water was unnaturally deep for that part of the coast.

Some time later, Geoff and his son surfaced from the dive. After removing his gear, Geoff's face told the bad news.

"Sorry, lads, but she's struck an outcrop of the reef and is badly damaged."

"How badly damaged? Can she be salvaged?" Bert asked.

"I'm afraid not," said Geoff. "She's broken in two for starters, and there is other damage. She's a wreck. I'm so sorry."

Bert was gutted, and the trip back to port was made in almost complete silence. Bert had also learned the nets were all ripped asunder and anything else on the boat was lost. Even the engine had been damaged with the boat's descent to the reef below.

Once back on shore, the men adjourned to The Anchor Inn for an inquest and for Bert to drown his sorrows.

Later that evening, Peter and Lulu Demelza stood outside the pub.

"Well, here goes, Lulu D. We have to do this some time."

Both of them plucked up the courage to enter her father's local.

Once inside, they immediately saw him, Oppo and the usual suspects playing euchre.

Halifax saw them first and nudged Al on the arm. Lulu's father turned to look at the pair.

Peter suddenly wondered if this was such a good idea. Much to his surprise and relief, Al didn't explode and tear the pub and him apart at the seams with his bare hands.

"Mine's a pint if you're buying, Peter," said Al, almost civilized.

He returned to playing his game.

Peter was mightily relieved. It was Al's way of saying he was OK about the situation.

"So, you're not maized, Dad?" said Lulu Demelza sheepishly.

"I'm just pleased you didn't come in here with a German," said Al without looking around and still playing his game of euchre.

Peter remained quiet and had a good reason for doing so, while Lulu Demelza also kept quiet, she too having an equally valid reason.

Peter got the drinks in for himself, Al and Lulu D, and they joined the others on the fringes of their game.

By the end of the week, the newspapers and other media had tired of Porth Branven and its German tales, and news of the town was now chip papers. A consensus had been reached that Porth Branven had pulled off a stupendous public relations stunt to aid its tourist trade. Only the incident involving the mine washed up there had any factual basis.

It was the morning of Friday the 13th - in this case, August, 1971 - and Commander Carrington, staying at a London hotel, had been summoned to appear before the Navy top brass at The Admiralty.

Carrington was looking forward to the meeting. Normally, appearing in front of the bigwigs of the Navy could be a daunting experience, much like attending one's own court martial.

For once, Commander Carrington was impeccably dressed in best uniform. He waited patiently outside the oak panelled room that displayed portraits of past British naval heroes such as Bligh and Nelson, and battles on the high seas of the past.

Carrington was summoned through a security cleared steward, and entered the grandiose and imposing room.

They were all there; The First Sea Lord, more Navy top brass, and even The Minister of Defence.

"Good morning, Commander Carrington. Do come in. Take a seat. Tea or coffee?"

Carrington obeyed the order and dreamt that one day his oil painting portrait would adorn these hallowed walls, up there with Nelson.

He opted for tea and awaited The First Sea Lord's praise for his work in Cornwall.

The Navy's top man stood up and turned his back to Carrington, his hands clasped behind his back as he looked out of the window. The others present all fixed Carrington with cold stares and showed little emotion. Without turning around, the senior officer spoke.

"Commander Carrington, you were ordered to Cornwall on an important mission and my colleagues and I have studied your submitted report. I must say, it is detailed and you have covered a lot of ground in a short space of time."

The First Sea Lord turned around to face Carrington and paced slowly up and down behind his heavy desk.

A prepared map on the wall depicted Cornwall, with map pins placed in certain places.

The senior naval man went on to say that the defence mechanisms on board HMS *Bosun* did appear to have been compromised, but matters were in hand to rectify perceived problems. Then he got on to Carrington's more detailed submitted report.

"A U-boat was allegedly spotted off the fishing port of Porth Branven. This U-boat's crew boarded a small Cornish fishing vessel, scuttled it, stole the catch and took the crew prisoner. Later on, these prisoners were released unharmed. The name of this scuttled fishing boat? *The Two Inbred Sisters*."

There was a small outbreak of guffaws from those present, but they ceased when they saw that The First Sea Lord did not share the joke.

"And who were these people who saw, or were victims of, these would-be German pirates? Bert, a Cornish fisherman, as dodgy as they come and of more interest to HM Customs and Excise than us, plus his two crew members, who are equally as guilty of carrying on the traditions of their ancestors on the coast.

Then we have a retired army Major who lives in a residential home for the elderly, and whose memory comes and goes more often than the train from Paddington to Penzance. This same retired Major likes his drink and wanders out on to the cliff tops most days to look at the sea with his telescope. His companion is an old lady, ninety if she is a day, and is called, apparently, the Countess Trovanovich, also resident at this home and a good friend of the Major. She has two passions; one being the Bolsheviks and the second being ships and all things nautical. It's been a hobby of hers for years, apparently. She's not the only one with a passion for ships, is she, gentlemen?"

It was the cue for those present to have a legitimate laugh. Only Carrington declined. He suddenly didn't like the way this was going.

The First Sea Lord continued with his summing up of Carrington's report.

"So, we have these Cornish fishermen, AKA smugglers, plus the Major and the Countess, all apparently deeply involved in this alleged Soviet spy ring. The information is obtained by the agent known as Boras in Falmouth, who I shall come to in a moment.

"Boras is a long term Russian agent who lives near the docks in Falmouth and who obtains information on the port's shipping movements, both Navy and merchant vessel alike. He passes the information on to the Countess Trovanovich, another, more obvious sounding Russian agent, who has been in Cornwall for more years than its pasties.

"The information is then passed on to Moscow, possibly through France on fishing vessels, after rendezvousing with drop-offs in specially adapted crab and lobster pots hoisted up and dropped off by the Cornish fishermen.

"So, where do the U-boat and the Germans fit into the equation? Well, we know there was a twinning ceremony between Porth Branven and the West German port of Bremerstunghaven. This provided obvious cover for potential East German spies. However, none were discovered. Meanwhile, the Mayor of Porth Branven does his bit to cement, shall we say, Cornubian-Germanic relations, by defecting with the German lady organiser of this twinning celebration.

"Commander Carrington, the Navy, like myself and, I suspect, most persons here, does not believe in ghost ships or, indeed, ghost U-boats. If any submarine was spotted in those waters, it would be the diesel powered boat, HMS *Barracuda*. And when I last looked, she was, and still is, one of ours."

More guffaws came from those present.

"Your U-boat, AF9, struck a mine on Thursday, 7th August, 1941, after sinking a merchant vessel. She went down with all thirty-four hands in a position approximately five miles north-west of Porth Branven. Our people have received confirmation from West German naval sources of this. Here, Commander. There's the file with an updated Admiralty chart showing its position, which has not yet been made public. See for yourself."

Carrington picked up and perused the file, and all was as his superior had said.

"Commander Carrington, with all this German activity going on, it was obvious that someone would play the practical joker. Armed German sailors? Ghosts?"

The First Sea Lord forced a smile.

"I think the tabloid newspapers have got this story pretty much well covered, old man. It was a clear hoax by persons unknown to drive up interest in tourism in that part of Cornwall. You know how important tourism is to some of these people."

Carrington interrupted his superior.

"Sir, sir, please listen to me. I insist. There were witnesses to the armed German sailors, including police officers. They were even captured on film."

The Sea Lord paused before answering Carrington.

"Police officers witnessed these armed Germans, you say? Well here are the relevant police officers statements, Commander. Look through them, if you like. I don't think you will see any reference to any armed German sailors in any of them."

Carrington was gobsmacked.

"Sir, they were captured on film."

The senior officer studied Carrington, who was feeling decidedly uncomfortable as his case for spies in Cornwall appeared to be crumbling around him.

"Ah, yes, the film. Let us take a look at this footage, shall we, Commander?"

A projector had been set up ready and the steward started the film rolling.

"Watch carefully, Commander Carrington. As you can see, a good time is being had by all. Lots of drinking and no doubt some whoring as well. Lots of Germans but none that are armed, and no sailors either. Our experts have gone over every single frame of this footage, and no German sailors can be seen in any of them. You are welcome to sit and look through the entire film, Commander, if you wish."

Carrington declined the offer.

"Discounting German involvement in this business, the story of the Soviet spy ring in Cornwall sounds much like a work of fiction so bizarre that it might even be true. This whole business has gone so high as to involve even the Cabinet Office and The Prime Minister himself. Mr Heath, himself being a keen yachtsman, was extremely interested and concerned about this whole business.

"As it turned out, and with some persuasion from myself, a high powered dawn police swoop was ordered to arrest all of the people you allege to be involved in this spy ring. However, the raids were called off at the last possible minute."

Carrington was now deeply mystified.

"Why, sir? The link was well established from coast to coast, from the fishermen to Boras in Falmouth."

The First Sea Lord went quiet for a few seconds, went to the table and slammed down his fist in a rage, startling those seated.

"Boras? Boras the Russian agent in Falmouth? Boras in league with the Countess Olga Trovanovich? Commander Carrington, you blithering idiot! A marker buoy in the Solent has more common sense than you! What were you thinking of, man? This report of yours is only fit to be used to wrap up chips."

The senior naval man paced a bit more.

"We managed to abort the police raids just in time, which was just as well, before you single-handedly made the senior service a laughing stock."

Carrington was even more confused. To him, the whole thing concerning the Soviet spy ring made perfect sense.

"Commander Carrington, Boras, AKA Mr John Trebannan of 4 Barrangwaneth Row, Falmouth, Cornwall. He drives a green 1964 Hillman Super Minx estate car, has a wife called Valerie and two grown up children, one of whom is a merchant Navy officer, the other a second Lieutenant in The 1st, The Queens Dragoon Guards.

"Boras hands over files of shipping to his Russian fellow, or, more accurately, lady spy, the Countess Trovanovich. Well, Commander Carrington, are you aware of a weekly Cornish newspaper called *Cornwall Weekly*?"

Carrington considered what the man had said. He sounded more like a spy than ever before.

"I did come across this local rag during my few days in Cornwall, sir."

The senior officer was exasperated.

"Well, man, if you had bothered to investigate by actually reading this rag, as you call it, you would have discovered that it runs a weekly shipping movement column. And, Commander, if it's a rag, well, being from that part of the world myself, I have it sent to me regularly.

"Basically, the correspondent catalogues shipping movements in Truro, the Fal and other, smaller ports in Cornwall. The column is written by one Mr John Trebannan; yes, that same one."

"The perfect cover," thought Carrington.

The First Sea Lord went on.

"Mr John Trebannan, a librarian and noted authority on oyster fishing who writes under the name of BORAS, which stands for 'boats on river and sea'."

The Senior Naval Officer looked highly annoyed. The incompetence of this man, Carrington!

As for Carrington himself, he was completely deflated and saw his promotion and Queen's honour disappearing before his very eyes.

"All the expense, the time and resources to unearth a set of people who would be thrown out of a lunatic asylum for being too stupid. Get out of my sight, Commander! Go sit outside until I summon you after I decide what to do with you, you complete and utter… There is no appropriate word at hand right now."

Carrington rose to his feet, came to attention and put on his peaked cap and saluted his superior. Doing a smart about turn, he marched off out of the room, his ears burning, feeling eyes boring into the back of his head, and still smarting from the words of the Navy's senior man. He took a seat outside the room and felt thoroughly dejected.

Back inside the room, The First Sea Lord sighed and sat back down. He addressed the people present.

"Well, gentlemen, that concludes this business. Could have made the whole service a complete laughing stock and sent shock waves across the world for the government as well. Lord knows what the Soviets would have made of this. Ghosts of German submariners, elderly Russian lady spies and a lunatic who flies an aeroplane across the Cornish countryside and is obsessed with asbestos. The World of Asbestos? I ask you. Who visits such a place?"

Those present were already aware of the reference to the man who claimed to have had his aeroplane shot at by the crew of a World War Two U-boat. Apparently, the man had had his pilot's licence revoked, which was a good thing according to The First Sea Lord.

"I think I have had enough for one day, gentlemen. Let's adjourn to my club for some refreshments. This business has been nipped in the bud, but it has left a sour taste in my mouth."

As the senior Navy men and the Minister left the room, they passed the thoroughly miserable Carrington, who stood up to attention.

"Commander Carrington, my office, first thing Monday morning. Bring your passport with you."

"Sir! Yes, sir!" replied Carrington, wondering if he was going to be shipped off out of the way to the Far East.

Chapter Nineteen

It was Friday evening at The Bluebells in Porth Branven, Cornwall.

The Countess Olga Trovanovich was getting ready to go out for the evening, which was a rare occasion. She went to see the Major and twisted his arm to accompany her.

The Anchor Inn was busy, as was usual for a Friday night. All the fishermen, except for those out on the water, were present, including Halifax, Bert and his mates. Big Bert had still not got over the loss of *The Two Inbred Sisters*. He was very surprised to see the elderly couple from The Bluebells arrive at the pub. They were made to feel welcome and joined the fishermen.

"Let me buy you both a drink," said Bert, getting up from his seat.

The Countess placed a shaking bony hand on the big man's arm.

"Mr Bert, it is I who will be buying you and your fisherman's friends some drinks. You have suffered a terrible injustice with the loss of your craft, *The Two Twin Sisters*."

The name was close enough for Bert, who forced a smile.

"Come with me, Big Bert, to the bar rail, and help me carry back the drinks. I also want to talk to you in your own self."

The two, who made an unlikely couple, stood at the bar. Bert was intrigued.

The Countess ordered the drinks, helped by Bert, who remembered what the lads all drank.

"Bert, you have been so good to me and the Major with fresh fish and some of the strong stuff with questions asked so little. So now I wish to help you. I am a rich woman and I will not take no for an answer. I want to buy you a new craft to replace your lost one that the Bosch scuttle-fished."

Bert forced another laugh. He didn't know what to say.

The Countess was adamant. She was going to buy him a new boat. He was to go and find one and she would pay for it and would be very pleased to do so.

They got their drinks and Bert toasted her good health, and said thank you by way of kissing her on both cheeks and on the hand.

"I have told the Major and he is in complete agreement with my plan, but keep this between yourself and myself for now," she said, finishing the conversation.

Carrington had suffered a troubled weekend. Having gone from hero, or so he thought, to zero, he had the daunting prospect of appearing again before the Sea Lords at the Admiralty on Monday morning. Monday came around far too quickly.

"Enter!"

The order from inside the room sounded cold and uninviting. Carrington did as ordered and saw that the Navy's senior man, plus one other Officer, was present.

"Good morning, Commander Carrington."

"Good morning, sir. Good morning, gentlemen."

Carrington wasn't sure what was to happen to him. He was soon to find out. Traditionally, when someone had fucked up as he undoubtedly had, they were posted to HMS *Oban* in the out-of-the-way highlands of Scotland.

"Commander Carrington. You are to be taken off intelligence duties and assigned a new posting starting two weeks today."

Carrington had vivid mental images of HMS *Oban*, which he had had the misfortune to visit once many years before. His fate was to be worse than expected.

"You have the option of two posts, Commander. The first being a public relations officer at HMS *Raleigh*, which you know is at Torpoint in Cornwall. I know how you love Cornwall, Commander. Your second option is to accept a newly created position as a Naval Liaison Officer at a West German naval base near to the port of Bremerstunghaven. I've pulled a few strings with our NATO friends over this one. The duration of the posting, whichever one you accept, will be three years. The choice is yours. Please let my secretary know by 5pm today. You know the number to ring."

"Oh, by the way, Captain Carrington - yes, you are being demoted in rank to Captain - I require you to hand over the keys to your Navy issued car. Any questions, Captain Carrington?"

Carrington hadn't any. He was seething. He had lost his rank, his reputation and his car, to add to the indignity of it all. And he was being posted to his nemesis, whichever option he chose.

"That will be all, Captain Carrington. Good day to you."

Carrington replaced his cap, saluted and left the two senior Navy Officers to discuss events without his presence.

"Well, that's the matter of Carrington sorted out, sir. He's sure to stay out of mischief, wherever he chooses to be posted. Now I shall have words with the relevant people in The West German Navy about making sure no dead German sailors are ever seen in Porth Branven again."

The First Sea Lord had one last observation to make.

"Rupert, make sure the woman agent and the Cornish policemen's original files are put somewhere safe so they never see the light of day. There's a good chap."

"Consider it done, sir," came the decisive reply.

A few days later, the Matron of The Bluebells sought out the Countess Olga.

"You have a visitor, Countess. It's Bert, the fisherman from down at the harbour, with that ghastly pick up truck of his. He wants you to accompany him down to the harbour. Says he has something to show you. Oh, and he wants Major Beere to go as well. Just what are you lot up to?"

The Matron knew that no information was forthcoming.

"I'll go and get the Major."

While she did this, the Countess made sure she looked her best.

Bert drove the pair down to the harbour and the Countess beamed when it came into view. They got out of the truck and went up to where Bert's usual berth was.

"Mr Bert, she is absolutely beautiful! Just like me. What a grand craft she looks. You have chosen well, my fisherman's friend."

The Countess and the Major were invited on board and shown around the boat. The Countess had noticed something missing.

"She doesn't have a name, Bert."

Bert smiled, went into the wheelhouse and came out with two wooden hand-painted name boards. A tear came to the Countess's eye.

"You have chosen a wonderful boat and have also chosen a wonderful name for her."

The Countess was handed one of the name boards. She showed it to the Major. He read the name out loud.

"*The Countess Olga*. By Jove, how splendid!"

He could see how pleased the old woman was to have the new boat named after her.

"I'm having your name hand-painted on the stern as well, when her registration number comes through," said Bert.

A few days later they all gathered down at the harbour. *The Countess Olga* was a fitting vessel to take the party on the ten-mile round trip out to the site of the wreck.

Bert had made sure that there was plenty of food and drink on board for his guests. Bad weather was forecast for the next day, and Peter was due to return to the Middle East, so it was right that he should pay his respects.

Apart from Bert and his two crew members, Arthur Pengelly and John Thomas, the party consisted of the Major, the Countess and Lulu Demelza, who was representing Al and Oppo. There were also Molly, Peter and the West German Navy padre, who had arrived from London specially to conduct the service.

The passengers and crew on Bert's boat were in a solemn mood and hardly spoke on the choppy trip out to the wreck.

When they reached the position on Bert's chart, he cut the boat's engines and Molly dropped the specially prepared black, red and gold reef in the swirling waters above the wreck.

The Lutheran pastor proceeded to conduct a short ceremony of dedication in memory of the thirty-four crew members of U-boat AF9 who had perished in their steel coffin some way below them.

All present had their own thoughts and Molly shed a discreet tear and mouthed a silent goodbye as she dropped a single red rose, which floated alongside the wreath.

Peter felt cut up inside but kept his emotions in check; well, after a hug from Lulu D.

The German Navy pastor finished the service with some heartfelt words in German, which were translated into English for the benefit of most of the congregation.

"May the crew of the U-boat, AF9, sleep in everlasting peace in their grave of the Mother Ocean. God bless every one of them. Amen."

Bert restarted the engines and *The Countess Olga* started out on a course back to the harbour.

When they arrived back and Bert and his lads had secured the boat, they adjourned to The Anchor.

"Things should be a lot quieter now," said the pastor. "I have time for one more drink with you wonderful people before my taxi gets here."

The man was off to Penzance to get the train back to London. His task, sanctioned by the British naval hierarchy, was completed. Hopefully, no more spirits of World War Two German submariners would be seen again.

"Right, good people of Porth Branven, and you as well, Herr Pastor Schnell," said the Major, raising his glass of Irish whiskey aloft. "I want you all to join me in a toast to Kapitanleutnant Otto Von Diesel and every member of his crew. It's time to put these hostilities to bed for good. Here's to them and to a peaceful future for all of us. May they rest in eternal peace. God bless them all!"

Those present joined the Major in his toast to the dead submariners and chinked their glasses together.

And there the story ended; or did it?

A few weeks later, Bert and the boys had been out fishing and had done well. On the way in, they checked out the pots placed just off the Spurdog reef. Bert and John Thomas hauled in the pots while Arthur idled the engine. Bert was in for a surprise.

"Well, what have we got here? I don't believe this! Isn't he an absolute beauty? I never thought I'd see him again. It's Herman! I have caught him twice. I would recognise Herman anywhere. His markings and his size are absolutely unique. The last time I caught him, well, boys, you know what happened then."

Arthur Pengelly and John Thomas studied the grand specimen of a lobster that Bert held aloft. He then secured the creature's fearsome claws with elastic bands and tape, such were their size.

"So, what are you going to do with him?" asked Arthur. "He'll fetch a lot of money."

Bert studied the creature carefully.

"Herman's been in the sea a long, long time, lads. He's not being sold to anyone or going in anybody's pot. He's a grand old man like the Major and he deserves a second chance. He's going to live out his days at the Porth Branven aquarium. I'm sure Lulu D will be delighted to home such a prize specimen. Herman will outlive all of us, and he will be the main attraction there for years to come. He's a reminder of what we all know really happened. Make sure we have a bucket of sea water to keep him fresh and healthy."

That night, the biggest moon that anyone could ever remember seemed to sit out low over the sea off Porth Branven.

As Molly and Peter slept in their respective bedrooms, Otto leaned over and kissed her softly and then went to place a loving, firm father's hand on his sleeping son. Lulu D stirred from her sleep and felt her partner's comforting arm curl around her.

Otto paid a visit to Herman as well, in the darkened confines of the aquarium.

His duty was fulfilled. Now he could enjoy a drink with his comrades aboard the pride of the German Kriegsmarine. He and his crew were at peace at last.

UB-AF9 Crew List

Kapitanleutnant Otto Von Diesel
Leutnant Franz Spiegel
Leutnant Hans Krieger
Engineer Fritz Köln

Erhard Schwartz
Bernhard Schultz
Ralf Holsteig
Karl Horst
Klaus Baumgarten
Helmut Wolf
Heinz Breitner
Dieter Khone
Gunther Koller
Adolf Freund
Franz Schelling
Johann Pedersen
Reinhard Schwartz
Sebastian Voller
Manfred Von Krauch
Heinrich Lundt
Wilhelm Sturm
Ernst Schmidt
Torsten Kiss
Gebhard Steinfeld
Uwe Baur
Horst Schein
Lars Friederick
Wolfgang Eppel
Siegfried Culpman
Axel Jungst
Gottfried Scharnschloss
Lothar Luntz
Kristian Gernhardt
Ulf Gernhardt

Herman

Printed in Great Britain
by Amazon